Mystical Moments

AND UNITIVE THINKING

Mystical Moments

AND UNITIVE THINKING

DAN MERKUR

State University of New York Press

Published by
State University of New York Press, Albany

© 1999 State University of New York

For information, address State University of New York
Press, State University Plaza, Albany, N.Y., 12246

Production by Diane Ganeles
Marketing by Patrick Durocher

Library of Congress Cataloging-in-Publication Data

Merkur, Daniel.
     Mystical moments and unitive thinking / Dan Merkur.
          p.   cm.
     Includes bibliographical references and index.
     ISBN 0-7914-4063-X (alk. paper). — ISBN 0-7914-4064-8 (pbk. :
alk. paper)
     1. Mysticism—Psychology.   2. Psychoanalysis and religion.
I. Title.
BL625.M375   1999
291.4'22—dc21   98-20221
                                                              CIP

10 9 8 7 6 5 4 3 2 1

And behold, the Lord passed by, and a great and strong wind rent the mountains, and broke in pieces the rocks before the Lord, but the Lord was not in the wind; and after the wind an earthquake, but the Lord was not in the earthquake; and after the earthquake a fire, but the Lord was not in the fire; and after the fire a still small voice.

—1 Kings 19:11b–12

CONTENTS

PREFACE

The psychoanalysts Hans Loewald (1951, 1978, 1988), Donald W. Winnicott (1963), and Hal J. Breen (1986) advanced the theory that the order of unitive thinking that manifests consciously in mystical experiences functions as an unconscious core of the human personality throughout life.

This book explores, revises, and extends their thesis.

The revision includes acceptance of the current consensus among developmentalists who engage in direct infant observation, that people are born with innate abilities to communicate with our care-givers. There is no neonatal developmental phase of primary narcissism, or monism, or subject-object non-differentiation, when infants naively mistake their care-givers for parts of themselves (Lichtenberg, 1983; Stern, 1985). Although people's ideas of their "selves" assuredly change and mature from infancy onward (Stern, 1983), the knowledge to engage in communication with care-givers is inborn (Bråten, 1988; Murray, 1991). The subject-object distinction is implicitly innate. Accordingly, the traditional psychoanalytic theory of mysticism is simply wrong. Mystical experiences of nondifferentiation may not be explained as regressions to infantile modes of ego functioning. There is no neonatal stage of nondifferentiation to which to regress (Harrison, 1986).

In developing a psychoanalytic theory of mysticism that speaks not of regression but of sublimation, I have suggested that mystical moments are conscious manifestations of a general type of thinking that also proceeds unconsciously. Unitive thinking may be conceptualized, from a mixed Freudian and Piagetian perspective, as a category of cognitive development, akin to time perception, mathematical reasoning, and moral development. Mystical experiences occur when recent achievements of unconscious unitive thinking manifest consciously as momentary inspirations.

Although the changes that I have urged in psychoanalytic theory are individually small, their cumulative implication places a novel spin on the view, shared by Loewald and Winnicott, that in some sense we are all of us mystics. Working with a theory of infantile regression, they viewed mysticism as natural but irrational. Its conscious manifestation could have only limited value.

A theory of sublimation has radically different diagnostic implications. Unlike symbol-formation, sublimation occurs in the absence of conflict and resistance. It is inherently and inalienably healthy. If unitive thinking is indeed a form of sublimation, psychoanalysis must maintain the view that unconscious unitive thinking has a natural and healthy tendency to manifest as conscious spirituality. The clinical question then becomes the conditions in health and pathology under which unitive thinking manifests, or is resisted and diverted into symbolic compromise formations.

This book is the second part of a project that began as my M.A. work in Interdisciplinary Studies at York University in 1981–82. *The Ecstatic Imagination: Psychedelic Experiences and the Psychoanalysis of Self-Actualization* discussed the data of LSD, psilocybin, and mescaline experiences. It focused on the psychedelic state and its implications for the theories of the psyche and its integration. *Mystical Moments and Unitive Thinking* depends chiefly on the additional data of spontaneous "peak" experiences and meditation states. It addresses the unitive thinking that manifests, albeit with minor differences, in the several alternate states.

The project has benefited immeasurably from the contribution of Keith Haartman, who has been my student, good friend, and most careful critical reader for many years. I would also like to thank my former teachers, Jordan Paper, David Bakan, and Christopher Nichols, for their friendship and continuing conversations. My thanks also to William W. Meissner and Laurence Nixon for their comments on earlier drafts of this book.

Chapter 1 is a revised version of "Unitive Experiences and the State of Trance," which appeared as a chapter in *Mystical Union and Monotheistic Religion: An Ecumenical Dialogue*, edited by Moshe Idel and Bernard McGinn (New York: Macmillan, 1989).

ACKNOWLEDGMENTS

Thanks are due to the following authors, publishers, and publications for permission to reprint materials from the following publications.

Arthur J. Deikman, Experimental meditation, *Journal of Nervous and Mental Disease* 136 (1963): 329–73. Copyright 1963, Williams & Wilkins. Reprinted by permission of the publisher.

Paul Horton, The mystical experience: substance of an illusion, *Journal of the American Psychoanalytic Association* 22 (1974): 364–80. Reprinted by permission of International University Press, Publishers.

Inglorious Wordworths, by Michael Paffard. Copyright 1973, Michael Paffard. Reproduced by permission of Hodder and Stoughton.

The Spiritual Nature of Man, by Sir Alister Hardy. Copyright © 1979, Sir Alister Hardy. Reprinted by permission of Oxford University Press.

Tales of the Hasidim: The Early Masters, by Martin Buber, translated by Olga Marx. Copyright 1947, 1948, and renewed 1975 by Schocken Books. Reprinted by permission of Schocken Books, distributed by Pantheon Books, a division of Random.

Watcher on the Hills, by Raynor C. Johnson. Copyright 1959, Raynor Johnson. Reproduced by permission of Hodder and Stoughton.

ONE

Some Varieties
of Mystical Union

Upon the rise of medical psychiatry in the mid-nineteenth century, various Christian mystics—including several traditional saints—were diagnosed as morbid personalities. The diagnoses were challenged, firstly by Roman Catholic writers, and next by Anglicans, who simultaneously revived the practice of mysticism in their churches after a lapse of some two hundred years (Butler, 1922, pp. xiii–xiv; Knowles, 1967, pp. 9–10). Due to the discontinuity of the living practice throughout most of Western Christendom, modern knowledge of traditional Catholic mysticism depends on historical reconstructions. As may be expected, factual errors have not been few (for a critique, see: Arbman, 1963, pp. 418–515).

Comparative perspectives played an understandably large role in the Christian mystical revival. Living mystical traditions were investigated for insights that would elucidate the writings of Christian mystics. Due to the Romantics' fascination with India (Willson, 1964; Figueira, 1994), the Hindu Yogic emphasis on the Atman-Brahman equation and the Buddhist preoccupation with nirvana were compared with the emphases that some Christian mystics had placed on *unio mystica*. The problem of discerning spirits, that is, of deciding whether a vision or voice is divine, angelic, demonic, or a natural product of the body, has led to categorical avoidance of visions and voices at various times in Christian history, from the fourth-century Evagrius Ponticus (1981, pp. 71, 74) onward. Although apparitions and visions had been classified in Western Christianity since St. Augustine (1982) as corporeal and imaginative visions, the modern mystical revival endorsed the Eastern standard. Catholic and Anglican theologians privileged *unio mystica* but discourage the revival of other Christian mystical experiences because they were no longer prepared to defend their religious validity (Inge, 1899, pp. 15–19; Poulain, 1910, pp. 299, 320–48; Maréchal, 1927, p. 111).

Academic studies of comparative mysticism arose late in the nineteenth century in furtherance of Christian concerns and favored comparably restrictive definitions. In an influential formulation, Evelyn Underhill (1910) suggested that "mysticism, in its pure form, is . . . the science of union with the Absolute, and nothing else, and . . . the mystic is the person who attains this union" (p. 72). Emphasis was placed on experience to the exclusion of ideology, but at the expense of a value judgment that denied spiritual authenticity to experiences other than union. The inherently theistic implications of the term *mystical union* were later avoided by references, for cross-cultural purposes, to "the mystical experience." The definite article perpetuates the assumption that only one variety of religious experience is properly termed *mystical*.

When Gershom Scholem (1954, pp. 4–7, 40–118) pioneered the academic study of Jewish mysticism, he adopted a contrary position, claiming that whatever the historical Jewish mystics experienced was, by definition, mystical. Scholem emphasized that visionary practices had dominated Jewish mysticism from its origins through the twelfth century. Comparable arguments may readily be mounted on the evidence of Christian, Muslim, Hindu, and Buddhist mysticism. In no culture have mystics been limited to unitive experiences. Neither have unitive experiences been limited to mystics. For example, although shamans favor visionary and/or auditory experiences that suit the needs of their séance practices (Hultkrantz, 1978; Merkur, 1992a, pp. 109–68), shamans occasionally have unitive experiences (Paper, 1980, 1982) and may even base part of their worldviews on them (Merkur, 1991b, pp. 41–71).

Academic research also inherited a second unearned premise from the Christian mystical revival: the assumption that mystics' writings about unitive experiences referred to an experience that is everywhere one and the same. In his classic but rudimentary account of mysticism, William James (1902) proposed six invariants of mystical experience: a sense of union (p. 321); a "consciousness of illumination [that] is . . . the essential mark of mystical states" (p. 313, n. 28); and the much-remarked subsidiary features of ineffability, noetic character, transiency, and passivity (pp. 292–94). By ineffability, James referred to mystics' claims that they cannot adequately explain their experiences in words. Because language is inherently contextual and referential, mystics are at least partially unable to explain their experiences to the initiated, but only in the same sense that the blue of the sky cannot be explained to the unsighted, nor the melody of a symphony to the deaf, nor the taste of a pear to a person who has never eaten the fruit.

James's claim that mystical experiences invariably have a noetic—in modern idiom, a cognitive—aspect has been much disputed; I shall return to the problem in the next section. Passivity is definitely a variable feature. It is found in Christian mysticism but not, for example, in Buddhist meditation (Gimello, 1978). As for transiency, most mystical experiences vary in duration from several minutes to perhaps as much as two hours; but a few mystics have known unitive states that were continuous during all of their waking hours for periods of years (e.g., Brother Lawrence, 1977, p. 56).

James (1902, pp. 387–88) maintained that mystical experiences were highly variable and contingent on what he termed *overbeliefs:* religious conceptions that a person brings to a religious experience, not only postexperientially in the process of its interpretation and reportage, but also preexperientially as a contribution to the contents of the experiences.

> The mystical feeling of enlargement, union, and emancipation has no specific intellectual content whatever of its own. It is capable of forming matrimonial alliances with material furnished by the most diverse philosophies and theologies, provided only they can find a place in the framework for its peculiar mood (p. 326).

All in all, James referred the "common core" of mysticism to the "subconscious." Mystics' conscious experiences were highly variable because their overbeliefs were integrated within "the mystical feeling of enlargement, union, and emancipation" (pp. 316–17).

The older psychologists of religion fostered a debate between the uncommunicating positions of medical psychiatry and academic theology. James wrote in explicit refutation of the hysteria theory of mysticism, while George Albert Coe (1916), James Bissett Pratt (1921), Robert H. Thouless (1924), and J. Cyril Flower (1927) allowed that mysticism and hysteria sometimes overlapped. The psychological consensus arose in response to theologians' emphasis of a neglected fact. Many Catholic mystics had actively engaged in detailed and protracted practices of meditation, in whose consequence they had experienced progressively increasing oblivion to both the perceptible world and the interior life of the mind. At the height of their meditations, the mystics passively experienced contemplations that subjectively seemed to "infuse" consciousness in spontaneous and involuntary fashions. The psychologists translated these findings into the language of their own discipline. They concluded that although mystical union is sometimes a spontaneous symptom of psychopathology (Boisen, 1936; Lowe & Braaten, 1966; Bradford, 1984), it is not necessarily pathological, because its occurrence can also be induced through meditation. Meditation was recognized as a religious form of autosuggestion. Mystics' psychic state was identified as self-hypnosis, and passively experienced ("infused") contemplations were comprehended as self-hypnotic automatisms.

An example of the type of experience that the "common core" hypothesis addressed may be observed in the following self-report by Alfred, Lord Tennyson.

> I have never had any revelations through anaesthetics, but a kind of waking trance—this for lack of a better word—I have frequently had, quite up from boyhood, when I have been all alone. This has come upon me, as it were out of the intensity of the consciousness of individuality, individuality itself seemed to dissolve and fade away into boundless being, and this not a confused state but the clearest, the surest of the surest, utterly beyond words—where death was an almost laughable impossibility—the loss of personality (if so it were) seeming no

extinction, but the only true life. I am ashamed of my feeble description. Have I not said the state is utterly beyond words? (as cited by James, 1902, p. 295, n. 3).

Tennyson induced his experience through monotonous, repetitive meditation—a classic technique for the induction of both hypnotic trances and mystical experiences. During his experience, consciousness of both external reality and personal identity disappeared. What remained was a sense of "boundless being." It was an experience of existing, an experience not that "I am," but simply of "am." All else was forgotten.

The Phenomenological Approach

The rise of the phenomenological school of the history of religions (*Religionswissenschaft*) ruled out of court all references to the unconscious and returned academic research to the status quo ante James. Serious attention was accorded, however, to the varieties of mystical experiences.

Friedrich Heiler (1932) understood mysticism as an introvertive experience during which the body is fixed in "cataleptic rigidity and complete anaesthesia" (p. 140). There is "a perfect cessation of the normal conscious life" (p. 139). Neither the world of external sense perception, nor the mystic's "human personality" are experienced. The soul is wholly "absorbed in the infinite unity of the Godhead" or, in Buddhism, nirvana (p. 136). Heiler distinguished between two major types of mysticism on the criterion of the absence or presence of emotional content during the experiences.

> Ecstasy is the highest pitch of emotion. Although the suppression of the normal emotional life is its presupposition . . . it shares with the normal emotional experience the element of spontaneity, passivity, involuntariness, impersonality, brevity, and lasting effect. . . . Nirvana, on the contrary, is complete disappearance of emotion, a continuous, permanent state of profound quiet and perfect solitariness, a blessedness without excitement, transport, or storm, not a being possessed, but a being utterly self-absorbed (p. 140).

As an illustration of what Heiler meant by "nirvana," let us consider a self-report by Agehananda Bharati (1976), a Viennese-born social anthropologist and a Hindu tantric monk.

> One night when I was about twelve, it happened for the first time. I was falling asleep, when the whole world turned into one: one entity, one indivisible certainty. No euphoria, no colors, just a deadeningly sure oneness of which I was the center—and everything else was just this, and nothing else. For a fraction of a minute, perhaps, I saw nothing, felt nothing, but was that oneness, empty

of content and feeling. Then, for another five minutes or so the wall with the *kitschy* flowers reappeared, and the fire crackled in the large brick stove. But I knew it was One, and I knew that this was the meaning of what I had been reading for a year or so—the Upanisadic dictum of oneness, and the literature around and about it. I did not think in terms of God, *atman*, *brahman*, nor, strangely enough, in terms of having found fulfillment—I was just struck by the fact that I had not known this oneness before, and that I had kept reading about it very much as I read about Gaul being divided into three parts, or elementary Sanskrit grammar. Then after some time, no longer than half an hour I would think, things returned to whatever had been normal before (p. 39).

Although he appears to have stated that he felt an ultimate oneness or unity at the climax of his experience, Bharati (personal communication, 1986) denied that his published self-report is so to be understood. The climactic moments of his "zero experience" consisted of a conscious state that was entirely lacking in cognitive contents. His published account asserts that the moments of zero experience were "oneness" and "One," not because they were so experienced, but because Bharati so understood their significance. His understanding arose immediately after the moments of zero experience, during the waning phases of the experience, when he resumed cognitive thinking and external sense perception.

Bharati (1976, pp. 40–41) also had a second zero experience in which euphoria was present. It was Heiler's contention that the difference is significant. A conscious state that lacks both cognitions and affects is not the same experience as a conscious state that lacks cognitions but involves euphoria. As an example of the purely affective experience that Heiler meant by "Ecstasy," let us consider a self-report by the German Dominican, the Blessed Henry Suso (d. 1366).

He went into an ecstasy and saw and heard what is ineffable. It was without form or shape, and yet it bore within itself all forms and shapes of joyous delight. His heart was hungry and yet satisfied, his mind joyous and happy, his wishes were calmed and his desires had died out. He did nothing but gaze into the brilliant light, in which he had forgotten himself and all things. He did not know whether it was day or night. It was a sweetness flowing out of eternal life, with present, unchanging peaceful feeling. He said then: "If this is not heaven, I do not know what heaven is, for all the suffering that can ever be put into words, could not enable anyone to earn such a reward and for ever possess it." This blissful ecstasy lasted perhaps an hour, perhaps only half an hour; whether his soul remained in his body, or was separated from his body, he did not know. When he came to himself he felt just like a man who has come from another world (1952, pp. 19–20).

During its climactic phase, Suso's experience lacked all cognitions, but had an intensely positive affect. Cognitive thought resumed before the experience ended.

Rudolf Otto (1950), to whom a Buddhist monk had described Nirvana as an experience of "bliss—unspeakable" (p. 39), treated both of Heiler's categories together as "the Inward Way" or as "Mysticism of Introspection." He contrasted introspective mystical experiences with "the Outward Way" whose "unifying Vision" apprehends the perceptible world (1932a, pp. 57–88). The following self-report from James's (1902) collection is an instance of Otto's "Outward Way."

> I felt myself one with the grass, the trees, birds, insects, everything in Nature. I exulted in the mere fact of existence, of being a part of it all—the drizzling rain, the shadows of the clouds, the tree-trunks, and so on (p. 310, n. 12).

The waning phase of Bharati's experience, when he saw the phenomenal world in all its multiplicity but understood it to be One, is a further example of the "Outward Way."

W. T. Stace (1960) proposed the terms *introvertive* and *extrovertive* mysticism, respectively, for Otto's two categories. He explained that "the introvertive [experience] looks inward into the mind . . . from which all the multiplicity of sensuous or conceptual or other empirical content has been excluded," while "the extrovertive experience looks outward through the senses" (pp. 61, 110).

As varieties of introspective mysticism, Scholem (1971) distinguished mystical union and communion. Abraham Joshua Heschel (1962, II, pp. 99–104) expressed the same distinction by contrasting *unio mystica* with *unio sympathetica* (see also: Corbin, 1969). Johannes Lindblom (1962) rephrased the distinction by contrasting the impersonal and personal character of the two experiences. The goal of "*mysticism of unity* or *impersonal mysticism* . . . is complete oneness with the divine conceived of as a more or less impersonal substance." In personal mysticism, however, "the personality is preserved, both the personality of the divine and the personality of the religious man" (p. 302). What is at stake in Lindblom's formulation is personality, not personhood. Mysticism is not personal simply because the divine is conceived theologically as a personal being. Martin Buber (1958) observed that our experience of another person in the second person as a "Thou" differs from an experience of the same person in the third person. The failure to be engaged with another person's personality denies much of his or her personhood, reducing "Him" or "Her" to an "It." The converse is also true. Through their treatment in the second person, inanimate phenomena can be accorded personality, personalized, or personified. So understood, mysticism is personal whenever it involves both an "I" and a "Thou," but impersonal whenever an "I-It" relationship occurs.

The following self-report is an instance of personal mysticism.

> I was reading the words telling of the ever-present and all-pervading quality of Brahman, when suddenly my whole being was seized by an acute state of awareness, and immediately the words assumed a great significance. I knew somehow that they were true, that Brahman (at the time I suppose I translated it as God) *was* all about me, and through me, and in me. The knowledge did

not come from without, unmistakably it came from within. The state was one of extraordinary joy; I realised happiness was within me. (I believe I also felt that I controlled great power, so that I could have stopped the train just by willing it, but in writing of this afterwards as I do, I cannot be certain of this.) I can remember looking out at the countryside passing by, and everything, the trees, meadows and hedges, were all part of me, and I of them, and all were in a great unity through which was God. Everything was a whole.

The experience lasted a few minutes, and very gradually it ebbed away. But I *knew* with completely unshakable conviction that I had been in touch with Reality in those few minutes (Johnson, 1959, p. 24).

The sense of being united with all physical reality, which as a whole was united with God by being within God, preserved the distinction between self and God, even at the moments of most profound unity.

In some experiences of personal mysticism, the personalities not only remain distinct, but engage in interpersonal communications. F. C. Happold (1970) reported:

If I say that Christ came to me I should be using conventional words which would carry no precise meaning; for Christ comes to men and women in different ways. . . . There was . . . no sensible vision. There was just the room, with its shabby furniture and the fire burning in the grate and the red-shaded lamp on the table. But the room was filled by a Presence, which in a strange way was both about me and within me, like light or warmth. I was overwhelmingly possessed by Someone who was not myself, and yet I felt I was more myself than I had ever been before. I was filled with an intense happiness, and almost unbearable joy, such as I had never known before and have never known since. And over all was a deep sense of peace and security and certainty. . . .

The other experience of which I must tell, happened a little later in the same room. I have always thought of it as a continuation and completion of that I have described; it "felt" the same. This time, however, it seemed that a voice was speaking to me. It was not sensibly audible; it spoke within me. The words were strange: "Those who sought the city found the wood: and those who sought the wood found the city." Put into cold print they sound nonsensical. Yet I felt vividly that they meant something very important, that they were the key to a secret (pp. 133–34).

Personal mysticism may also occur as a vision in which unitive ideas are manifested in vivid pictorial forms. The Indian Sadhu Sundar Singh, who converted from Hinduism to Christianity in 1904, generalized about several such visions.

Christ on His throne is always in the centre, a figure ineffable and indescribable. The face as I see it in Ecstasy, with my spiritual eyes, . . . has scars with blood flowing from them. The scars are not ugly, but glowing and beautiful. He has a beard on His face. The long hair of His head is like gold, like glowing light. His face is like the sun, but its light does not dazzle me. It is a sweet face, always smiling—a loving glorious smile. Christ is not terrifying at all.

And all around the throne of Christ, extending to infinite distances, are multitudes of glorious spiritual Beings. Some of them are saints, some of them angels. . . . When they speak to me they put their thoughts into my heart in a single moment; just as on earth one sometimes knows what a person is going to say before he says it. . . .

In these visions we have most wonderful talks. . . .

Any one who has been there [in Heaven] for one second says to himself, "This is the place on which I have set my heart, here I am completely satisfied. No sorrow, no pain, only love, waves of love, perfect happiness. . . .

Streaming out from Christ I saw, as it were, waves shining and peace-giving, and going through and among the Saints and Angels and everywhere bringing refreshment, just as in hot weather water refreshes trees. And this I understood to be the Holy Spirit (Streeter & Appasamy, 1922, pp. 117–18, 120, 55).

In unitive visions of this type, the identities of the mystic and God remain distinct. Union proceeds through a bond of love, emanating from God, which thoroughly permeates the mystic.

Although the typological observations of phenomenologists were empirical and valid, they were rarely treated as a reason to acknowledge the historical diversity of mystical experiences. The complexity of the historical evidence was seen as a reason to adjust the common core hypothesis. It was not treated as a reason to abandon it. Perhaps because most scholars disbelieved that any experience could lack both cognitions and affects, they ignored the difference between zero and purely affective experiences, lumped their literary evidence together, and identified the resultant scholarly category as "the mystical experience" (Stace, 1960, p. 110; Bharati, 1976, pp. 32–61; Smart 1968, p. 42; 1983). The maneuver, which shifted the common core hypothesis from a Hindu standard of ultimate Selfhood to a Buddhist standard of ultimate nothingness, had a superficial plausibility. Mystical experiences had everywhere to be one and the same because, it was reasoned, complete absences of cognition cannot differ from experience to experience.

The Current Debate

Few scholars appreciated the irony that defining the *mystical experience* as an experience devoid of cognitions made the term mutually exclusive with unitive experiences, which involve cognitions of union. The common core hypothesis retained general subscription until Aldous Huxley (1954, 1956) claimed psychedelic experiences to be mystical. Although most writers on the topic agreed with Huxley, several theological writers responded prejudicially by abandoning the ecumenicism that had informed the common core hypothesis. Religious intolerance has since played an important role in shaping academic discussions of mysticism.

The current debate takes its point of departure from R. C. Zaehner's (1957, 1970, 1972) claim that differences among mystics' doctrines reflect actual differences in the phenomenologies of their experiences. Scholars had previously treated mystical experiences and religious doctrines as independent variables, with single types of experience accommodating several doctrinal interpretations, and vice versa. Zaehner's (1957) first category encompassed mystical experiences of the unity of external physical reality. Not content to characterize the experiences as extrovertive, Zaehner specified that "nature mysticism" in which "all creaturely existence is experienced as one and one as all" is a "pan-en-hen-ism," meaning "all-in-one-ism." It has no theistic content, is improperly termed *pantheism*, cannot constitute mystical union, but does account for psychedelic experiences (pp. 28, 168). Zaehner next distinguished as "monism" all experiences of "the soul contemplating itself in its essence." Monistic mystical experiences involve a "state of pure isolation of . . . the uncreated soul or spirit from all that is other than itself." These experiences of "detachment . . . from all purely physical and psychic, and . . . temporal elements" contain no theistic element (pp. 128, 168, 29). Theistic mystical experiences, by contrast, entail "the simultaneous loss of the purely human personality, the 'ego,' and the absorption of the uncreate spirit, the 'self,' into the essence of God, in Whom both the individual personality and the whole objective world are or seem to be entirely obliterated." In theistic mysticism, "the soul feels itself to be united with God in love." Zaehner reserved the term *unio mystica*, "mystical union," to theistic mystical experiences, for they alone entail "the return of the 'self' to God" (pp. 29, 168).

Zaehner's methodology, to invent psychological categories on the basis of doctrinal evidence, led him to err on all three counts. Extrovertive mysticism can indeed be theistic, as in the following self-report from the eighteenth century. Thomas Oliver (1779) had been asked at a meeting to join the society of Methodists and had been delighted to accept the invitation. The following experience occurred to him as he was walking home.

> A ray of light, resembling the shining of a star, descended through a small opening in the heavens, and instantaneously shone upon me. In that instance, my burden fell off, and I was so elevated, that I felt as if I could literally fly away to heaven. . . . I truly lived by faith. I saw God in everything: the heavens, the earth, and all therein, showed me something of him; yea, even from a drop of water, a blade of grass, or a grain of sand, I often received instruction (pp. 86–87).

Oliver perceived the perceptible environment but simultaneously enjoyed a faith that disclosed something of God in everything that he beheld.

The following self-report of extrovertive mysticism was offered by a contemporary Roman Catholic priest. The experience occurred while he was engaged in missionary work in Africa, "helping a medical team deal with a sudden epidemic that involved risking their lives to get people onto boats and down a dangerously swollen river" (Needleman, 1980, p. 70).

> I remember a broken-down boat—it would have been risky floating it in a swimming pool—charging down that river, people screaming and weeping; the crew—meaning myself and three other priests whose knowledge of how to handle a boat added up to half of nothing—managing somehow to pilot it to the neighboring village where the people not yet infected could be taken care of. We did that a dozen or so times within a forty-eight hour span, carrying the boat back on our shoulders through the jungle each time.

> Toward the end of the second night, there was a moment just before dawn when the river was quiet and the people were all quiet. Suddenly, everything in myself became still, including my body, which had been in agony from stress and exhaustion. I felt the presence of God. The smells of the jungle and the river, the night sounds, the sensation of heat in the air—everything seemed part of the Oneness of God. Everything was motionless in eternity. All the things I had been afraid of—the sickness, the danger of drowning, of failing; all my personal revulsions and resentments—and there were plenty of them—everything appeared before me also as part of God. I felt an overwhelming gratitude toward God that He had given me this work to do. I prayed in a way that I had never before prayed; I knew it was the Son praying to the Father through myself (pp. 70–71).

The perceptible world was united in God. "Everything seemed part of the Oneness of God." Fears, revulsions, and resentments were reconciled within the divine unity and replaced with "an overwhelming gratitude."

These examples of unitive experiences that were simultaneously theistic and extrovertive establish that Zaehner was mistaken to claim that extrovertive and theistic mysticism are mutually exclusive. His category of "monistic" mysticism was no less misinformed. The category is fairly applied to experiences of "boundless being." However, Ninian Smart (1965) rightly criticized Zaehner for treating both Hindu and Buddhist doctrines as "monistic" when the differences between the two are as great as those between "monistic" and "theistic" doctrines (pp. 75–87). Hindu doctrines can accommodate a variety of experiences, for instance, those of Tennyson, Bharati, and Suso. Buddhism is more restrictive and has historically debated whether nirvana is void of both cognitions and affects, or cognitions alone (compare: Conze, 1962).

As for "theistic" mysticism, Zaehner's methodology did not do justice to the complexity and subtlety of the mystics' accounts. A more convincing analysis of impersonal theistic mysticism was established by Ernst Arbman in a magisterial study of religious trance that is unfortunately marred by an extremely difficult English translation.

Arbman (1968) emphasized that mystical union has a gradual onset. The experience may commence quite early in the path to contemplation, while the mystic is still able to perceive external reality. It invariably climaxes in a deep trance, when both external perception of the sensible world and internal perception of the mind have been inhibited (p. 339). The process commences with the mystic experiencing a faint sense of the invisible presence of God. As the experience progresses, the divine presence becomes increasingly intense and compelling, until, at climax, it is the exclusive content of consciousness (pp. 310, 334). Concurrent with this intellectual and, to some extent, kinesthetic dimension to mystical union is its emotional side. Both the mystic's emotional devotion to God and God's love for the mystic increase until, at climax, God's love alone is experienced (p. 319). A self-report by Mechthild of Magdeburg (1210–97) will illustrate.

> My body is in long torment, my soul in high delight, for she has seen and embraced her Beloved. Through Him, alas for her! she suffers torment. As He draws her to Himself, she gives herself to Him. She cannot hold back and so He takes her to Himself. Gladly would she speak but dares not. She is engulfed in the glorious Trinity in high union. He gives her a brief respite that she may long for Him. She would fain sing His praises but cannot. She would that He might send her to Hell, if only He might be loved above all measure by all creatures. She looks at Him and says, "Lord! Give me Thy blessing!" He looks at her and draws her to Him with a greeting the body may not know (1953, p. 9).

Mechthild described an initial phase during which she experienced a process of being attracted to God. She cooperated in this process by remaining passive, giving herself to God, and avoiding speech. An impersonal union followed, but then ceased. During the "respite," she experienced not God's love for her, but her own for God. She was now sufficiently introverted that she was unable to sing. She was able, however, to conceptualize a wish, and then mentally to request God's blessing. Impersonal union then resumed.

The great systematizers of Roman Catholic mysticism developed generalizations which, as generalizations, are necessarily idealizing accounts. They attest, however, to similar transitions from personal to impersonal union, as the experiences proceeded from onset to climax. The following account is by Richard of St. Victor (d. 1173).

> The Beloved is forced to wait a moment and a moment in all of these places. . . .
> He is heard by memory; seen by understanding; kissed warmly by affection; embraced by applause. He is heard by recollection; seen by wonder; kissed warmly by love; embraced by delight. Or if this pleases you better, He is heard

by a showing; seen by contemplation; kissed warmly by devotion; drawn close for the infusion of His sweetness. He is heard by a showing when the whole tumult of those who make noise is quieted down and His voice only is heard as it grows stronger. At last that whole crowd of those who make a disturbance is dispersed and He alone remains with her [the soul] alone and she alone looks at Him alone by contemplation. He is seen by contemplation when on account of the sight of an unexpected vision and wonder at the beauty of it, the soul gradually glows, burns more and more, finally at last catches fire completely until it is thoroughly reformed to true purity and internal beauty . . . she melts completely in desire for Him with a kind of ineffable infusion of divine sweetness and that spirit which clings to the Lord is made one spirit (1979, pp. 285–86).

The differences between the beginning and the climax of mystical union were such that St. Teresa of Avila (1515–82) referred separately to the "Spiritual Betrothal" and the "Spiritual Marriage," respectively.

In the union of the Spiritual Marriage. . . . The Lord appears in the centre of the soul, not through an imaginary, but through an intellectual vision. . . . This instantaneous communication of God to the soul is so great a secret and so sublime a favour, and such delight is felt by the soul, that I do not know with what to compare it. . . . It is impossible to say more than that, as far as one can understand, the soul (I mean the spirit of this soul) is made one with God, Who, being likewise a Spirit, has been pleased to reveal the love that He has for us by showing to certain persons the extent of that love, so that we may praise His greatness. For He has been pleased to unite Himself with His creature in such a way that they have become like two who cannot be separated from one another: even so He will not separate Himself from her.

The Spiritual Betrothal is different: here the two persons are frequently separated, as is the case with union, for, although by union is meant the joining of two things into one, each of the two, as is a matter of common observation, can be separated and remain a thing by itself. This favour of the Lord passes quickly and afterwards the soul is deprived of that companionship—I mean so far as it can understand. In this other favour of the Lord it is not so: the soul remains all the time in that centre with its God (1946, II, pp. 334–35).

Teresa's Spiritual Betrothal was a personal mysticism that had intermittent moments of impersonal union. The Spiritual Marriage was a sustained impersonal experience.

The climactic moments of mystical union consist of a loss, not of consciousness, but of self-consciousness. It is this process that mystics have described, metaphorically, as death or annihilation (Arbman, 1968, pp. 371–73). As in a dream, or when absorbed in a book or a drama, the idea that one is having an experience is forgotten, and the whole of conscious attention is devoted to the experience itself. In mystical union, the experience happens to be the presence of God (1968, pp. 384–85, 390–92). Coinciding with the absorption of attention by the experience, so I suggest, is an identification with its contents. Just as, in a dream, one may observe one's image and feel it to be the locus of one's consciousness and self, so too, in mystical union, there is both an external observation of an experience and an identification with its content. Because the content happens to be the presence of God, the mystic feels at one with God.

Arbman emphasized that the union is invariably experienced as the mystic's own deification (Arbman, 1968, pp. 359–62, 370). St. John of the Cross referred explicitly to the soul's deification through experiences of mystical union (Butler, 1922, p. 151). St. John of the Cross (1973) wrote:

> They are indeed encounters, by which He ever penetrates and deifies the substance of the soul, absorbing it above all being into His own being (p. 594).

As further instances, Arbman cited *Sister Katrei*, Angela of Foligno, Madame Guyon, and Janet's patient Madeleine (Arbman, 1968, pp. 357–59). The evidence may readily be augmented. The Greek Fathers of Christianity conventionally spoke of the mystic's "divinization" (Bouyer, 1963, pp. 417–21). Symeon the New Theologian claimed that "by grace I am God." St. Catherine of Genoa spoke of being "changed completely into pure God." Maria Maddalena de'Pazzi saw herself "wholly united with God, transformed into God." Antoinette Bourguignon wrote that "the purified soul transforms itself into him" (Buber, 1985, pp. 41, 109, 110, 121). The "Brethren of the Free Spirit" of the fourteenth century, were said to have laid claim to deification through mystical union (Lerner, 1972, pp. 16, 18, 126, 144, 240, 241). Again, the Kabbalah and Hasidism speak literally and not euphemistically of the mystic's "divine soul." *Yehidah*, "union" or "unification," is considered an experience of the mere "comprehension" of the then self-evident fact (Dobh Baer, 1963, pp. 62–64, 94–97, 128, 130, 135–39).

The monotheistic religions have regularly interpreted the mystical experience of deification as falling short of identity with God. Christian mystics have spoken of "divinization by grace" and denied the reality of "divinization by nature." Kabbalists accept an identity of the soul with the *Sefirot*, the emanations of the divine within the creation, while categorically rejecting the possibility of an identity with the *En Sof*, the uncreated Godhead. It is important to emphasize, however, that mystics experience very little of a cognitive character during the moments of union. There is an unelaborated intuitive idea of deification, but sustained reasoning or discursive reflection forms no part of the experiential moment. St. Teresa (1946) explained that "the soul is wholly in the power of another, and during that period, which is very short, I do not think that the Lord leaves it freedom for anything" (I, p. 158). For this reason, the Sufi mystics of Islam distinguish between the soul's intoxication during union and its subsequent reassertion of sobriety. Catholic mystics speak of the soul's death during union and its rebirth upon God's withdrawal, and so forth (Arbman 1968, pp. 133–44, 371–73). It is only after the moments of deifying union, during the waning phase of the ecstasies, that measured intellectual observations become possible and theological interpretations begin to consider the sense in which deification took place.

For present purposes, it is not the claimants of mystical deification, but the apologists who most command attention. In polemic against the Free Spirit movement, Suso (1953) argued that because the self is experienced both before and after union, it cannot be destroyed, but must instead persist during the experience of Nothing (p. 184). The subjective experience and its objective reality consequently differ. "The powerful transport into the Nothing casts out all difference in the ground, not according to our essence, but according to our perception" (p. 192). Although the soul does not perceive itself, it is nonetheless present, as is proved by its capacity to perceive the experience. "Man can, in some measure, if he is rapt into God, be one in losing himself, and yet externally be enjoying, contemplating, and so on" (p. 194). For Nothing to be experienced, there must be a soul, an observing self, which experiences the Nothing.

Suso (1953) further denied that "the creative Nothing that is called God" (p. 192) is the same Nothing that the soul experiences in mystical union.

> A man may in this life reach the point at which he understands himself to be one with that which is nothing as compared with all the things that one can imagine or express in words. By common agreement, men call this Nothing "God," and it is itself a most essential Something. . . . But there is something more deeply hidden in Him. . . . As long as one understands thereby a unity, or such a thing as can be explained by words, one has to go farther inwards. The Nothing, however, cannot penetrate deeper into itself, but we can, as far as our understanding allows (pp. 191–92)

The soul may experience Nothing, but this Nothing is necessarily an essential Something. Hidden within it is what alone truly cannot be described in words: the hidden Godhead. Union with the essential Nothing is possible in this life, but union with the hidden and utterly Indescribable is not (Suso, 1953, pp. 195–96). During its absorption in the Nothing, the soul fails, however, to appreciate the distinction.

> The soul always remains a creature, but in the Nothing in which it is lost, it does not consider at all in what way it is then a creature, or what the Nothing is, or whether it is a creature or not, or whether it is united or not. But when one is able to reflect, one understands this, and it remains in us unimpaired (p. 194).

In addition to his extended discussion of impersonal mysticism, Suso also remarked briefly on personal mysticism, when self-perception persists.

These men who are rapt into eternity, consider themselves and all things for
ever as everlasting and eternal, because of their surpassing indwelling unity.

Question: Is there no otherness there?

Answer: Yes, he has it more than ever who knows it, and recognizes himself as
a creature, not as sinful, but as united (pp. 193–94).

Suso's account of mystical union was intended to explain experiences of
both impersonal and personal types. Because he had himself experienced purely
affective mysticism, he was not prepared to deny the actual phenomenon of impersonal mystical experiences, but he was adamant in rejecting its apparent
philosophical significance.

The Sufi mystics of Islam have similarly gone to the trouble of denying the
reality of mystical deification. The following passage is from Al-Ghazali (d. 1111),
the philosopher and mystic who first secured the public respectability of Sufism.

The mystics, after their ascent to the heavens of Reality, agree that they saw
nothing in existence except God the One. Some of them attained this state
through discursive reasoning, others reached it by savouring it and experiencing it. From these all plurality entirely fell away. They were drowned in pure
solitude: their reason was lost in it, and they became as if dazed in it. They no
longer had the capacity to recollect aught but God, nor could they in any wise
remember themselves. Nothing was left to them but God. They became drunk
with a drunkenness in which their reason collapsed. One of them said, "I am
God (the Truth)." Another said, "Glory be to me! How great is my glory",
while another said, "Within my robe is naught but God." But the words of
lovers when in a state of drunkenness must be hidden away and not broadcast.
However, when their drunkenness abates and the sovereignty of their reason is
restored,—and reason is God's scale on earth,—they know that this was not actual identity, but that it resembled identity as when lovers say at the height of
their passion:

"I am he whom I desire and he whom I desire is I;

We are two souls inhabiting one body" (as cited by Zaehner, 1957, pp. 157–58).

The testimony of Martin Buber (1965) provides further and unequivocal
evidence of the experience of deification.

Now from my own unforgettable experience I know well that there is a state
in which the bonds of the personal nature of life seem to have fallen away
from us and we experience an undivided unity. But I do not know—what the
soul willingly imagines and indeed is bound to imagine (mine too once did
it)—that in this I had attained to a union with the primal being or the god-

head. That is an exaggeration no longer permitted to the responsible understanding. Responsibly—that is, as a man holding his ground before reality—I
can elicit from those experiences only that in them I reached an undifferen-
tiable unity of myself without form or content. I may call this an original pre-
biographical unity and suppose that it is hidden unchanged beneath all
biographical change, all development of the soul . . . existing but once, single,
unique, irreducible, this creaturely one: one of the human souls and not the
"soul of the All"; a defined and particular being and not "Being"; the creaturely basic unity of a creature (p. 24).

The very fact that Catholic, Sufi, and Jewish mystics have apologized for
experiences that they did not wish to experience, indicates that the experiences
were real. Deification is not an overestimation but the actual phenomenon or
experience of impersonal theistic unions. Indeed, it cannot be otherwise. Impersonal theistic mysticism is invariably a conjunction of the senses of self and
God. The experience commences as an interpersonal encounter, but God ceases
to be felt as a distinct "Thou" when, at climax, one's normal or realistic sense of
oneself is replaced by an ideal self who is seemingly God.

Arbman (1968) further established that any or all of three subsidiary features
of unitive experiences may coincide with the climactic moments of deifying
union: an emotional experience of intense love (pp. 373–75), a visual experience
of brightness or light (p. 376), and an intellectual experience of ideas that seem
to the mystic to be thoughts of God that have now become his or her own (p.
377). These ideas, which may have either verbal form or nonverbal form, impart
an extensive cognitive content to the total experience, but should not be confused with the extremely limited cognitive contents of the actual moments of
union. St. Teresa (1946) stated that "we never . . . hear these words at a time
when the soul is in union . . . when this short period has passed, and the soul is
still enraptured. . . . Divine locutions" (I, p. 158). The ideas, which are highly
variable in content, may pertain to any topic of religious or theological interest.
Arbman emphasized that they frequently have moral content. St. Teresa wrote:
"They make us tremble if they are words of reproof and if they are words of love
fill us with a love that is all consuming" (ibid.).

Mystics who have written of the union of wills with God refer to their acceptance of moral values. Their own wills become one with, because subservient
to, the will of God. "Rebirth" and "passive transformation" are metaphors for
this moral regeneration (Arbman, 1968, pp. 372–73). This union of wills occurs
after the climactic moments of deification, during the waning, cognitively rich
phase of the total experience. Angela of Foligno (1966) stated:

When the soul is transformed in God and is in God, and hath that perfect
union and fulness of vision, it is quiet and worketh nothing whatsoever. But

when it cometh again to itself it striveth to transform itself into the will of God (p. 129).

Arbman emphasized that at no time during mystical experiences does the mystic's ego disappear. The conscious idea of self is forgotten, but the subjective experience of being an observer—the basic core of self—persists throughout. Nor is its experience vague or amorphous. Union is vivid, coherent, and completely memorable. It has been claimed to be vague and amorphous, but only by writers who have vague and amorphous understandings of the experience (Arbman, 1968, pp. 381–84).

Impersonal theistic union may also occur in the pictorial form of a vision. The following self-report is by Hadewijch (1980), a Flemish Beguine of the thirteenth century.

> The eagle, who had previously spoken to me, said: "Now see through the Countenance, and become the veritable bride of the great Bridegroom, and behold yourself in this state!" And in that very instant I saw myself received in union by the One who sat there in the abyss upon the circling disk, and there I became one with him in the certainty of unity. Then the eagle said, when I was received: "Now, behold, all-powerful one, whom I previously called the loved one, that you did not know all you should become, and what your highest way was, and what the great kingdom was that you as a bride should receive from your Bridegroom" (p. 296).

In the following self-report, Angela of Foligno (1966) described a vision of the same impersonal unitive type.

> Upon another occasion, as I was gazing at the Cross with the Crucified, and was looking at the Crucified with my bodily eyes, such a fervent love was suddenly kindled in my soul that even the members of my body felt it with great joy and delight. I saw and felt that Christ embraced my soul with the arm wherewith He was crucified, wherefore I rejoiced with a joy greater than I had ever had before.
>
> From this time forth there hath remained unto me a certain joy and clear enlightenment, whereby the soul knoweth and understandeth how it is that we see our flesh made one company with God (pp. 220–21).

Experiences of this type consist of a vivid vision that commences with the mystic beholding both himself or herself and God as discrete personal beings. As the vision proceeds, however, the two figures merge into one. What begins as personal mysticism thus ends as an impersonal union. God's personality abides but, in seemingly becoming an addition to the mystic's personality, ceases to be experienced in a personal manner as a "Thou."

Patanjali's Experiential Alternatives

Because Zaehner linked the psychological analysis of mystical union to the philosophical problem of mystics' truth claims, he sparked a heated debate among philosophers and theologians. The common core hypothesis had assumed that conflicting theological claims regarding mystical experiences had to be reconciled with one and the same experience. Zaehner instead suggested that there were several different types of mystical experiences. Each supported a different religious doctrine that was consistent with its own category of experience. Panenhenic and monistic mysticism differed both as experiences and as doctrines from the theistic mysticism that Zaehner privileged.

The ensuing debate did not proceed, as I have done, by citing empirical data in order to refute Zaehner. Rather, it addressed methodological innovation at a theoretical level. In the process, methodological issues were brought to the fore. Smart (1965) sought to invalidate Zaehner's conclusions by emphasizing that mystical experiences differ from the interpretations that mystics place on them, both during and after their occurrence. H. P. Owen (1971) added that the mystics' beliefs, practices, and expectations contribute interpretive content to the experiences themselves. James (1902) had made these points long before.

Once scholars began to distinguish between mystical experiences and their interpretations, it became possible to make sense of historical teachings in which mystics themselves discussed the issues at stake. Consider, for example, the *Yoga Aphorisms* of Patanjali. Its classical formulations of Hindu Yoga have been much discussed; but because they were seen through the lens of the common core hypothesis, the teachings could not be accurately understood. Patanjali based his practice of Yoga on the three elements of *dharana, dhyana,* and *samadhi.*

> Dharana Is The Mind's (Chitta's) Fixation On A Particular Point In Space.

> In That (Dharana) The Continuous Flow Of Similar Mental Modifications Is Called Dhyana Or Meditation.

> When The Object of Meditation Only Shines Forth In The Mind, As Though Devoid Of The Thought Of Even The Self (Who Is Meditating), That State Is Called Samadhi Or Concentration (Sutra III, 1–3; Aranya, 1981, pp. 249, 251, 252).

Dharana, "fixation," refers to the focusing of attention on an object, to the exclusion of other mentation. *Dhyana,* "meditation," refers to the subsequent maintenance of attention that is focused exclusively on the object. *Samadhi,* "concentration" or "absorption," refers to a loss of the sense of self, which causes the object of attention to occupy the place of self in the experience of the yogin. *Samadhi* is a term for the experiences that Western scholars have described as introspective unions. Patanjali characterized *samadhi* as a state of object-consciousness, to the exclusion of self-awareness, because he recognized that its further features are highly variable.

Patanjali stated that a yogin may achieve concentration in either of two manners: directly through personal action, or with the benefit of devotion to a transcendent deity named Isvara.

> Yogins With Intense Ardour Achieve Concentration And The Result Thereof Quickly.

> From Special Devotion To Isvara Also (Concentration Becomes Imminent).

> Isvara Is A Particular Purusa Unaffected By Affliction, Deed, Result Of Action Or The Latent Impressions Thereof (Sutra I, 21, 23–24; pp. 54, 56, 57).

A voluntaristic approach to Yoga, involving personal initiatives alone, is an effective alternative to a devotional approach that seeks the intervention of Isvara. Both types of meditation lead successfully to mystical experiences. Patanjali consequently asserted the functional equivalence of self and God in the performance of meditation.

Like the inductive meditations, the objects of *samadhi* are variable. A yogin has mastered the practice of *samadhi* when he is able to achieve object-consciousness of anything that he chooses. "When The Mind Develops The Power Of Stabilising On The Smallest Size As Well As On The Greatest One, Then The Mind Comes Under Control" (Sutra I, 40; p. 87).

Regardless of what a yogin chooses as the object of meditation, union is achieved with it.

> When The Fluctuations Of The Mind Are Weakened The Mind Appears To Take On The Features Of The Object Of Meditation—Whether It Be The Cogniser (Grahita), The Instrument Of Cognition (Grahana) Or The Object Cognised (Grahya)—As Does A Transparent Jewel, And This Identification Is Called Samapatti Or Engrossment (Sutra I, 41; p. 89).

Once again, Patanjali outlined practices by which yogins might experientially verify classical Hindu doctrines. When meditations on object after object consistently result in experiences in which the object comes to be experienced as timeless, infinite being, each object is revealed as an aspect of timeless, infinite being. For the yogin, discovery of unity behind plurality calls into question the nature of diversity, and the Hindu doctrine of maya, "illusion," is confirmed.

Among all possible unitive experiences, Patanjali distinguished *samadhi* in which verbal thoughts about the object persist, and *samadhi* that is limited to the object alone. In both cases, the objects of *samadhi* may be either gross or subtle.

> The Engrossment, In Which There Is The Mixture Of Word, Its Meaning (i.e.,
> The Object) And Its Knowledge, Is Known As Savitarka Samapatti.
>
> When The Memory Is Purified, The Mind Appears To Be Devoid Of Its Own
> Nature (i.e., Of Reflective Consciousness) And Only the Object (On Which It
> is Contemplating) Remains Illuminated. This Kind of Engrossment Is Called
> Nirvitarka Samapatti.
>
> By This (Foregoing) The Savichara and Nirvichara Engrossments Whose Ob-
> jects Are Subtle Are Also Explained (Sutra I, 42–44; pp. 92, 94, 98).

Patanjali stated that the experience of Nirvichara Samadhi culminates in
the Unmanifested: "Subtlety Pertaining To Objects Culminates In A-Linga Or
The Unmanifested" (Sutra I, 45; p. 102). Repeated experience of *samadhi* in and
through all manner of different things verified the doctrine of maya. It also
pointed beyond the manifest maya to an underlying or transcendent constant.
The Unmanifested did not become manifest. Rather, the culmination consisted
of the intellectual realization that there was a logical need to postulate a Latent
or Unmanifested. The latter remained latent and unmanifest.

Scholars working with the common core hypothesis have regularly missed
the significance of Patanjali's argument. It is because each and every meditation
may result in a *samadhi* that discloses a different phenomenon as all-being, that
experience of all-being must be recognized as maya. At the same time, explanation of the commonalities of different *samadhis* logically necessitates the postulation of the Unmanifested. If all mystical experiences were one and the same,
there would be no reason to question the experience of all-being nor to entertain the idea of the Unmanifested.

Patanjali regarded the outcome of Nirvichara Samadhi as a point of departure for further attainments. Once an intellectual distinction between the manifest and the Unmanifested had been attained, a yogin was to meditate fixedly on
the concept of the Unmanifested.

> By The Stoppage Of That Too (On Account Of The Elimination of the Latent
> Impressions of Samprajnana) Objectless Concentration Takes Place Through
> Suppression Of All Modifications (Sutra I, 51; p. 110).

Patanjali maintained that meditation regarding the Unmanifested leads to a
samadhi with the Unmanifested, in whose course the Unmanifested paradoxically
becomes manifest. In this teaching, Patanjali took for granted the validity of the
doctrine of maya. Having found that meditation may cause any idea to develop
into a unitive experience, Patanjali did not theorize that meditation on a concept
leads to *samadhi* with the concept rather than with what the concept represents.
A Western solution to the logical problem did not appeal to him. The doctrine of

maya instead calls into question the validity of distinguishing between signifiers and signifieds. Because signifieds, no differently than signifiers, are maya, all signifieds are themselves signifiers. The Unmanifested is no exception.

Finding ontological paradox logically necessary, Patanjali proceeded to explain a corollary.

> The Seer Is Absolute Knower. Although Pure, Modifications (Of Buddhi) Are Witnessed By Him As An Onlooker.

> To Serve As Objective Field To Purusa Is The Essence Or Nature Of The Knowable (Sutra II, 20–21; pp. 179, 185).

When a yogin experiences a *samadhi* in which neither passing thoughts nor modifications persist, the Unmanifested has displaced the yogin's self-awareness and the yogin is able to recognize a fundamental distinction between the knower and the known. That which continues to know, even when there is no thought to be known, is the Unmanifested. Pure Spirit (Purusa), it acts as an Onlooker that witnesses all things. Objects exist in order to function for this Knower as the known.

Interestingly, because different *samadhi* experiences culminate alike in the experience of the one transcendent Spirit, which is God, Patanjali also acknowledged that devotion directly to God is also a sufficient way to proceed.

> From Devotion to God, Samadhi Is Attained (Sutra II, 45; p. 227).

Patanjali implied that the more complicated yogic procedure of going to the trouble of having a great variety of unitive experiences has the virtue of demonstrating the validity of devotion directly to God. What devotion finds intuitively valid, skeptical voluntarism finds logically necessary. By whichever path one proceeds, logical reflection on *samadhi* necessitates the postulation of the Unmanifested. The longer voluntaristic procedure is necessary only in order to know that the shorter devotional practice is sufficient.

The Postulation of the Unconscious

The present consensus regarding the diversity of mystical experiences has been phrased in a manner that is one-sided and categorical. The recognition that religious doctrines contribute content to mystical experiences (James, 1902; Owen, 1971) was developed by Steven Katz (1978) into the general claim that there are no unmediated experiences. No differently than all other experiences, mystical experiences are partly or wholly shaped by the individuals who have them. A consensus has since developed that personal, cultural, and universal factors are interwoven in mystical experiences much as they are in nocturnal dreams (Pike, 1965, pp. 147–48; Garside, 1972, pp. 101–2; Almond, 1982, pp. 162, 173–74). With the arguable exception of moments of "zero" experiences (Almond, 1982, pp. 174–79), mystical experiences invariably contain "incorporated interpretations" that are rooted in the cultures and eras of the mystics. In the final analysis, "there are as many different types of mystical experience as there are incorporated interpretations of them" (p. 128).

Although two generations of historians of religion noted differences among introspective and extrovertive mysticism, personal and impersonal mysticism, experiences of pure affect and experiences of nothing, these phenomenological observations have been neglected by the current debate. Katz (1978) has made bold to assert that there "is no foundation for a phenomenology of mysticism or a typology of comparative mystical experience" (p. 56; compare: Katz, 1982, 1983). He maintains that mystical experiences are infinitely various. They vary not only from individual to individual, but also from occasion to occasion in the lives of single individuals. Katz opposes the subdivision of mysticism into types, categories, or varieties. Responsible discussion may be made of individual mystical experiences, but there can be no valid generalizations concerning either historical traditions or cross-cultural parallels.

For many scholars, myself among them, the emergence of the current consensus has been liberating. Topics that were formerly neglected, because they were not dignified as mystical, have been taken up as worthy subjects of research. Experiences of nothing have been clearly distinguished from unitive experiences and made a topic of historical and philosophical study (Forman, 1990). Historical practices of visions have been documented in Taoism (Kohn, 1991), in rabbinical Judaism and the kabbalah (E. R. Wolfson, 1987, 1994, 1996), and in gnosticism (Merkur, 1993a). At the 1995 congress of the International Association of the History of Religions, Western esotericism was recognized for the first time as a reputable area of scholarly specialization. Arguing from a Western occult perspective, Jess Byron Hollenback (1996) went so far as to define mysticism in terms of visionary experiences.

These gains in the understanding of mysticism have been won, however, at the expense of a considerable neglect of mystical union. Now that mystical union has lost its exclusive claim to the name of mysticism, it has ceased to monopolize the scholarly agenda. Attention has deservedly been devoted to a broader range of religious experiences. Unfortunately, if one expands the category of "mysticism" to encompass much more than unitive experiences, while refusing to subdivide "mysticism" into types or varieties, the topic of unitive experiences has been ruled out of court, and a host of intriguing questions about unitive experiences go unanswered. Granted that unitive experiences do not exhaust the phenomena of mysticism, what are they? Why do they occur? How may they be used and abused? What do they teach us about humanity?

Katz's refusal to countenance typological analyses is, I suggest, the product of a widely shared methodological fallacy. It is a necessary theoretical implication of the phenomenological method that has shaped the academic debate since Heiler. The limitation of phenomenological reasoning was most clearly exemplified by Arbman, who theorized that the belief-complex, or group of beliefs, which forms the content of the meditations prior to a trance, is converted by the trance state from an object of belief to an object of actual experience. Beyond its conversion of beliefs into experience, the alternate state contributes no doctrinal content to the experience. All differences among religious uses of trance states are consequently to be explained by reference to the pre-experiential belief-complex (Arbman, 1963, p. 347).

The flaw in Arbman's theory is its inconsistency with the facts. Were mystics' pre-experiential beliefs the exclusive determinants of their experiences, mystics disbelieving in self-deification would never experience it. They would not need to deny the apparent doctrinal consequences of their experiences. Some mystics have nevertheless experienced deification despite consciously held religious beliefs to the contrary.

An exclusively phenomenological approach is similarly unable to explain the affective content of the unitive experiences self-reported by Sundar Singh.

> When I used to practise Yoga there was no permanent refreshment, though the trance might be temporarily comforting. Indeed the great contrast between the state of Ecstasy and the Yogic states which I cultivated before becoming a Christian lies in the fact that in Ecstasy there is always the same feeling of calm satisfaction and being at home, whatever had been my state of mind before going into Ecstasy. Whereas in the Yogic state, if before the trance I was feeling sad, I used to weep in the trance, if cheerful I would smile. Also after an Ecstasy I always feel strengthened, invigorated, and refreshed. This result did not follow Yoga (Streeter & Appasamy, 1922, pp. 135–36).

The affective contents of Singh's experiences of Yoga varied in keeping with his emotions prior to the alternate state. After he converted to Christianity, however, he experienced a highly positive feeling regardless of his mood prior to the onset of his ecstasies. Singh's ecstatic euphoria may not be traced to his Christian beliefs and expectations. Because his Hindu beliefs did not take precedence over his pre-experiential mood during his Yogic states, we have no warrant to suppose that his Christian beliefs can have done so either.

Again, unitive experiences may be unanticipated and, as it were, adventitious consequences of trance induction. In a series of psychological experiments, Arthur J. Deikman (1963) had his subjects sit in comfortable armchairs, in a well-lit, neutrally painted, and decorated room. Before them was "a blue vase ten inches high, which stood on a simple brown end table against the opposite wall." The subjects were given the following instructions concerning the technique of meditation.

> The purpose of these sessions is to learn about concentration. Your aim is to concentrate on the blue vase. By concentration I do not mean *analyzing* the different parts of the vase, or thinking a series of thoughts about the vase, or associating ideas to the vase, *but rather, trying to see the vase as it exists in itself,* without any connections to other things. Exclude all other thoughts or feelings of sounds or body sensations. Do not let them distract you but *keep them out* so that you can concentrate all your attention, all your awareness on the vase itself. Let the perception of the vase fill your entire mind (p. 330).

The experimental subjects meditated for 5 minutes on the first day, 10 on the second, and 15 on the third session and thereafter. Subjects wishing to prolong the sessions were allowed to do so; the sessions then lasted from 22 to 33 minutes before the subjects terminated them spontaneously (p. 331).

One subject reported impersonal unitive experiences from the first session onward, but was frightened by the loss of her sense of reality.

> One of the points that I remember most vividly is when I really began to feel, you know, almost as though the blue and I were perhaps merging, or that vase and I were. I almost got scared to the point where I found myself bringing myself back in some way from it. . . . It was as though everything was sort of merging and I was somehow losing my sense of consciousness almost (p. 334).

The following is a report concerning the same subject's twenty-first session, when she briefly passed beyond union to a complete lack of cognitions.

> She reported that a diffuse blue occupied the entire visual field and that she felt merged completely with that diffuseness. She had a sense of falling, of emptiness, of loneliness and isolation as if she were in a vacuum. Her sudden realization that there were absolutely no thoughts in her mind made her anxious and she *searched* for thoughts to bring herself back. "It was as if I leaped out of the chair to put the boundaries back on the vase . . . because there was *nothing* there . . . the vase was going and I was going with it. . . ." (p. 337).

In her fifty-fourth session, the subject achieved a more complete union, together with a distinct impression of the presence of a unifying, metaphysical force.

> It was also as though we were together, you know, instead of being a table and a vase and me, my body and the chair, it all dissolved into a bundle of some-

thing which had . . . a great deal of energy to it but which doesn't form into anything but it only feels like a force (Deikman, 1966b, p. 105; compare: Deikman, 1966a, pp. 324–38).

Deikman's subjects were attempting to concentrate on their visual perception of the vase, while excluding all other thoughts from consciousness. The voluntary restrictions induced trance states that converted them into increasingly restricted automatisms. Complete emptiness of consciousness was once experienced directly. Because the meditations did no more than to restrict the normal contents of consciousness, the impersonal unitive experiences cannot be traced to the prior contents of consciousness. The meditation technique produced a psychic emptiness that the unitive materials filled. Their source must be sought elsewhere.

These examples of unwanted self-deification, unprecedented affects, and unanticipated unions amply refute the theory that mystical experiences can be explained by reference to beliefs or ideas that were consciously entertained prior to the experiences. Unitive experiences are not in perfect agreement with pre-experiential beliefs. Unitive experiences exhibit points of resemblance that cannot be explained by a theory that is limited to phenomenology. As Patanjali and William James both recognized, it is logically necessary to attribute some manifest contents of unitive experiences to the Unmanifested.

Patanjali, along with many other traditional mystics, postulated that the Unmanifested is metaphysical. With James, Freud, and many modern mystics, I shall instead assume that the Unmanifested is psychical. My assumption is not meant to preclude the possibility of metaphysical considerations. It is intended only to avoid attributing to grace what may reasonably be attributed to human nature.

Summary

In this chapter, I have reviewed the phenomenology of mystical union or, more precisely, unitive experiences. In the process, I argued with the present consensus against the older view that all mystical experiences are one and the same; but I also argued against the current claim that they are infinitely various. Unitive experiences, so it seems to me, form a distinct subset of mystical experiences. With Patanjali, Suso, Buber, and modern depth psychologists, I also hold that a theoretical explanation of unitive experiences obliges us to move beyond phenomenological methods and to postulate the unconscious.

TWO

Unitive Experiences
and Unitive Thinking

Because unitive experiences are not all one and the same, it becomes important to question whether cross-cultural data that compare with the *unio mystica* of Christianity exhaust the varieties of these experiences. Perhaps the varieties of unitive experiences are more than the varieties of *unio mystica* that were recognized historically by Christianity. The conventional, cross-cultural extension of a culture-bound theological category may be useful for ecumenical purposes, but does it meet the criteria of psychological science? On the evidence of psychedelic experiences, I have elsewhere argued that if unitive experiences are considered as a naturally occurring class of psychological phenomena, there are many more varieties than have been recognized as instances of *unio mystica* (Merkur, 1998a).

In this chapter, I also want to make a further point. Because the explanation of unitive experiences necessitates the postulation of the unconscious, we may infer that unitive thinking both occurs unconsciously and sometimes manifests consciously in the form of an experience. Perhaps it also manifests in other forms as well. This enlargement of our topic from a narrow concern with unitive experiences to a general consideration of unitive thinking brings with it a significant shift in perspective. We cease to be addressing a rare and marginal topic of the psychology of religion. We prove instead to be discussing a central concern of general human psychology.

Consider the following evidence.

Unity and the Self

The Solitary Self

One type of unitive experience discovers unity in the solitude of the self. There may be a sense of timeless, infinite being.

A complete absence of a sense of specific time and place, complete involvement of one's whole being, at the same time a loss of the sense of being yourself (Laski, 1962, p. 389).

The sense of timeless, solitary being may coincide with sense perception of the external world, resulting in an assimilation of the physical environment to the imagined solitude of one's timeless being.

The air was clear and still. I looked up and watched the flight of a big bird, probably a vulture. It glided on the air.

Suddenly I felt totally transfixed. Time simply stopped. Nothing else existed. I was one with the bird and the sky as I sat on the boulder (E. Hoffman, 1992, p. 38).

Donald W. Winnicott (1963) likely was referring to experiences of the solitary self when he suggested that mystical experiences provide access to a hidden core of the personality.

I suggest that in health there is a core to the personality that . . . never communicates with the world of perceived objects, and that the individual person knows that it must never be communicated with or be influenced by external reality. . . . Although healthy persons communicate and enjoy communicating, the other fact is equally true, that *each individuate is an isolate, permanently noncommunicating permanently unknown, in fact unfound.*

In life and living this hard fact is softened by the sharing that belongs to the whole range of cultural experience. At the centre of each person is an incommunicado element, and this is sacred and most worthy of preservation (p. 187).

Winnicott noted that threats to the incommunicado element cause it to be hidden as a secret self, a syndrome that psychoanalysts had noted in a variety of pathologies. "Traumatic experiences that lead to the organization of primitive defences belong to the threat to the isolated core, the threat of its being found, altered, communicated with. The defence consists in a further hiding of the secret self" (ibid.). Implicitly, unitive experiences in which the incommunicado element emerges out of hiding and becomes known to consciousness would be nondefensive, which is to say, healthy.

Incorporation

Another type of unitive experience extends the unity of the self to the perceptible world without denying the finite separateness of perceptible phenomena. The result is an experience of oneself as a cosmic being or, in psychoanalytic terminology, an experience of *incorporating* the cosmos. In both of the following self-reports, as the ecstasy commences, the idea of self expands enormously to include the entire environment.

> The thing happened one summer afternoon, on the school cricket field, while I was sitting on the grass, waiting my turn to bat. I was thinking about nothing in particular, merely enjoying the pleasures of midsummer idleness. Suddenly, and without warning, something invisible seemed to be drawn across the sky, transforming the world about me into a kind of tent of concentrated and significance. What had been merely an outside became an inside. The objective was somehow transformed into a completely subjective fact, which was experienced as "mine," but on a level where the word has no meaning; for "I" was no longer the familiar ego. Nothing more can be said about the experience, it brought no accession of knowledge about anything except, very obscurely, the knower and his way of knowing. After a few minutes there was a "return to normalcy." The event made a deep impression on me at the time; but, because it did not fit into any of the thought patterns—religious, philosophical, scientific—with which, as a boy of fifteen, I was familiar, it came to seem more and more anomalous, more and more irrelevant to "real life," and was finally forgotten (Happold, 1970, p. 130).

> It was as if I had never realized before how lovely the world was. I lay down on my back in the warm, dry moss and listened to a skylark singing as it mounted up from the fields near the sea into the dark clear sky. No other music ever gave me the same pleasure as that passionately joyous singing. It was a kind of leaping, exultant ecstasy, a bright, flame-like sound, rejoicing in itself. And then a curious experience befell me. It was as if everything that had seemed to be external and around me were suddenly within me. The whole world seemed to be within me. It was within me that the trees waved their green branches, it was within me that the skylark was singing, it was within me that the hot sun shone, and that the shade was cool. A cloud rose in the sky, and passed in a light shower that pattered on the leaves, and I felt its freshness dropping into my soul, and I felt in all my being the delicious fragrance of the earth and the grass and the plants and the rich brown soil. I could have sobbed with joy (Reid, 1912, p. 42).

The distinctive ideas of an experience of incorporative union may be described by the formula, "I contain all." Incorporation is well-known to psychoanalysis as an unconscious mental process. Its precise nature has never been established, however, because the concept of a "psychical mechanism" has never been translated out of metaphor into prosaic explanation. For present purposes, it will suffice to treat incorporation as a schema or general pattern for the production of what Freud termed *typical* fantasies. Schemas are ordinarily considered to be "cognitive structures of organized prior knowledge, abstracted from experience with specific instances" (Fiske & Linville, 1980, p. 543). I am suggesting that the mind develops some fantasies into schemas, just as it does with knowledge based on sense perception.

Fantasies of incorporation are ordinarily unconscious. Their exclusion from consciousness is possibly due to a reality-testing process that rejects them as unrealistic, impossible, and absurd.

When a fantasy of incorporation becomes conscious with the intensity and immediacy of a creative inspiration, a unitive experience occurs. By definition, a creative inspiration "is always accompanied by the 'aha' phenomenon, the feeling of sudden fit, the feeling of closure, a mingled sentiment of surprise and gratification, and elation" (Bellak, 1958, p. 374). A creative inspiration seems subjectively to enter a passive consciousness from without (Lee, 1948). It has the character of a completed pattern or logical structure, yet its manifestation creates a gap in conscious thought by leaping well beyond previous attainments (Patrick, 1937; Cohn, 1968). Despite its speculative character, it is attended by a subjective sense of certainty, of perfect confidence and absolute conviction in its validity (Lee, 1948; Kris, 1950).

Consider, for example, the testimonies of Albert Einstein, the composer Johannes Brahms, and the British poet laureate John Masefield.

> It's a sudden illumination, almost a rapture. Later, to be sure, intelligence analyzes and experiments confirm (or invalidate) the intuition. But initially there is a great forward leap of the imagination (Kirk, 1971, p. 142).

> Straightway the ideas flow in upon me, directly from God, and not only do I see distinct themes in my mind's eye but they are clothed in the right forms, harmonies and orchestration. Measure by measure the finished product is revealed to me when I am in those rare, inspired moods (Abell, 1955, p. 21).

> This illumination is an intense experience, and so wonderful that it cannot be described. While it lasts, the momentary problem is merged into a dazzlingly clear perception of the entire work in all its detail. In a mood of mental ecstasy, the writer (and sometimes the painter also) perceives what seems to be an unchangeable way of statement, so full, and so insistent, that he cannot set down one half of what there is to utter (Freemantle, 1964, pp. 257–58).

Creativity does not always involve an experience of inspiration. Even when it does, the inspiration is only one aspect of a larger process. For purposes of analysis, Joseph Wallas (1926) divided inspired creativity into four phases: preparation, incubation, illumination, and verification. Preparations consciously identify a problem and gather materials toward its solution. The ideas are incubated outside consciousness where they undergo development into a solution. Once incubated, the developed ideas erupt into consciousness as inspirations or intuitions in a moment or period of illumination. The final phase, which is better described as elaboration than verification, begins when the sense of certainty yields to critical analysis and the inspirations are reexamined, tested, revised, crafted, or otherwise employed in conscious reasoning and behavior.

Wallas acknowledged that creative work often involves a considerable number of inspirations developing concurrently at different paces. Partial solutions may manifest consciously at intervals prior to the culminating inspiration of a definitive solution (Patrick, 1935, 1937, 1938). Single creative projects may involve a series of inspirations that build one on another in sequence (Vinacke, 1952). These qualifications do not significantly alter the theoretical analysis of any single inspiration.

In likening unitive experiences to creative inspirations, I leave open the question whether unitive experiences are instances of inspired creativity that happen to pertain to topics of existential concern, or are instead a closely similar but finally distinct process of unconscious inspiration. Existing research on inspired creativity is, if anything, even more meager than the history of research on unitive experiences.

Inclusion

Another variety of unitive experience, which I term *inclusion*, is similar to incorporation in content, but differs in being more closely in agreement with reality.

> One evening when I was sixteen it broke over me so strongly and lasted so long that I was awed into giving it a name.
>
> I was sitting alone, in a boat beached at the back of the island in the throat of the tidal lagoon, called the Basin, behind Montrose; the sun was setting before me and the Basin was full. Except for a distant curlew's call there was no living sound. The "feeling" came upon me like a tide floating me out and up into the wide greening sky—into the Universe, I told myself. That was the secret name I gave it: Belonging to the Universe. Like Thoreau, I felt myself "grandly related" (Muir, 1968, p. 14).

> It seemed as though the sky and the stars were reaching right toward me. Suddenly I had a warm and joyful sense of being absorbed into this enveloping scene. Though I certainly lacked the vocabulary at the time [age 3], I absolutely *knew* that I belonged there, and was somehow integrally connected (E. Hoffman, 1992, p. 22).

Unlike solitary and incorporative unions, unitive experiences of inclusion do not deny the externality of the perceptible world. Inclusive unions portray the world as a single unified reality that contains the self within it. In this manner, they imagine the world's unity while accommodating a realistic sense perception of the differentiation of external phenomena. As defined for psychoanalytic purposes by Hanna Segal (1991), imagination has a "what-if" quality, whereas fantasy is "as-if." "Imagination does not deny reality to produce an 'as-if' world, but explores possibilities" (p. 107). Imagination is speculative and may be inaccurate, but it is neither a flight from, nor a substitution for, reality.

A pattern, in Piaget's terms, of assimilation and accommodation can be seen in unitive experiences of incorporation and inclusion, respectively. Incorporation *assimilates* the idea of an external world to the fantasy of a solitary self by locating the world within the self. Inclusion readjusts the fantasy of incorporation in a manner that *accommodates* reality by recognizing that the perceptible world is external to the self. The perceptible world retains the unity, however, which was imposed on it through its incorporation within the self.

Identification

The pattern of assimilation and accommodation can also be seen in two types of unitive experience that pertain to an individual person, rather than to the perceptible world as a whole. Mystical moments of identification consist of a vivid experience of the identity and, in some cases, the physical existence of an external reality. Part or all of the identity of another person or thing is experienced as the identity of the subject. The identification may pertain to any person, animal, or thing that is subject to sense perception during the unitive experience.

> Suppose I happen to be walking up Brandy Hole Lane, on a summer evening, and see a fat girl painting a garden gate. Nothing extraordinary, just that. She is bending at the knees a little, to get down to it, so she bulges in different places. Suddenly I know what she feels like, laying that paint on thick, and black, watching it settle down into a smooth coat, with an enjoyment that is almost sensual; and adding to the pleasure by thinking, at the same time, about what she is going to have for supper. I know, because in a way I am her, that she thinks there is nothing better than being a fat girl painting a gate on a summer evening and thinking of what she is going to have for supper (Hillyer, 1966, pp. 140–41).

Like incorporation, identification is well-known to psychoanalysis as an unconscious "defense mechanism." It is frequently employed in everyone's everyday thought. When an identification assumes the experiential immediacy of a creative inspiration, a unitive experience occurs.

In the following self-report, a mystical identification was made with percept after percept, as though a general schema were being applied with ecstatic intensity wherever the person happened to look.

For those minutes, and I have no notion how many they were, I had the
heightened sensibility of one passionately in love and with it the power to
transmute all that the senses perceived into symbols of burning significance. . .
. The bells [of the caravan] came nearer and another sound mingled with theirs;
a low, monotonous chanting. I looked behind me for a moment and saw the
dark procession swaying out from behind the last bend in the wadi, then I
turned back so that the column should pass me and enter my world of vision
from behind. I found myself comprehending every physical fact of their passage
as though it were a part of my own existence. I knew how the big soft feet of
the camels pressed down upon and embraced the rough stones of the path; I
knew the warm depth of their fur and the friction upon it of leather harness
and the legs of the riders; I knew the blood flowing through the bodies of men
and beasts and thought of it as echoing the life of the anemones which now
showed black among the rocks (Hawkes, 1954, pp. 16–17).

Resonance or sympathy that is so very vivid as to obliterate consciousness of
one's own identity, by portraying the identity of another person or thing as one's
own, must be counted as fantasy. The assimilation to oneself of the identity of
another person is a fantasy. It lacks the realistic moderation of empathy. Its pri-
oritizing of self lends an unrealistic dimension to the fantasy.

Relatedness

In a closely similar variety of unitive experience, the solitude of the self is
applied to the reality of other individuals in a more realistic manner. Instead of
a sympathy that is so complete as to identify self with other, the experiences
preserve a sense of difference. The union of self and other manifests as a sense of
relatedness.

Once, a few weeks after I came to the woods, for an hour I doubted whether the
near neighborhood of man was not essential to a serene and healthy life. To be
alone was somewhat unpleasant. But, in the mist of a gentle rain, while these
thoughts prevailed, I was suddenly sensible of such sweet and beneficent society
in nature, in the very pattering of the drops, and in every sight and sound around
my house, an infinite and unaccountable friendliness all at once, like an atmosphere, sustaining me, as made the fancied advantages of human neighborhood
insignificant, and I have never thought of them since. Every little pine-needle expanded and swelled with sympathy and befriended me. I was so distinctly made
aware of the presence of something kindred to me, that I thought no place could
ever be strange to me again (Thoreau; abr. James, 1902, p. 218).

My grand object was to get off for lonely walks in the country. All my life I have
been like this. I have always regarded my existing domicile . . . as a resting-place

from which I could walk *into the country*. . . . What I am revealing to you now is the deepest and most essential secret of my life. My thoughts were lost in my sensations; and my sensations were of a kind so difficult to describe that I could write a volume upon them and still not really have put them down. . . .

A mysterious satisfaction . . . seems to well up from the inner being of old posts, old heaps of stone, old haystacks thatched with straw. . . . What I would like to emphasize just here is that the pleasure I got from these things of my solitary walks did not present itself to me as an *aesthetic* pleasure, nor did it call up in my mind the idea of beauty. What gave me these sensations seemed to be some mysterious "rapport" between myself and these things. It was like a sudden recognition of some obscure link, some remote identity, between myself and these objects. Posts, palings, hedges, heaps of stone—they were part of my very soul (Powys, 1934, pp. 168–69).

Like the sense of inclusion, the sense of relatedness is a normal part of human experience that has presumably escaped clinical remark because it is healthy. It is not the content but the intensity of the sense of relatedness that causes it to become a mystical moment.

Concluding Reflections

Five types of unitive experiences base their senses of unity in the unity of the self. In these experiences, either the self alone exists, or the self is extended to other phenomena that thereby become imbued with its unity. We may speak of incorporation and identification in Piagetian terms as schemas that *assimilate* sense perceptions to the schema of the solitary self, while inclusion and relation are schemas that *accommodate* the previous assimilations to reality. The assimilations are frequently discussed by psychoanalysts as unconscious psychic "mechanisms" because they are patently fantastic. The accommodations have been overlooked, presumably because they are imaginative without being absurd.

The very fact that two types of unitive thinking are well-known as unconscious thinking processes suggests a general theory: that unitive experiences are rare moments when unitive thinking manifests consciously with the intensity of a creative inspiration. William James (1902) and Evelyn Underhill (1910) made the same point, but without going on to probe the nature of unitive thought.

Unity and the All

Jean Piaget suggested that children construct their worldviews by commencing, more or less in Freudian fashion, with attention to bodily imperatives.

Atop the categories that are instinctually determined, children predicate open-ended series of assimilations and accommodations—first an assimilation, then an accommodation, then another assimilation, then another accommodation, and so forth. Cognitive development consists of a cumulative move away from the categories of instinctual selection toward a realistic appreciation of the world. Freudians refer to the same process as one of adaptation to external reality.

One point in dispute—and it may not be a negligible one—is whether, once a more accommodating or adaptive schema has been developed, the assimilation out of which it emerged remains active unconsciously. Cognitive theorists tend to ignore schemas that have been outgrown. Psychoanalysts acknowledge that more advanced schemas may undergo an "automatization" (Hartmann, 1939) that makes them independent of their sources in earlier thought. However, psychoanalysts also assert that early schemas may remain dynamic unconsciously, under a variety of conditions.

A third alternative may also be considered. If older schemas are ordinarily outgrown and forgotten, there may be circumstances under which they become relevant and active once again, without having been dynamically unconscious in the interval.

These general circumstances of how we construct our worldviews apply, I suggest, not only to the familiar topics of Piagetian and Freudian studies, but also to unitive thinking. A great deal of everyone's everyday thinking is unitive. Much of what passes for rational thought is either explicitly or unconsciously unitive. Most of us do not ordinarily think of ourselves as mystical; but mysticism is nevertheless universal in our species.

Consider a further variety of unitive experiences in which unity is found, not by extrapolation from the self to the all, but simply in the totality of the all. In these experiences, it is as though the idea of union in experiences of incorporation and inclusion has been accommodated even further to a realistic perception of the external world. The role of the self is diminished not through a loss of the idea of its relatedness, but through an extension of the idea of relatedness to anything and everything.

> When I was on holiday, aged about 17, I glanced down and watched an ant striving to drag a bit of twig through a patch of sun on a wall in the graveyard of a Greek church, while chanting came from within the white building. The feeling aroused in me was quite unanticipated, welling up from some great depth, and essentially timeless. The concentration of simplicity and innocence was intensely of some vital present. I've had similar experiences on buses, suddenly watching people and being aware how *right* everything essentially is (Hardy, 1979, p. 21).

Acute attention to the moment—an experience "intensely of some vital present"—disclosed the "simplicity and innocence" of things as they are, that is, "how *right* everything essentially is." In this context, "right" meant correct, proper, or appropriate.

In another self-report, closely similar ideas manifested together with a visual experience of light. Here, however, the sense of rightness combined a judgment of correctness or propriety with a feeling of safety or security.

> I was a girl of 15 or 16, I was in the kitchen toasting bread for tea and suddenly on a dark November afternoon the whole place was flooded with light, and for a minute by clock time I was immersed in this, and I had a sense that in some unutterable way the universe was all right. This has affected me for the rest of my life, I have lost all fear of death . . . because this light experience has been a kind of conviction to me that everything *is* all right in some way (Huxley, 1962, p. 49).

In both self-reports, the unifying sense of rightness was global in scope. It encompassed "everything" or "the universe." In a further example, again attended by fantasies of light, the ideas of the experience were simultaneously scientific and religious.

> In 1945 I was in Chemistry class. We were being introduced to the Table of Elements. It was a sunny day. Then the light seemed to flood into me—I was it and it was me. I never lost the view of being in the class, but suddenly I understood everything, how the world was made, how terribly important it was for the sciences to join together, that biology would have to involve chemistry and physics in order to be completely studied (these were just fragments of thoughts coming out of the experience). The feeling was of looking on at the ecstasy of those worshipping God. I seemed to be at once amongst them and yet a long distance away. While I was in this state I had a feeling of wholeness, and of sympathy and love for everyone in the room, and afterwards this feeling lingered (Prince, 1979–80, p. 173).

The experience was triggered by the subject's introduction to the table of atomic elements, and consisted of unitive ideas that pertained to "everything," to "the world," to "the sciences . . . join[ing] together," and to "a feeling of wholeness." In this moment of understanding, everything found its proper place within the whole. This understanding of scientific principles aroused wonderment and a sense of participating among "those worshipping God."

In another self-report, Roger Bannister (1955), the athlete who first ran a mile in less than four minutes, recounted the childhood experience during which he first discovered the joy of running.

> I remember a moment when I stood barefoot on firm dry sand by the sea. The air had a special quality as if it had a life of its own. The sound of breakers on the shore shut out all others. I looked down at the regular ripples on the sand,

and could not absorb so much beauty. I was taken aback—each of the myriad particles of sand was perfect in its way . . . there was nothing to detract from all this beauty.

In this supreme moment I leapt in sheer joy. I was startled, and frightened, by the tremendous excitement that so few steps could create. . . . A few more steps—self-consciously now and firmly gripping the original excitement. The earth seemed almost to move with me. I was running now, and a fresh rhythm entered my body. No longer conscious of my movement I discovered a new unity with nature. I had found a new source of power and beauty, a source I never dreamt existed (pp. 11–12).

In this self-report, unitive ideas were extended from the particular to the universal as the sense of perfection was applied, in turn, to the sand, to the act of running, and to nature. The sense of propriety was extreme. There was "so much beauty" that all of the sand "was perfect in its way." The emotion precipitated motion, but the motion was encompassed by the unitive schema. The boy "discovered a new unity with nature . . . a new source of power and beauty."

A similar shift from the particular to the universal may also be noted in another self-report.

I was sitting on the seashore, half listening to a friend arguing violently about something which merely bored me. Unconsciously to myself, I looked at a film of sand I had picked up on my hand, when I suddenly saw the exquisite beauty of every little grain of it; instead of being dull, I saw that each particle was made up on a perfect geometrical pattern, with sharp angles, from each of which a brilliant shaft of light was reflected, while each tiny crystal shone like a rainbow. . . . The rays crossed and recrossed, making exquisite patterns of such beauty that they left me breathless. . . . Then, suddenly, my consciousness was lighted up from within and I saw in a vivid way how the whole universe was made up of particles of material which, no matter how dull and lifeless they might seem, were nevertheless filled with this intense and vital beauty. For a second or two the whole world appeared as a blaze of glory. When it died down, it left me with something I have never forgotten and which constantly reminds me of the beauty locked up in every minute speck of material around us (A.E. [George Russell], cited in Huxley, 1956, p. 77).

Here again there was reference to "exquisite beauty" and to the scientific idea of "a perfect geometrical pattern, with sharp angles." These particulars led on, however, to a more complete manifestation of the unitive schema. "I saw in a vivid way how the whole universe was . . . filled with this intense and vital beauty" and "appeared as a blaze of glory."

Unlike sense perception, which finds perceptible realities to be themselves, unitive experiences of propriety discover that things are right and perfect in being themselves. The unitive schema attributes unity to the perceptible world, treating it as a unified whole, without violating the sense of reality. The experience of unity accommodates sense perception of plurality by restricting the element of unity to a value judgment that is imposed atop the experience of sense perception. Either the perceptible world as a whole, or a particular perceptible thing, is valued as proper, functional, and/or perfect.

Unitive experiences of propriety are mystical moments. The moments do not differ from ordinary sobriety in their ideas and feelings. The very same ideas and feelings might occur during sobriety without warranting remark. Moreover, the concept of the perceptible world's unity that is vividly experienced in unitive experiences of propriety is consistent with the concept of its unity that is postulated by Western science. Unitive experiences of propriety can celebrate scientific concerns without strain or distortion.

What is distinctive about mystical moments of propriety is the *increased attention* that is given to their ideas and feelings. The unitive experiences differ from sobriety in two major respects. They have an intensity comparable to creative inspirations; and their intensity precipitates self-consciousness about the experiences. The result is a *heightened awareness* of *otherwise ordinary*, everyday unitive thinking.

Cosmic Anthropomorphism in Scientific Thinking

There is no inherent or necessary inconsistency of science and mysticism (Bakan, 1966b). The relevant questions are what sorts of mysticism and what types of unitive experiences are under discussion.

I would like to suggest that the unconscious fantasy of a macroanthropos is an integral component of scientific thinking about perceptible reality. Scientific thought unconsciously anthropomorphizes the cosmos, unwittingly treating it as a cosmic self. The unconscious fantasy of the cosmos as a macroanthropos causes the relationship between science and mysticism to be a necessary one. Science proceeds as though the schema of incorporation, which manifests in unitive experiences of incorporation, also undergoes an accommodation that unconsciously preserves the role of a self while deleting its identity with the subject. In this manner, unconscious thinking imagines the cosmos as a self that exists objectively in its own right, independently of the subject.

Consider, for example, some basic propositions that scientific research has endorsed. David Hume established that there is no empirical evidence of causality. All that we know empirically is a succession of events. We do not witness any actual process of causation. The assumption that successive events have an unobservable connection, termed *causation*, is not physical but metaphysical. The unempirical nature of the proposition becomes all the more obvious when we consider all of the many efforts to impose a causal or deterministic model not only on the physical events of nature, but also on the willed regularities of historical human behavior, from politics and history to economics and ecology. We know ourselves to be willful and sometimes capricious beings, yet we try to conceive of ourselves as though we were uniformly subject to causal determinism. From Calvin and Knox to Marx and Durkheim, the presumption of determinism, in the individual as in the group, attests to an unconscious equation of unity and anthropomorphism. Consciously, we attribute impersonal causality throughout the universe, because unconsciously we attribute the unity of a willful, causally active self to the plurality of perceptible phenomena. The idea of causality is an accommodation to reality of an unrealistic anthropomorphic fantasy of cosmic will. Science postulates causality because unconsciously the psyche postulates will. The scientific concept is an unconscious mysticism.

A second scientific axiom is well-known to have originated historically as a mystical doctrine. On what basis do we postulate the universality of any natural law? What evidence have we that the very limited quantity of regularity that we are able to observe empirically is properly developed into generalizations regarding all similar events everywhere in the cosmos? Aristotle postulated the division of the cosmos into two domains: the perfect domain of circular motions above the moon, and the sublunary world of generation and decay in which we live. He suggested that only the former was orderly and lawful. The Stoics instead maintained the unity and perfection of the entire cosmos. They claimed that the *Logos*, the sum total of coherence, structure, thought, and wisdom in the cosmos, was God, whom they believed to be omnipresent in matter (Sandbach, 1975). Christianity endorsed the Stoic idea of the *Logos* in the first verse of the Gospel of John, and it was not until the twelfth century that Latin schoolmen decided that the structure of the world is not God Incarnate. They considered Nature—Wisdom and the Madonna Intelligenza—to be God's impression on matter, in the sense that a signet ring leaves its image on wax (Economou, 1972). This concept of Nature as a reflection of the Incarnation of Christ was embraced by the protoscientific thinkers of the fourteenth through sixteenth centuries (Jaki, 1988) and remains, as it were, an implicit content of the scientific concept of natural law. Once again, an anthropomorphic fantasy underlies a fundamental axiom of science. The concept of the unity of the cosmos was derived historically from the concept of the unity of God.

An equivalent argument may be mounted for the scientific premise of the objective or external character of reality. We are inherently and unavoidably subjective beings. Objectivity is humanly impossible. We none of us directly experience anything outside our individual mental representations. Whether there is a reality beyond the psyche, an objectively existing external reality that is represented by mental contents, we do not experientially know. We have faith in our reasoning on the topic, but we have no experiential proof.

What we experience as objectivity when we try to be objective or adopt an objective perspective, are moments of self-observation, when we think of ourselves from a perspective seemingly other than our own. The perspective is an imaginative one. What we mean by objectivity is the imagined perspective of a subjective being of cosmic extent. Objectivity is the imagined perspective of a cosmic self, a God. Whenever we contemplate an objective perspective, we are unconsciously reconciling the world of sense perception with the same subjective perspective that occurs in unitive experiences of incorporation.

The assumptions, as articles of scientific faith, that natural processes are causal, objective, and everywhere and forever valid, have unquestioned utility in facilitating technological invention. The argument from technology is no disproof, however, of the imaginative or unempirical nature of the axiomatic propositions. It is merely an argument for the success of the biological adaptation of human imagination to life in the cosmos that we know.

Useful though the axioms may be, they do not have their basis—as, for example, logic and mathematics do—in abstractions from empirical observations of reality. They are not mental representations of observable quiddities. They are overinterpretations of the evidence of sense perception and anthropomorphizing speculations beyond the empirical data.

What we experience consciously as causality, objectivity, and universality are the will, subjectivity, and scope of a cosmic self, as the unconscious anthropomorphism is accommodated to the sense of reality. Like unitive experiences of incorporation, which fantasize a cosmic subject, scientific thinking imagines the cosmos as a self, but it is a self that exists objectively in its own right. Unlike the mystical moments, scientific thinking accommodates reality by restricting the full anthropomorphizing logic of the unitive thinking. Scientific thinking concerns a cosmos whose self is not a person but a thing. The unconscious idea of the personal will of the cosmos is accommodated to the idea of the impersonal through the development of the idea of impersonal causality. The idea of cosmic subjectivity is reduced to impersonal objectivity, and internal consistency is revised as universality. In each instance, the censorship of the unconscious anthropomorphic fantasy is incomplete. Part of each unconscious anthropomorphism manifests. Another part does not.

Conventional contrasts of science and mysticism are fallacious. Unconscious anthropomorphisms are as integral to scientific thinking as conscious anthropomorphisms are to mystical moments (Loewald, 1951). The anthropomorphisms accommodate reality more closely and so have greater access to consciousness when they are impersonal rather than personal; but the scientific schema presupposes the mystical one. Incorporation assimilates the idea of an external world to the idea of a solitary self. Scientific thinking accommodates the idea of a cosmic self to the impersonalism of the external world.

The unconscious anthropomorphisms of scientific thinking are normative in our species. They are normally experienced by all people, commencing at an extremely early stage of psychological development. They are the stuff of common sense—and yet they are accommodations of mystical ideas.

We are all of us unconsciously mystical. Because we are scientific, we cannot be otherwise.

The Unitive Basis of Morality

The universal mysticism of the unconscious psyche is most easily and conclusively argued from the nonempirical aspects of scientific thinking. A parallel argument can be mounted, however, regarding humanistic thinking.

Let us examine some further self-reports of mystical moments. In some unitive experiences, the sense of perfection sometimes has an aesthetic dimension. What is proper, right, functional, and/or perfect is simultaneously beautiful.

> In the middle of the forest there was a clearing. As I stepped into it, I was suddenly overwhelmed by the greenness of the overhanging young leaves and the lush meadow shining under a brilliant sun. I experienced an indescribable state of happiness, with an intense feeling of beauty, fullness, and perfection (E. Hoffman, 1992, p. 34).

As with unitive experiences whose dominant idea is perfection, those experiences whose dominant idea is beauty include variants in which a single or particular object of sense perception has the idea of universal beauty attached to it. The one object then epitomizes or becomes metaphoric of the whole.

> The sight of a spring bulb in flower . . . has always remained in my mind as a strange experience. The flower arrested my attention and as I gazed at it, its beauty seemed to become more profound every second and for some moments I couldn't speak. Perhaps this may seem imaginative, but for some moments it seemed the magnificent centre of the whole world (Paffard, 1973, p. 105).

In this experience, an extrapolation from the particular to the universal is implicit but unconscious.

In further cases, the sense of beauty has a distinctly ethical or moral quality.

> I had chanced on this graveyard quite unexpectedly one morning when out for a walk. The season was spring, but a spell of summer seemed to have fallen on this place: the winds were hushed, the air mild and caressing. And as I sat on a sun-warmed, fallen headstone, I felt that I had wandered into the very heart of Peace. Thrushes and rooks and starlings flitted about the church tower, while directly in front of me was a mass of flaming crimson blossom, where a flowering currant had found a root-hold among the crumbling stones. I know not

what there was about the place that so entranced me. It was a beauty that seemed mingled with innocence and simplicity; it had a definitely *moral* quality, which dropped deep down into my soul and made me feel good. I very seldom felt good. I very seldom *was* good, though I loved goodness in other people. But as I sat in that churchyard all my restless thoughts and impulses sank away: I was like one of Wordsworth's little boys or little girls, and could have held a dialogue with the sage precisely in their manner had his mild old ghost come woolgathering by. . . . (Reid, 1926, p. 199).

Just as scientific thinking rests on an unconscious fantasy of a macroanthropos, morality too has its basis in unconsciously unitive thinking (Breen, 1986). Adding to the older psychoanalytic view that moral scruples are internalized on the basis of parental examples in a psychic agency that Freud (1923) termed the *superego*, Hans Lichtenstein (in Goodman, 1965) postulated "the decisive, though not exclusive, role of an inherent factor, not derivable from transvalued outside demands, in the formation and function" of moral thinking. He suggested

three main reasons why it is difficult to trace the sense of urgent "oughtness" to internalized outside demands: first, the logical *non sequitur* existing between the proposition of identification with parental demands and the development of self-imposed moral rules; second, the fact that historically great moral decisions seem typically to dispense with the very outside demands that the individual had at one time accepted without questioning; third, the problem of the individual selectivity of identifications (p. 177).

Another proof that moral thinking has its basis in an innate, autonomous factor is the striking convergence of moral systems cross-culturally. What needs explanation is not the divergence of different moral systems, but the fact that they show any resemblances at all. Summarizing anthropologists' findings, Heinz Hartmann (1960) asserted:

According to Kluckhohn, murder, unlimited lying and stealing are everywhere valued negatively; also something like a principle of "reciprocity" is recognized everywhere. Montagu states that murder is generally considered a crime; some incest regulations are universal; nowhere is cannibalism regular practice. Also, the duty of the adults to take care of the children is generally accepted; a certain respect for private property is, too, and so is respect for the dead of one's own group (p. 83).

Géza Róheim (1943–44, p. 99) added that the principle of reciprocity is common to all cultures. Ernest A. Ticho (1972) inferred that moral universals must be based on an innate and unvarying aspect of the human psyche.

The values of a mature, autonomous superego may be different from society to society, but it is surprising how similar are the ideals of many religions, whatever the ritual or the credo: e.g., overcoming self-centeredness and a concern for other human beings are universal goals, and as such can be seen as of universal autonomous superego content (p. 221).

Freud (1914, 1921, 1933) postulated the existence of the superego in order to explain the nonego or "ego-alien" character of conscience. To issue in judgments of conscience, the psyche must observe the ego, possess values, and apply those values as ideal standards against which the ego is measured. Freud consequently attributed the three psychic functions of self-observation, ego ideals, and judgments of conscience, to a single psychic agency, which he repeatedly renamed, settling eventually on the term *superego* (1923).

Hal J. Breen (1986) has emphasized the unitive character of moral thinking. He locates the origin of morality in the infant's identification with the mother. To hurt the mother is to hurt oneself. I would like to suggest, however, that the universal extension of morality implies an unconscious fantasy of a macroanthropos, precisely as scientific thinking does. A fantasy in which all other people are parts of one's cosmic self entails the logical corollary that to hurt others is to hurt parts of oneself. Occasional mystics have consciously articulated the macroanthropic foundations of moral reasoning. St. Paul wrote:

> Just as the body is one and has many members, and all the members of the body, though many, are one body, so it is with Christ. By one Spirit we were all baptized into one body—Jews or Greeks, slaves or free—and all were made to drink of one Spirit. . . . If one member suffers, all suffer together; if one member is honored, all rejoice together (I Cor 12:12–13, 26).

The Hasidic Rebbe Shmelke of Nikolsburg taught:

> Love your neighbor like something which you yourself are. For all souls are one. Each is a spark from the original soul, and this soul is wholly inherent in all souls, just as your soul is in all the members of your body. It may come to pass that your hand makes a mistake and strikes you. But would you then take a stick and chastise your hand, because it lacked understanding, and so increase your pain? It is the same if your neighbor, who is of one soul with you, wrongs you for lack of understanding. If you punish him, you only hurt yourself (Buber, 1947, p. 190).

Due presumably to the irrationality of incorporation, the schema does not ordinarily manifest in its entirety, except in a mystical moment. Moral thinking ordinarily depends on an accommodation of the unitive schema to reality that acknowledges the otherness of other people. Unconscious unitive thinking provides a foundation for morality, but no type of morality traces directly and solely to unitive thinking. Moral decisions always involve intellectual recognition of the existence of at least two people. Morality is unconsciously unitive, but it is never exclusively so.

Due to the compromise between the unconscious unitive fantasy and its accommodation, the manifest content of moral thinking is invariably arbitrary. People are to be treated as though they were oneself. Their happiness is to be promoted and their distress minimized even though they are consciously known to be autonomous individuals. The manifest illogic rests, however, on an unconscious fantasy of self-interest. Moral behavior is felt to be advantageous and desirable because the beneficiaries of moral behavior are unconsciously imagined to be oneself.

Moral thinking has its conscious basis in the extension of empathy to others (Furer, 1967). Empathy consists of feeling badly about hurting others, and about their pains, as well as feeling good about benefiting others, and about their happiness. The link between how one makes others feel and how one feels about oneself is unconscious. It is an irrational fantasy of incorporation or identification, but its conscious manifestation as empathy accommodates the schema to reality. Empathy remains an imaginative exercise, but its prosocial consequences have had sufficient evolutionary advantage that we experience morality as rational.

The arbitrariness of the conscious portion of moral thinking is increased when the emotional content of empathy is excluded from consciousness. Only the attendant ideas then manifest: it is wrong to hurt others, wrong for others to hurt, good to benefit others, and good for others to be happy.

Unitive Experiences and Metaphysics

Both science and morality are predicated on the unconscious assumption of unitive thinking. Because both scientific and moral thinking issue in practical and productive behavior, they are conventionally diagnosed as rational, wholesome, and integral to mental health. Whether the unitive aspects of science and morality are considered from a philosophical perspective as metaphysical, or from a psychoanalytic one as fantasies, their utility keeps them from attracting the controversy that so often surround further varieties of unitive thinking, whose greater abstraction causes them to be categorized apart from science and morality, as "metaphysics" and "religion."

Consider the following varieties of unitive experiences.

Vitality

In these unitive experiences, a metaphysical power of vitality permeates the environment. Reality is experienced as the receptacle of an omnipresent power that is engaged in motion. It is not a vitality inherent within things, but a power that may enter, act upon, and leave things. Because the power is engaged in specific motions, it has both substance and structure.

> I prayed for help from out of the darkness, and there, behold, as a flash, the scene changed. All became alive, the trees, the houses, the very stones became animated with life, and all became vibrant with the life within them. All breathed effulgent light, vivid sparkling light, radiating out and in every direction; and no only that, but everything seemed to be connected with everything else. Although all separate forms, and all vibrating with their own intensity of life, yet they all seemed to be connected by their vibrations into one whole thing, as the different coloured parts of a picture are yet of the same picture, although when one is near to it each different object can be viewed separately.

> So in the same way with natural objects—by which I mean every common and ordinary thing of which we are conscious, including our bodies—they are but parts of one intensive radiant activity, every particle endowed with life and light of a quality that cannot be conceived of, for, although of the power of the arc lamp, there is no sense of glare or strain. And we are surrounded by this glorious world of light all the time! (Johnson, 1959, p. 64–65).

Unitive experiences of vitality portray an impersonal metaphysical force. In some self-reports, the force is conceptualized secularly as equivalent to the abstract concept of "life." In other cases, vitality is venerated religiously as divine; and the anthropomorphism at the unconscious foundation of unitive thinking may even contribute to its personification as a god or God. In all cases, the experiences portray the immanence of vitality within the physical environment. Physical reality seems to be permeated by vitality, but the power is unrealized. It does not move, and it does not issue in activity. The vitality is static. It is possessed rather than employed. Also notable is the extension of the vitality to both animate and inanimate external realities despite the organic implications of vitality.

Energy

In another variety of unitive experiences, a metaphysical power is again felt to unify physical reality, but the power is conceptualized more realistically as inorganic energy. In the following self-report, the energy permeated both the surround and the subject.

> One day, when I was four, I found myself standing at the beach, alone. The sea touched the sky. Breathing with the waves, I entered their rhythm. Suddenly there was a channeling of energy: the sun, the wind, the sea were going right through me.

> A door opened, and I *became* the sun, the wind, and the sea. There was no "I"
> anymore. "I" had merged with everything else. All sensory perceptions had be-
> come one. Sound, smell, taste, touch, shape—all melted into a brilliant light.
> The pulsating energy went right through me, and I was part of this energy (E.
> Hoffman, 1992, pp. 38–39).

The experience had three phases. First was a perception that the energy in the
sun, wind, and sea was permeating the subject. Next was a phase of solitary
union, when the solitude of the self was extended to the environment, and all
became one. Next, as the assimilation to the self yielded to an accommodation
to reality, the energy was experienced as both external and internal.

The unitive schemas of vitality and energy may perhaps be considered, respectively, as an assimilation and an accommodation of a common idea. More
anthropomorphic, vitality is more fantastic. More accommodating of reality, energy is imagined to be impersonal.

Loving Presence

William James's (1902) classic discussion of "the sense of presence" was
based on data that I prefer to divide into two varieties of unitive experiences
(compare: Stark, 1965). The first, to which I restrict the term *sense of presence*, entails the human subject's one-sided awareness of a metaphysical presence. The
other experience is two-sided or mutual. The presence is reciprocally aware of
the human subject. The following self-report concerns a one-sided awareness.

> I was completely aware that there was some sort of unseen but very real presence
> lovingly surrounding me. I had no question as to what it was. Obviously it was
> my perception of a Higher Power . . . there was no denying His presence—the
> source of all power and energy and love—love which I could feel streaming out
> of light and color along with something that felt vaguely like a transmitted feel-
> ing of care passing through me (Hoffer & Osmond, 1968, p. 121).

Although the sense of presence has been named in a fashion that emphasizes its
anthropomorphism, its theoretical understanding is better approached by seeing
it in series with unitive experiences of vitality and energy. Like unitive experiences of vitality and energy, the sense of presence pertains to a metaphysical
power that is immanent within space and time, but transcendent of matter. In
the sense of presence, the metaphysical power that is the concern of the experience happens to be love.

Love differs from vitality and energy, however, because it is necessarily felt
as a personal experience, rather than as an impersonal one. The intimate sense of
being the recipient of love is felt to imply not only love but a lover. However, it

is the experience of being loved, rather than the identity of the lover, which is the unitive element of the experience. The idea of a presence arises as a corollary to the unitive sense of being beloved. The presence is experienced indirectly, as it were, in the third person, in what Buber (1958) termed an *I-It* relation. The presence belongs to an implicitly personal being, but the personality of the presence is not directly experienced. Only one presence is ever felt at a time; it is not necessarily believed to be unique.

The very intimacy of the sense of presence is a unitive factor. Love is a bond that unites the subject and the metaphysical power in a dyadic unit. It is a relationship.

Omnipresence

Related to the sense of presence, but more abstract, are unitive experiences of a metaphysical omnipresence. Unlike vitality, energy, and love, which are immanent in space, the omnipresent power is both immanent and transcendent.

> I know an officer on our police force who has told me that many times when off duty, and on his way home in the evening, there comes to him such a vivid and vital realization of his oneness with this Infinite Power, and this Spirit of Infinite Peace so takes hold of him and so fills him, that it seems as if his feet could hardly keep to the pavement, so buoyant and so exhilarated does he become by reason of this inflowing tide (James, 1902, p. 302).

> One sunny day in autumn I was coming through a dark passageway between two old houses in my town. Holding on to the gate's latch, I was suddenly brought to a stop by the sight of the house's warm, old brick wall jutting against the blue of the sky.

> For some reason I immediately thought of God—being out there, up there, in the dazzling blue sky. In the very next instant I was overwhelmed by the awareness that God was also in the bricks, and everywhere—in everything that I saw, everything that I sensed, and everything that I touched. I felt that God surrounded me, and though I surely wouldn't have verbalized it at the time in these words, I knew that God was good, He was love (E. Hoffman, 1992, pp. 94–95).

Because only one metaphysical power can be omnipresent, this variety of unitive experience is intrinsically monotheistic.

In these self-reports, unitive experiences of an omnipresent power proceeded in company with sense perception of the physical environment. It is presumably the same type of unitive thinking whose occurrence in deep states of trance, when sense perception is inhibited, manifests as the theistic mystical union that Ernst Arbman analyzed in close detail.

Unitive experiences of vitality, energy, love, and omnipresence are neither more nor less anthropomorphic, fanciful, and speculative than the unitive ideas intrinsic to science and morality. All are metaphysical. None are falsifiable. However, unitive ideas concerning metaphysical powers do not have readily demonstrable practical consequences that restrict unitive speculations to a narrow margin of error. Scientific speculations are limited by technological achievements, and moral imagination by the effectiveness of prosocial behavior. Religious ideas and behavior are more difficult to evaluate. They permit a greater margin of error to go unchallenged and may consequently be less reliable.

For psychoanalytic purposes, we must judge speculations all of one piece. Scientific axioms, moral convictions, and religious faith are all inherently and inalienably speculative. The speculative features of science, morality, and religion need to be reality-tested and properly bounded as speculations. They must be kept, on the one side, from slippage into "excessive fantasy formation" whose reification leads to the "flagrant disregard of the obvious features of outer reality" (Pruyser, 1974, p. 115). Speculations must equally be kept from an "overdone realism" that "can lead to smothering the imagination and thereby truncating human potentialities." People "too fearful of the autistic fantasy going rampant" may fear speculation and seek its abandonment or suppression as nonsense (Pruyser, 1983, p. 176).

As long as metaphysical propositions are properly bounded and maintained as speculations that may be correct but can neither be demonstrated nor falsified, psychoanalysis can have no objection to them. Religion is as valid and psychologically healthy as morality. It is neither more nor less rational to maintain that good and evil exist, than that life, energy, and love exist, or that a transcendent God creates them all.

Summary

Discussions of mystical union within the comparative study of religion conventionally define the topic along ecumenical lines. When the topic is instead approached, so far as possible, on scientific principles, unitive experiences prove to be a limited part of the more general psychological phenomenon of unitive thinking.

Unitive experiences of the solitary self may be associated with the core of the sense of self that Winnicott (1963) termed an *incommunicado element.* The distinctive contents of unitive experiences of incorporation and identification are well-known to psychoanalysis as the products of so-called defense mechanisms that ordinarily generate unconscious fantasies.

Unitive experiences of incorporation and identification may be treated as assimilations, in a Piagetian sense, of cognitive ideas to subjective fantasies. Incorporation can be seen as an addition of perceptible reality to the content of the solitary self. The self expands to incorporate perceptible reality. Identification can be seen in parallel as an equation of the self with another person. Corresponding to these two assimilations are two unitive experiences that accommodate their ideas to the perceptible world in a more realistic way. Unitive experiences of inclusion and relation contain ideas that are normal parts of everyday thinking.

Because the individual varieties of unitive thinking manifest both as unitive experiences and in other contexts, they may each be conceptualized as schemas, of mixed cognitive and affective content. Unitive experiences consist of unitive thinking that manifests with the intensity of creative inspirations.

Single unitive schemas may apparently undergo different accommodations. The fantasy of incorporation generates the idea of a macroanthropos by incorporating the perceptible world within the self. When the subjective element of the fantasy is deleted, the result is a fantasy of a macroanthropos that exists in its own right, independently of the subject. As it is accommodated to the perceptible world, the unconscious fantasy of a macroanthropos underlies scientific thinking about causality, objectivity, and the universality of natural law. Moral thinking is predicated on a slightly different version of the macroanthropos fantasy, which conceives of the macroanthropos as a personal rather than an impersonal being.

In addition to these three orders of unitive thinking—personal, scientific, and moral—each with its own subtypes, unitive experiences and unitive thinking are also extended to topics of increasing abstraction, including such metaphysical powers as vitality, energy, love, and omnipresent power.

THREE

A Theory of
Unitive Experiences

In order to explain the unitive experiences that occur as symptoms of schizophrenia, Freud (1905) suggested that consciousness of a differentiated, external world is a secondary acquisition which, in schizophrenia, is apparently reversed. Freud speculated that self-love, or narcissism, has two main forms. Originally the infant naively assumes that all perceptible phenomena are parts of the self. Later the infant comes to restrict the idea of self to the limits of the body, while treating the balance of reality as an external world. Infantile solipsism thereafter remains an unconscious significance of the perceptible world. Freud (1905) wrote:

> Narcissistic or ego-libido seems to be the great reservoir from which the object-cathexes are sent out and into which they are withdrawn once more; the narcissistic libidinal cathexis of the ego is the original state of things, realized in earliest childhood, and is merely covered by the later extrusions of libido, but in essentials persists behind them (p. 218).

Freud suggested that the attitude to the self ("ego-libido") has chronological priority over the attitude to external reality ("object-cathexis"). Object-love does not exist initially but is a secondary developmental attainment. When the difference between self and object is recognized and love toward objects comes into being, primary narcissism dwindles to become secondary narcissism, which is the form of self-love that abides throughout life.

Freud held to his theory of primary narcissism throughout his career. The theory was embraced by most psychoanalysts. It was also endorsed by Jean Piaget (1951), who wrote of "the complete ego-centrism of the first year, during which the universe and the ego are one, because there are no permanent external objects" (p. 185).

In 1920, Cavendish Moxon explained mystical union as "nothing less than a return to the intra-uterine condition." The God with whom mystics unite "is a projected image of the narcissistic libido . . . a regression to the mother" (p. 330). One unstated assumption in Moxon's theory was its preservation of the structure of traditional religious doctrines on mysticism. The theory shares with all doctrines of mystical attainment the basic assumption that unitive experiences are moments of access to phenomena that are always present but ordinarily unknown. The transformation, in Freud's (1901) phrase, of "metaphysics into metapsychology" (p. 259) psychologized one term of the theory but preserved its overall structure. It replaced the idea of God with the idea of the unconscious, but continued to think in terms of a return to a lost primary state. The religious claim of access to metaphysical reality was replaced by a psychologizing claim of access to unconscious materials; but both theories shared the basic idea of momentary access to something fully formed and preexisting that is ordinarily outside conscious experience. Religious doctrines, no differently than the theory of psychological regression, conceptualize unitive experiences as a going back toward a prior state of things, in order to recover the original condition of the mind or soul.

Moxon (1920) was followed by Theodore Schroeder (1922) and Alfred Carver (1924) in treating unitive experiences as intrauterine regressions. Although Freud (1930) gave his predecessors no acknowledgment, he was the fourth psychoanalytic writer to publish a theory of mysticism as psychological regression. He depended for his data base on a fragmentary self-report of mystical union in a letter written to him by Romain Rolland, dated 5 December 1927. The letter referred to

> the simple and direct *sensation of the eternal* . . . subjective in character . . . without . . . in any way harming my critical faculties and my freedom to exercise them—even if against the immediacy of this internal experience. . . . I add that this "oceanic" feeling has nothing to do with my personal aspirations. . . . But the sensation that I feel is thrust upon me as a fact. It is a *contact* (Fisher, 1976, pp. 20–22).

In reporting what he termed the *oceanic feeling*, Freud (1930) equated the eternal and oceanic aspects of the experience and so arrived at a concept of "something limitless, unbounded." He wrote: "It is a feeling which he [Rolland] would like to call a sensation of 'eternity', a feeling as of something limitless, unbounded—as it were, 'oceanic'" (p. 64). To explain the oceanic feeling, Freud offered his most detailed account of neonatal solipsism.

> An infant at the breast does not as yet distinguish his ego from the external world as the source of the sensations flowing in upon him. He gradually learns to do so, in response to various promptings. . . . Or, to put it more correctly, originally the ego includes everything, later it separates off an external world from itself. Our present ego-feeling is, therefore, only a shrunken residue of a much more inclusive—indeed, an all-embracing—feeling which corresponded to a more intimate bond between the ego and the world about it. If we may assume that there are many people in whose mental life this primary ego-feeling has persisted to a

greater or lesser degree, it would exist in them side by side with the narrower and more sharply demarcated ego-feeling of maturity, like a kind of counterpart to it. In that case, the ideational contents appropriate to it would be precisely those of limitlessness and of a bond with the universe—the same ideas with which my friend elucidated the "oceanic" feeling (pp. 66–67, 68).

Moxon, Schroeder, and Carver had described mystical experiences as an *intrauterine* regression. Freud made no acknowledgment of their precedence presumably because his own theory of the "oceanic feeling" postulated a *neonatal* regression.

From Primary Narcissism to Unconscious Merger Fantasies

Writing in Freud's lifetime, Michael Balint (1937) disputed the theory of primary narcissism for three reasons. The theoretical construction about infancy has no direct evidence from infancy. Complete or perfect narcissism that contains no traces of object relation is never in evidence later in life, even as a symptom of psychosis. Lastly, primary narcissism is logically inconsistent with object relations, which can be observed "indisputably as early as the first week of . . . life and certainly in the first month" (p. 87). Balint's appeal to the criterion of parsimony went unheard for forty years, but it has since won general support.

In the last twenty years, a consensus has emerged that endorses Balint's position. Emanuel Peterfreund (1978) began by challenging conventional psychoanalytic methodologies that apply clinical concepts as yardsticks and so evaluate normal infant behavior for failing to meet adult standards. To say that an infant is narcissistic, since lacking in concern for others, is to impose an adult model that tells us what is not present. It does not explain what is. Equally inappropriate are the various linkages between infancy and the pathologies of later life. The premise has never been earned that psychopathology consists of fixation in, or regression to, an earlier developmental stage. It is equally possible and considerably more likely that pathology consists of a tragic distortion of normal developmental achievements. Following Peterfreund's methodological broadside, Milton Klein (1981) criticized Margaret Mahler's (1952, 1958) concepts of infantile autism and symbiosis, and Thomas M. Horner (1985) falsified Sandor Ferenczi's (1913) concept of infantile omnipotence.

Psychoanalytic writers soon began to submit the theoretical issues to the test of direct infant observation. Theodore J. Gaensbauer (1982) demonstrated that newborns have differentiated experiences of affects. Joseph D. Lichtenberg (1983) suggested and Daniel N. Stern (1983, 1985) amply demonstrated that subject-object differentiation is in evidence immediately upon birth. In one experiment, newborns, only hours after birth, were shown a moving object whose trajectory took it behind another object, out of the infants' sight, before it emerged into view once again. The infants' eyes were observed moving across the obscuring object, to await the reappearance of the hidden object at the appropriate place. The infants intuitively knew that the moving object was an object that continued to exist even when it was out of sight.

Cognitive psychologists began to postulate the inborn, genetically determined basis of an infant's knowledge of the objective, external existence of the mother (Bråten, 1988; Murray, 1991). Kernberg (1991) articulated the emerging consensus with the summary that

> It is probably fair to say that early psychoanalytic theories that considered the newborn infant an isolated, self-contained entity have given way to considering the infant a "wired-in" participant in a dyadic relationship. Within the infant-caregiver relationship, as contemporary infant researchers have convincingly demonstrated, the infant evinces a surprisingly early capacity to differentiate objects from each other and to develop a specific object relationship with the primary caregiver. The highly discriminating quality of early sensory perceptions reinforces the impression of a much earlier sense of self and of object than was formerly assumed. By the same token, the contemporary concept of affect as a phylogenetically recent neuropsychological system having as its primary function the establishment of an early and urgent communication system between infant and caregiver also points in the same direction (pp. 112–13).

What is to be rescued from the wreckage of the theory of infantile solipsism? In conceding the inaccuracy of the concept of neonatal undifferentiation, Mahler's coworker, Fred Pine (1981, 1986, 1990) transferred Mahler's theory of separation-individuation from the cognitive development of the child, to his or her fantasy life. Pine (1990) suggested that "the emergence of self and other as well as the laying down of vague memory traces of merger experiences are both occurring simultaneously from the beginnings of life" (p. 238). Pine supposed that infants engage in subject-object differentiation when performing realistic tasks, but also enjoy experiences of "wished-for-merger in the setting of moments of intensely gratifying 'oneness' experience" such as falling asleep while nursing at the breast (p. 205).

Object relations theorists are in close agreement. James Grotstein (1980–81) suggested that "the infant experiences himself as being separate as well as nonseparate from the very beginning of life" (p. 394). Otto F. Kernberg (1991) proposed that "the early differentiation of self and object representations takes place simultaneously with the setting up of fused or undifferentiated self and object representations under conditions of peak affect activation" (p. 113).

These formulations take for granted the fundamental psychoanalytic distinction between the pleasure principle that governs fantasy and the reality principle to which rational or "secondary process" thought conforms. Freud's theory of primary narcissism had maintained that infantile solipsism was the earliest stage of cognitive realism. Because we now know that newborns differentiate self and object, clinical observations that were formerly interpreted in terms of solipsistic infantile realism are being reinterpreted in terms of infantile fantasies about merger or fusion with their mothers. A theory of infants' general perception of reality has been replaced with a theory of infants' occasional fantasies about their mothers.

Interestingly, Ferenczi (1913) long ago suggested the universal occurrence in infancy of a nostalgia for intrauterine life. Although the whole of human development is assuredly driven by an instinct to emerge from the womb and to acquire maturity, Ferenczi may have been right to suggest that the aspiration for autonomy retains the self-sufficiency of the womb as its high-water mark throughout life. Just as finding a spouse has its neonatal precedent in bonding with the mother (Freud, 1905), the ideal of self-sufficiency can be understood as a fantasy that is suggested by intrauterine memories. Ferenczi's concern with fantasies of intrauterine life was overshadowed, however, by Moxon and Freud's theories of realistic cognitive regression. Discussion of fusion, merger, or unitive experiences as the content of fantasies, rather than as regressions of the ego's sense of reality, was not resumed until Bertram D. Lewin's (1951) study of mania. Edith Jacobson (1954b) expanded the argument with the generalization that "the earliest wishful fantasies of merging and being one with the mother (breast) are the foundation on which all future types of identification are built" (p. 98). In accounting for psychotic identifications, Jacobson (1954a) focused on neonatal sources of infantile fantasies: "The baby's wish for oneness with the mother, founded on fantasies of oral incorporation of the love object, will easily bring about refusions between self- and love-object images whenever the child experiences gratifications, physical contact, and closeness with the mother" (p. 242). Sylvan Keiser (1962); Eugenio Gaddini (1969); Lloyd H. Silverman (1978, 1979); and Silverman, Frank N. Lachmann, and Robert H. Milich (1982) offered similar interpretations of their patients' fantasies of fusion or merger with their mothers. They suggested that merger fantasies are regressions to early infantile fantasies of nondifferentiation or symbiosis. Martin S. Bergmann (1971) added "that love revives, if not direct memories, then feelings and archaic ego states that were once active in the symbiotic phase" (p. 32).

The Collapse of the Theory of Mystical Regression

Irving B. Harrison (1986) was the first author to relate the new consensus in direct infant observation to the psychoanalytic theory of mysticism. Unitive experiences cannot be regressions to the worldview of prenatal or neonatal ex-

periences, he concluded, because there is no solipsistic stage of infantile cognition to which a regression might proceed. Unitive experiences contain no element of regression whatever.

> There is no basis for the assumption that the oceanic feeling exists in normal
> infants or children, nor in the presumed intrauterine tranquillity of absolute
> (i.e., never disturbed) primary narcissism. . . . Nothing is returned to, in the ex-
> treme regression of the oceanic feeling, except in fantasy" (p. 156).

Harrison suggested that unitive experiences are to be regarded as fantasies.

The interpretation of unitive experiences as fantasies had initially been proposed by Edith Jacobson. In distinguishing mysticism from psychosis, Jacobson
(1964) wrote:

> Since normal experiences of ecstasy do not aim at destruction but are founded
> on a fantasy of libidinal union between self and object world, they result in a
> transitory sense of self-expression and the feeling that the self and the world are
> rich. Such experiences of merging, which may briefly retransform the images
> of the self and the object world into a fantasy unit vested with libidinal forces,
> permit an immediate reestablishment of the boundaries between them. By
> contrast, pathological regressive fusions caused by severe aggression may result
> in an irreparable breakdown of these boundaries and hence of the self and ob-
> ject representations (p. 69).

Jacobson argued that loving merger fantasies are followed by the resumption of
realistic knowledge of separation and serve to facilitate object-relations. Merger
fantasies are pathological when, through aggression, the fantasies become
chronic and interfere with object-relations.

W. W. Meissner (1992), who is both a Jesuit and a psychoanalyst, echoed Jacobson's position. "The mystical immersion rides on a grandiose fantasy of
union with an omnipotent and infinite love object . . . mystical experiences uni-
versally have the quality of wish-fulfillments—like dream experiences that satisfy
unconscious desires" (p. 339).

There are cogent grounds, however, for rejecting all theories that mystical
moments are regressive fantasies. It does not matter whether the theories pertain
to intrauterine or neonatal periods. It does not matter whether the theories concern pathological regressions or potentially wholesome "regressions in the service of the ego" (Geleerd, in Solnit, 1959; Prince & Savage, 1965; Fauteux,
1994). Regression is the wrong theoretical concept to account for what occurs.
Neither in realistic cognition nor in fantasy has an infant the intellectual capacity to conceptualize a unitive experience. Horner (1992) emphasized that "symbiotic states, which emphasize unions, mergers, and the like, convey only
metaphorically what it might be like, even as an infant, to achieve closeness to
and security with another" (p. 41). The distinction is an important one.

There are manifest differences between fantasies of mother–infant fusion and unitive experiences. Consider, for example, the following self-report of an LSD experience.

> I was sucking. Sucking. Sucking at mother's breast, I suppose. I had her big tit in my mouth and it felt like a cushion over my face. I could smell her stinking sweat. It was tickling my nostrils. Still it felt good. I was peaceful. . . . And then I was floating, swirling. Floating all over the universe. I was all over. Not happy, not sad. Just being—all over . . . being, just being (Easson, 1973, pp. 65–66)

The drug-taker's experience began with an Isakower phenomenon, the fantasy (Isakower, 1938) or dream (Blaustein, 1975) of a large, roughly textured, often dry, roundish lump of an object in the mouth, sometimes together with a feeling of pressure against the outside of the lips. In most cases the Isakower phenomenon is simply experienced without being understood; but in some cases, as in the case cited by William M. Easson, the experience is immediately understood as the act of sucking on a nipple. In addition, in this drug-taker's experience, the concrete fantasy of nursing suddenly underwent transformation into a unitive experience of the solitary self.

The discrete representations of self and other in the Isakower phenomenon were derived from infantile sense perception. This phenomenon was not followed by an equally concrete fantasy of blending into the mother's body, but by a unitive experience that portrayed the self in solitary self-sufficiency as the totality of being.

Experiences of self in solitude are probably the closest that unitive experiences come to portraying intrauterine self-sufficiency, but they remain at a considerable remove from a regression *ad uterum*. The blissful passivity of unitive experiences is inconsistent with the busy fetal activity that ultrasound technology has disclosed. In unitive experiences, there is no proprioception of a fetal body that is capable of arm and leg motion, swallowing, bringing the hands to the face and mouth, and so forth. There is no concrete sense perception of amniotic fluid in the throat and outside the skin, nor is there representation of the umbilical cord that fetuses have been observed to clutch, to rub sensuously against, and to swing from in play (Piontelli, 1992). Whatever faint memory of intrauterine solitude may contribute to unitive experiences is considerably reworked, partly through the additions of abstractions—timelessness, boundlessness, and so forth—and partly through the denial of discrete bodily sensations in favor of a vague, amorphous notion of being. The unitive experience is, as it were, a mental image or portrait of the abstract concept of being—an effort to depict the abstract concept of being in the medium, as it were, of a waking dream.

The discrepancy between the theory of regression and the empirical evidence of unitive experiences was emphasized by Paul C. Horton (1974), who analyzed the following self-report of a patient's experience.

That day I was headachy. I had a sense, an anticipation of something about to happen. In fact, I felt like I was going to explode. I hadn't been eating much for several weeks and had fasted the whole day before going to church. I was scared when I went in, but it was a beautiful morning and the church was full of people praying. I began praying—I don't remember what—and, all of a sudden, I was filled with brilliant white light. I was it. It was me. My whole body felt tingly and radiant, and I felt like I was part of everything and everything was part of me. I was overcome with love and joy. I was ecstatic. I had never experienced anything like that before in my life. It was like a mental orgasm. I was ecstatic for a long time, and the church was empty when I left. Slowly, I began coming down. The world, which had been so sparkling and dazzling just hours before, now became dull and miserable, and I could see all of its imperfections. I had no idea what had happened to me. All that I knew was that both worlds could not be true. And I *knew* that the experience I had just had was the most real possible experience (p. 368).

Horton asserted that even though mystical experiences are "derivative of, or based on, the child's internalization of the mother figure," they are "not . . . reducible to the mother-child symbiosis" (p. 373). Different aspects of his patient's unitive experience exhibited many other psychological processes and motives.

The worldly reality of being utterly and agonizingly alone was transiently *denied*. Oral sexual longings, which had been repressed, were now *intellectualized* and *sublimated* (she analogized her experience to a "mental orgasm"). Her rage at the world's failure to gratify her oral dependency needs was stringently *repressed*. The beauty of the church with the warm sun pouring through the glowing, stained glass windows was *distorted*. This distortion consisted in a transmutation of a concrete, physical experience (sunlight, vivid colors, soothing hymns, etc.) into an inner, emotional experience (p. 377).

The inadequacy of theories of regression was subsequently argued by the psychologist Ralph W. Hood Jr. (1976). Writing from a Lacanian standpoint, Julia Kristeva (1987) made a related observation regarding theistic unitive experiences, when she emphasized that mystical experiences transpose fusion "from the mother's body to an invisible agency."

Overcoming the notion of irremediable separation . . . reestablishes a continuous fusion with an Other that is no longer substantial and maternal but symbolic. . . . What we have here is fusion . . . transposed from the mother's body to an invisible agency. . . . This is quite a wrench from the dependency of early childhood, and it must be said that it is a compromise solution, since the benefits of the new relationship of dependency are entirely of an imaginary order, in the realm of signs (p. 24).

In Kristeva's view, the transposition of the idea of fusion from the mother's body to an invisible agency utilizes the latent idea of the mother's body as a *metaphor* that refers to God as Other.

Theories that unitive experiences are regressions to mother-infant symbiosis have never been able to explain why unitive experiences are not simply nursing fantasies. Theories of regression to intrauterine solitude are similarly unable to account for the metaphoric character of the portraiture of the abstract concept of being. Unitive experiences are plainly not relivings of early fantasies. Their manifest contents do not replicate sense perceptions, but instead portray abstractions in the concrete form of dreamlike experiences. Whatever role nostalgia may have in their motivation, there is little evidence of actual memory in their manifest content.

A Theory of Creative Sublimations

The relation of mother-infant merger fantasies to unitive experiences is better conceptualized, I suggest, by reference to the psychoanalytic concept of "sublimation" (Arlow, 1995, p. 253; Neubauer, 1995, p. 343; for recent discussions of sublimation, see: Loewald, 1988; Gay, 1992). Melanie Klein suggested that for nonclinical purposes we may reverse the conventional clinical psychoanalysis of practically everything as symbols of unconscious sexuality. Cultural symbols may be understood more fully by regarding symbols of unconscious sexuality as building blocks with which we construct our worldviews. For example, it is not simply that an infant will mouthe things in the environment as though they were breasts, but that the category "breast" functions as the infant's criterion for developing a worldview. Klein (1936) wrote:

> The breast of the mother which gives gratification or denies it becomes, in the mind of the child, imbued with the characteristics of good and evil. Now, what one might call the "good" breasts become the prototype of what is felt throughout life to be good and beneficent, while the "bad" breasts stand for everything evil and persecuting (p. 291).

External realities can be treated as symbols of the breast, reducing their psychological significance to the latter (M. Klein, 1937); but experiences pertaining to the breast can also be used to generate ideas with which a worldview may begin to be constructed. Freud introduced the term *sublimation* to name the circumstance when symbolic ideas, such as good and evil, are abstracted from concrete experiences in interpersonal relations. In a symbol, a reality other than the breast is invested with the significance of the breast. In a sublimation, the reality is treated in its own right, by investing it with the metaphoric significance of the

breast. The two processes should not be confused. In sublimation, concrete sensorimotor images, closely tied to instinctual desires, have undergone generalization, abstraction, and—most importantly—metaphoric application or adaptation
to the reality of the perceptible world.

Most psychoanalytic references to fantasies, including the distinction between fantasy and imagination in the last chapter, are broad and generic. A more
precise and nuanced theory of unitive experiences, consistent with their treatment as sublimations, was offered as early as 1923 by Gustav Bychowski, who associated mystical and creative experiences. Bychowski (1951) suggested that
both alike "aim and at time succeed in grasping, experiencing and occasionally
expressing something like the eternal truth and essence of things" (p. 404). Ernst
Kris (1939) concurred. "The driving of the unconscious toward consciousness is
experienced as an intrusion from without—an attitude of passive nature *par excellence*. . . . In ecstasy, the process results in an emotional climax only; in states of
inspiration, it leads to active elaboration in creation" (p. 302). The equivalence
of creative and mystical experiences won broad acceptance, however, only when
it was restated by Gilbert J. Rose (1964).

> Aesthetic, religious, and empathic experience may all be conceptualized as cre-
> ative expansions of ego boundaries with id, superego and external world. They
> may all be associated with some temporary fusion and loss of differentiation which
> has been variously labelled according to whether it has occurred during aesthetic,
> religious, or empathic experience, but has been almost invariably traced to sepa-
> ration anxiety and the attempt to restore the mother-child symbiotic bond (p. 76).

The new perception of mystical experiences had important consequences
for clinical diagnoses. Nathaniel Ross (1975) suggested that the unitive experiences that occur spontaneously as symptoms of acute schizophrenia are com-
pensatory in function. "It is quite common for schizophrenics to experience
mystical ecstasies briefly before they plunge into the psychic depths. This would
appear to represent a last desperate attempt to cling to the object world" (p. 91).
Ross cautioned against facile equations of mystical experiences with psychosis.
Not only do "symbiotic" states occur in psychosis, but "partial and reversible"
symbiotic states are frequent and varied aspects of normal experiences.

> It is characteristic of a wide range of satisfying experiences that there is a loss of
> self-consciousness with the retention of self-awareness. One is "immersed,"
> "lost," "absorbed," "possessed," by a person, a book, a drama, a cause, an idea, a
> piece of music, an intellectual discovery, a beautiful painting, an enchanting
> child, etc. I believe that such "immersions," passionately sought by men in a
> great variety of ways, are partial and reversible symbiotic states. There is a subtle
> alteration of consciousness in such "immersions." There is no loss of identity:
> the sense of self is continuously enriched by experiences of this nature (p. 91).

Rose (1972) retained Jacobson's diagnostic distinction between temporary and permanent fusion states. He was consequently generously disposed even to unitive experiences in which the sense of self is momentarily lost. He suggested that "fusion" states are themselves normal and may contribute to psychological growth at all developmental levels. In his view, the diagnostic question is whether recovery occurs.

> The capacity for effecting at least a fleeting oneness with objects is never completely lost. The boundaries between the self and object representations within the ego may remain somewhat fluid and interchangeable even into adult life. . . . To merge in order to re-emerge may be part of the fundamental process of psychological growth at all developmental levels. Although fusion may dominate the most primitive levels, it contributes a richness of quality and texture to the others (pp. 182, 185).

Following these improvements in the psychoanalytic understanding of mysticism, compatible theories were advanced in other schools of psychology. Discussing religious experiences in general, the social psychologists C. Daniel Batson and W. Larry Ventis (1982) likened the four stages of inspired creativity—preparation, incubation, illumination, and verification (Wallas, 1926)—to the religious processes of an existential crisis, self-surrender, achieving a new vision, and making a new life (pp. 82–87). Whether creative or religious, the unconscious thought of the second phase accomplishes a reorganization of cognitive structures. Depending on whether the new cognitive Gestalt, which emerges in the moment of illumination, is an improvement or not, "religious experiences may be noncreative as well as creative" (p. 87).

The creative nature of mystical moments may be better appreciated by considering them in the context of spiritual awakenings. I have elsewhere (Merkur, 1997) presented the theoretical model as follows.

1. Preparation. With a spiritual awakening, the establishment of the religious problem might occur in any of several manners: for example, through education, an existential crisis, or a growth in intelligence, such as the developmental acquisition of the capacity for generalization around age six, or for abstraction around puberty. The problem tends to concern the origin, meaning, and/or purpose of personal existence.

2. Incubation. The unconscious incubation of the problem's solution formulates or activates an unconscious unitive schema (based perhaps on infantile merger fantasies) and develops an unconscious solution.

3. Illumination. The creative solution manifests as the content of one or more religious experiences. A spiritual emergency (Grof & Grof, 1990) then tends to occur. Unconscious resistance to the emergent spirituality is responsible, among other matters, for requiring the unconscious spirituality to undergo symbol-formation ("dream-work") prior to its manifestation. Other symptoms may include acting-out behavior (Merkur, 1995–96).

4. Verification. A spiritual emergency may be resolved in any of several manners. The spiritual insights may be denied. They may instead be accepted in a partial manner, leading to one or another compromise (e.g., normative devotion to a traditional religion). In cases that lead to self-actualization, however, eagerness for spiritual insights reduces the resistance and permits the unconscious spirituality to manifest with increasing clarity, that is, with less recourse to symbolism. As the initial insights manifest with increasing clarity, new insights continue to be attained. Eventually the resistance may be more or less completely dissolved and a spirituality may manifest that is nonsymbolic in a psychoanalytic sense. The spirituality does not consist simply of insights. For self-actualization to occur, the creative insights must additionally be integrated within the sense of self and actualized as a way of faith and behavior.

The transpersonal psychologist Ken Wilber offered a different but complementary theory. He viewed the *via mystica* as a process of cognitive development, in whose course the mystic conceptualizes a series of metaphysical propositions. Wilber (1983) suggested that mystical experiences depend on the formulation of "basic structures [that] are essentially cognitive structures" that have never previously been attained. If the "cognitive maps or worldviews" emerge from the unconscious, they are recent achievements of "successively new and higher structures." Each represents an advance beyond the previous reach of cognitive development (p. 275). In Wilber's model, a mystic's development is analogous to a child's progress in mastering mathematical ideas. Advances in the understanding of reality produce a more or less predictable series of cognitions. The experiences express increasingly correct understandings of an unvarying truth. In the case of mysticism, Wilber privileges the Zen Buddhist doctrine that All and Nothing are one (p. 301). Empirical studies of single mystics' development falsify Wilber's claim that mystics progress from personal mysticism to impersonal introspective union to mystical nothingness (pp. 90, 97). Wilber's metaphysical claims notwithstanding, his treatment of unitive experiences as a series of creative cognitive achievements has much to recommend it.

Some Developmental Considerations

The mother-infant fusion fantasies that undergo sublimation into unitive schemas may originate early in neonatal life, but their sublimation into unitive schemas presupposes a capacity for metaphoric thinking that is achieved developmentally only somewhat later. Because unitive experiences have been reported as early as age three (E. Hoffman, 1992), Horner's (1992, p. 40) suggestion cannot be correct that unitive experiences presuppose the type of metaphoric thought that children acquire only in latency. Unitive experiences necessarily depend on an earlier and simpler form of symbolic thought. The problem is a difficult one, however, and I am unable to resolve it. I strongly suspect that the collapse of the theory of infantile solipsism calls into question Piaget's (1937) notion of a sensorimotor stage and its dramatic supercession by symbolic thought. Communication between infant and mother is instinctual. In some sense at least, symbolic thinking is inborn and active immediately following birth.

In the absence of a reliable understanding of how symbolic thought develops, I can suggest when but not why unitive thinking first comes about. The onset of consciously *symbolic thought*, in Piaget's sense of the term, is indicated definitively by the "no" headshake (Spitz, 1957) in advance of the acquisition of speech. The capacity to respond "no" facilitates an intellectual distancing from others and increases self-awareness (McDevitt, 1979, p. 332). There soon arises a self-conscious concept of the self, a capacity to entertain a symbol for the self (compare: Stern's [1985] concept of the "verbal self"). The formation of a self-representation or idea of the self occurs typically around the seventeenth month: seeing a mark on their foreheads as reflected in a mirror, children know for the first time to touch their own faces (Amsterdam & Levitt, 1980). Self-recognition presupposes a developed capacity for generalization that is able to organize discrete memories of sensorimotor self-perceptions into a generalized self-representation, complete with an identity that is constructed out of fantasy and speculation (W. I. Grossman, 1982).

The conditions for the cognitive achievement of a would-be realistic self-representation are presumably the minimum conditions necessary for the development of the simplest unitive schema, the schema of the solitary or "secret" self. The idea of an endless, timeless, solitary self has less content than any other schema and may be treated *ex hypothesi* as the foundational schema atop which all others build (Merkur, 1998a). As a metaphoric extrapolation from the idea of self, it cannot antedate the latter, which originates typically around the seventeenth month.

On the other hand, the commencement of moral thinking only a few weeks later indicates the completed developmental origin of at least one fairly advanced mode of unitive thinking. Sandor Rado (1928) suggested that morality originates in the oral-sadistic stage of development through the child's fear to offend the mother by biting her. Klein (1933, 1937) endorsed Rado's position and added guilt and reparation to the oral-sadistic dynamics of love and fear. Basing himself on direct infant observation, Manuel Furer (1967) dated the origin of empathy and, with it, morality, specifically to the rapprochement subphase of development, during the fourteenth to eighteenth month after birth. Furer argued that empathy is responsible for the origin of guilt in the child. In cases of the empathic "experience [of] the painful quality of an affect in the other person that . . . [has]

been evoked in the observed person by an act of the observer," it sometimes happens that 'either the child ends up saying, "I am sorry," in actual words, or else this is to be understood from the nature of his consoling behaviour toward the object' (p. 277). What Furer observed was indeed a transmuting of empathic pain, through self-observation, into the knowledge of having caused hurt. Due to the child's love, the knowledge of responsibility led to sorrow, guilt, remorse, and reparation. Most writers concerned with developmental issues date the origin of empathy to the same period, which is understood theoretically as the rapprochement subphase of the so-called separation-individuation process (Schafer, 1959; M. L. Hoffman, 1978; McDevitt, 1979; Buie, 1981; Bergman & Wilson, 1984; Emde, 1988). With the collapse of the theory of infantile solipsism, the term *separation-individuation* is no longer tenable; but the empirical observations of the rapprochement subphase remain reliable.

These considerations connect the unitive schemas with the ego ideal. When Freud introduced the term *ego ideal* in 1914, he referred to a set of values that conscience applies in its deliberations, both as a model for aspiration and as a criterion for self-assessment (compare: Morrison, 1983; Milrod, 1990; Tyson & Tyson, 1990, p. 202). Freud changed the term's definition in 1921 to denote the psychical agency, previously called conscience, to which he attributed the functions of self-observation, conscience (including dream censorship), and maintaining ideals (Parkin, 1985). In order to cut short the confusion that he had caused in 1921, from 1923 onward Freud referred to the psychical agency as the superego and wrote of the ego ideal only in its original sense as a set of values.

Under all of its names, the psychical agency had the same functions of self-observation, conscience (including dream censorship), and maintaining ideals (Freud, 1914, 1921, 1933). However, Freud's account of the agency under the term *superego* involved an increase in understanding. The chief theoretical innovations were two. Freud initially thought of the agency as a conscious structure. However, when Freud (1916–17) reexamined his theory of dream-censorship, he came to recognize it as an unconscious activity of the psyche's moral agency. The other major innovation was developmental. Where Freud had considered the ego ideal to be "the substitute for the lost narcissism of childhood," he dated the superego to the onset of latency.

Where Freud replaced his ego ideal theory of 1914 with the superego theory of 1923, Herman Nunberg ([1932] 1955) treated both theories as valid and restated them in a developmental sequence. "The predominantly maternal ego ideal starts to develop as early as the pregenital stages, but the predominantly paternal superego is observed first in the genital stage" (p. 146). Nunberg's distinction was largely ignored when it was first published, but it became a permanent part of mainstream psychoanalytic thinking upon its revival by Annie Reich (1953). She wrote:

> The deep longing to become like the parent creates a constant inner demand upon the child's ego: an ego ideal is formed. . . . The ego ideal, on the other hand, is based upon the desire to cling in some form or another to a denial of the ego's as well as of the parent's limitations and to regain infantile omnipotence by identifying with the idealized parent. . . . One can describe the ego ideal as the earlier structure, as the precursor of the superego (pp. 188–89).

Although Reich called the ego ideal a "precursor" of the superego, she portrayed the ego ideal as a developmentally early nucleus of the superego that is radically different from what it becomes at the beginning of latency under the influence of increased reality-testing.

Building on the work of Reich, Edith Jacobson (1954b; see also: 1964) articulated a coherent theoretical link between the positions of Freud and Nunberg.

> The insufficient distinction between object and self during the beginning constitution of an ego ideal, or rather of its precursors, explains why in its deep, unconscious kernel we may detect fusions of both early infantile images of the love object and of the self, and why at bottom the superego and the ego ideal harbor the grandiose wishes of the preoedipal child as well as his belief in the parental omnipotence. In fact, parental demands and prohibitions can probably become internalized only by joining forces with the child's own narcissistic, ambitious strivings to which they give a new direction (p. 106).

Jacobson's reference to "the insufficient distinction between object and self" was an equivocal phrasing that accommodated both Jacobson's own position and the then widely held theory that infants are initially unable to distinguish self from loved objects. Jacobson (1954a) herself maintained what is now the accepted position, that "the baby's wish for oneness with the mother, [is] founded on fantasies of oral incorporation of the love object" (p. 242). She suggested that a single psychic agency matures from an original lack of subject-object distinctions, into the ego ideal of the oral stage, and later into the latency superego. Its core of unitive thinking has its basis, however, not in infantile misunderstandings of reality, but in "wishful fantasies of merging and being one with the mother (breast)" (Jacobson, 1954b, p. 98).

Jacobson's formulation provides a basis for integrating my findings with the main body of psychoanalytic theories. The lack of subject-object differentiation at the superego's core has its basis in unitive fantasies. It is in these fantasies—but not in infants' realistic knowledge—that subject-object distinctions disappear or do not exist.

Because infant-mother merger fantasies undergo sublimation into unitive schemas, some of which portray ideals of the self—as solitary, as cosmic, and so forth—; because the same fantasies underlie the formation of the ego ideal or superego of the oral stage; and because unitive schemas accomplish moral thinking, which is conventionally attributed to the classical superego of latency, I suggest that unitive schemas are functions of the superego. At least some of them, for example, identification, are responsible for internalizing specific values within the superego. Others presumably generate individual ego ideals.

The Structure of Unitive Thinking

As a provisional model, I suggest that the development of unitive thinking is not unilinear, but multilinear. There is a scientific line of unitive thinking, a moral line, and so forth. All presumably develop from a common origin, but each develops separately. (Neurochemical differences may perhaps be involved. MDMA experiences [Adamson, 1985] apparently affect the empathic line without going on, as LSD, mescaline, and psilocybin experiences do [Merkur, 1998a], also to the metaphysical lines.)

For heuristic purposes, I imagine the unconscious organization of the unitive schemas by analogy to a tree of directories and files in a computer. If *ex hypothesi* each variety of unitive experiences is attributed to a different unitive schema, the schemas can be arranged in the multiply branching pattern of a computer directory tree. The solitary self, for example, would be analogous to a root directory. Incorporation and identification would be subdirectories; and their accommodations, inclusion, and relation, would be sub-subdirectories. The scientific line of unitive thinking presumably branches off incorporation in a different direction, while moral thinking branches off identification.

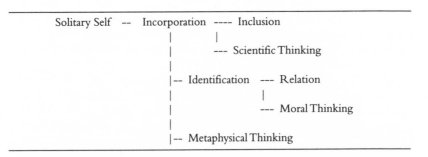

Working with such a model, it becomes possible to speculate that a person who has developed scientific and moral thinking into a highly differentiated series of subschemas may eventually reach a logical problem whose solution can be developed only by backtracking to the root directory, and by starting to develop a new branch of the directory tree. For example, exhaustion of the possibilities of scientific materialism to generate a sense of meaning and purpose may precipitate an existential crisis that is resolved through a religious conversion. Because the birth of spirituality may require a return to basic unitive schemas, before more advanced or sophisticated subschemas can be developed in the spiritual line, the initial conversion experiences may seem "regressive." However, the return to simple ideas is in fact developmentally progressive. There is regression in form, but progress in overall unitive development.

A directory tree model has far-reaching implications for the understanding of spiritual awakening. It seems clear that in the course of a spontaneous spiritual awakening, the reversion to a simple schema in a highly fantastic mystical moment is normally followed by the rapid elaboration of a more or less predictable series of sublimations (Grof & Grof, 1990; Merkur, 1995–96, 1997). The initial awakening involves a cognitively simple insight, which is elaborated into a cognitively more complex, nuanced, and complete spirituality as developmental progress is made. The discrepancy between the lived actuality of spiritual development and the tripartite scheme of purgation, illumination, and union, was already common knowledge among medieval Sufis. In the eleventh century, Al-Ghazali divided the "mystic way" (tariqah) into "the purification of the heart," "the recollection of God," and "complete absorption" (fana) in God. However, he went on to state:

> At least this is its end relatively to those first steps which almost come within the sphere of choice and personal responsibility; but in reality in the actual mystic "way" it is the first step. . . .
>
> With this first stage of the "way" there begin the revelations and visions. The mystics in their waking state now behold angels and the spirits of the prophets; they hear these speaking to them and are instructed by them. Later, a higher state is reached; instead of beholding forms and figures, they come to stages in the "way" which it is hard to describe in language. . . . In general what they manage to achieve is nearness to God (Watt, 1994, p. 64).

The reduction of thought to the simplicity of union with God is not the summit of the mystical path. It is the moment of a breakthrough to a new line of unitive thinking. Not yet elaborated, the new developmental line is as yet simple and rudimentary. It is nevertheless the condition for further progress along the same metaphysical line.

The puzzle of psychotic mysticism is not solved, but is advanced by interpolating the theory that a spiritual awakening progresses, more or less sequentially, from cognitively simpler to cognitively more complex spiritual insights. Psychotic mysticism, no differently than spiritual awakenings, is characterized in part by its inclusion of idiosyncratic symbolic elements. In optimal development, insight is gained into the idiosyncrasies, the need for symbolization is reduced, and the intersubjective constants of spirituality are explored increasingly fully. Pathological complication of a spiritual awakening typically involves the reification and fixation of some idiosyncratic symbolism—an isolation within consciousness, rather than a repression from it. Once the unitive materials are isolated, the process of reality-testing, accommodation, and cognitive development is skewed, if not also slowed and halted. Fixation at or near the root schema is not infrequent. Many schizophrenics, for example, identify with God not only for the duration of a mystical moment, but as a chronic feature of their psychosis.

Another puzzle that may open to solution is the so-called dark night of the soul that Underhill (1910), in my view wrongly, suggested was a typical or regular feature of the *via mystica*. St. John of the Cross invented the phrase in reference to a period of "spiritual dryness." He had already successfully achieved mystical union when he underwent a prolonged period during which no mystical moments occurred. His "dark night" consisted of frustration, resentment, anger, and mourning. Underhill added the dark night as a regular feature to Proclus' tripartite division of the *via mystica*, which pseudo-Dionysius had introduced within Christianity. The resultant four-part model consisted of purgation (preparatory moral reform, ascesis, etc.); illumination (mystical visions, voices, theological insights, etc.); the dark night; and union. Contemporary discussions of the dark night often extend the term from desolation and anger at the failure to have religious experiences, to include desolation and anger in response to the content of religious experiences. Kevin Fauteux (1994, pp. 70, 115) has plausibly analyzed the dark night as a transference onto God of unconscious anger at infantile abandonment by a care-giver. My present concern, however, is with the failure of access to religious experiences that provokes the transference. Why should someone who has already successfully enjoyed mystical moments undergo a subsequent period of their nonoccurrence? If it were only a case of projecting parental abandonment as a Divine rejection, there would be no mystical experiences at all. For mystical moments both to occur and then to cease, something more must be happening unconsciously. In this context, I would draw attention to the fact that the dark night occurs in a world-rejecting mystical tradition that uses self-hypnotic trance states in efforts to fixate unitive development in the root schemas, which they prioritize doctrinally (compare: Committee on Psychiatry and Religion, 1976). Other historical instances are Vedantin Yoga and the Neoplatonic trends in Sufism. Mystics who favor the root schemas that these traditions promote may become engaged, in my view, in a kind of spiritual Peter Pan-ism. In fidelity to received doctrines, they may attempt to remain developmentally simple, rejecting spiritual progress to unitive schemas of greater complexity and realism. Refusing to allow themselves consciously to experience the progress that they have already begun to achieve unconsciously, they experience a "dryness" of their own making.

Healthier or nonconflicted attitudes to the integration of mystical moments within spiritual development is available in several mystical traditions. The theosophical trend within Sufism and, to a lesser extent, within both the kabbalah and Christian theosophy in the tradition of Jacob Boehme (Merkur, 1998b) have a long history of attempting to map the further stages of spiritual growth. Good advice on how to work with the "dark night" is presented, I suggest, in the following Hasidic teaching.

> A disciple asked the Baal Shem: "Why is it that one who clings to God and knows he is close to him, sometimes experiences a sense of interruption and remoteness?"

> The Baal Shem explained: "When a father sets out to teach his little son to walk, he stands in front of him and holds his two hands on either side of the child, so that he cannot fall, and the boy goes toward his father between his father's hands. But the moment he is close to his father, he moves away a little, and holds his hands farther apart, and he does this over and over, so that the child may learn to walk" (Buber, 1947, p. 65).

My understanding of progress and fixation in spiritual development is consistent with the psychoanalytic approach of Harold F. Searles, who contrasted solipsistic mystical moments with other experiences of relatedness in which a realistic sense of individuality was preserved. Searles's clinical insight remains valuable even though it was articulated with reference to the theory of mystical regression, which is no longer tenable. Searles (1960) wrote:

> Deeply pleasurable though such [mystical] experiences are, and however essential they may be to normal personality development during childhood and adolescence, I believe that they are not the characteristic *mature* orientation toward the nonhuman environment. Portrayed in the above account is an experience of dissolution of ego boundaries, a loss of identity as an individual human being and a perception of oneself, in an infantile-omnipotent fashion, as being at one with the totality of one's environment. Such experiences, which as I say hold great appeal even for mature human beings, are very different from the experience of *relatedness* to the nonhuman environment. . . . In this latter experience, by contrast, the person feels a sense of real and close kinship, but does not lose his awareness of his own individuality; that awareness is, instead, deepened (pp. 106–7).

Searles considered solipsistic unitive phenomena normal during childhood and adolescence, but only the sense of relatedness fully mature. "The former experience, however joyous, is, I believe, basically an infantile experience of sensing oneself to be in union with the Good Mother, an experience no more mature than that of the melancholiac who feels himself to be in union with the Bad Mother" (pp. 107–8). Searles cited Martin Buber's rejection of introspective union in favor of I-Thou relatedness as a precedent for his own diagnostic stance (pp. 118–19).

Summary

Speculating on the basis of the data of unitive experiences in schizophrenia, Freud suggested that newborns are initially solipsistic and only gradually learn to recognize the externality of the perceptible world. He later used his theory of "primary narcissism" to explain unitive experiences as regressions to a neonatal "ego feeling." The circularity of his argument escaped attention until advances in direct infant observation established that object relations are inborn. Clinical phenomena that were previously interpreted by reference to the theory of neonatal solipsism have since been reinterpreted in terms of unconscious fantasies of mother-infant fusion or merger. These fantasies occur *ex hypothesi* during the first two years of life.

The replacement of Freud's theory of infants' general perception of reality with Jacobson's theory of infants' occasional fantasies about their mothers makes nonsense of the theory that unitive experiences are regressions. Unitive experiences are incommensurate with their ostensible sources in infancy. The transformation of concrete fantasies of being one with the maternal breast, for example, into a sense of oneness with all-being, presupposes a sophisticated process of generalization, metaphorization, abstraction, and so forth. Unitive experiences may instead be seen as creative inspirations that depend, at minimum, on the sublimation of unconscious merger fantasies.

The earliest possible date for the origin of unitive thinking is likely the rapprochement phase, in the middle third of the second year of life, when the idea of the self originates and empathy, guilt, and reparation first make their appearance. Clinical observation of the nondifferentiation of self and loved objects in the deepest levels of the ego ideal suggest that unitive schemas are constituent functions of the oral superego. A detailed account of the development of unitive schemas is not presently possible. The question is an empirical one and awaits solution through direct infant observation. It seems clear, however, that the schemas do not develop each out of the last in a unilinear fashion. Rather, the data exhibit a complicated multilinear relation that is possibly analogous to the organization of directories and subdirectories in a computer.

Working with a directory tree model also helps explain the differences between mysticism of the One and the postunitive mystical orientation of theosophy. It may also explain why the "dark night of the soul" is not a problem for the latter.

FOUR

Unity, the Transcendent, and Death

Interpreting unitive experiences as products of sublimation raises not one but several corollary problems. Let us proceed immediately to the fundamental question of the relation to reality. Sublimations may be described as adaptations of instinctual desires to nonsexual realities. Aggression may be sublimated, for example, in competitive sports; anal retention in quality control; and coitus in a roller coaster ride. Through sublimation, the psyche assigns meaning and value to objective realities that exceed the scope of its instinctual endowments. The psyche can assign no inborn values to realities of which it has no inborn knowledge. Sublimation is the process by which the values attached to the inborn knowledge of the infant are extrapolated to the circumstances of realities unanticipated by our innate cognitive endowment.

Accordingly, to tell us that it is fantasies of mother–infant fusion that undergo sublimation is to provide us with only half of a theory of mystical moments. Another question must also be asked. What are the nonsexual realities that are being given psychosexual value through the process of sublimation? What is the rational component of mystical moments, which compares with the prosocial behavior that morality values through identification and the perceptible world that scientific thinking unconsciously anthropomorphizes? Mother–infant fusion fantasies are sublimated in all three cases. Morality results when the sublimations concern prosocial behavior, and science in the case of the perceptible world. What realities do mystical moments concern?

The Rational Component in Religion

To define religion, not nominally but in a manner that reflects its natural compass, the phenomenological school of the history of religions (*Religionswissenschaft*) has traditionally endorsed the position of Rudolf Otto (1931, 1950), who proposed that the holy and the demonic be treated together as "the numinous." Otto regarded the numinous as a "non-rational" factor in the conception of the divine. Otto (1932b) also argued that historical religions have all known the *sensus numinus*, for which reason the sense of the numinous may be treated as a defining characteristic of religion.

Otto wrote generically of the holy or numinous in the singular, but he invoked Romantic dualism (Merkur, 1993b) in classifying numinous experiences. As a Christian theologian, Otto did not advocate duality within God. He tacitly acknowledged, however, that the dualistic classification of religious experiences in late Romanticism could readily be reconciled with his account of the numinous. Borrowing a technical term from J. J. Bachofen and Friedrich Nietzsche, Otto (1950) explicitly discussed "the Dionysiac element in the numen" (p. 31) under the term *fascinans*. The Apollonian element was implicitly to be understood as the other components of the numen, *mysterium* and *tremendum*.

Otto described the *mysterium tremendum* as a sense of the holy as awesome, majestic, urgent, and mysterious (pp. 13–28). In connection with the *mysterium*, Otto introduced the phrase "the Wholly Other," which he expressly identified as an affirmation of the *via positiva*.

> Not content with contrasting it with all that is of nature or this world, mysticism concludes by contrasting it with Being itself and all that "is," and finally actually calls it "that which is nothing." By this "nothing" is meant not only that of which nothing can be predicated, but that which is absolutely and intrinsically other than and opposite of everything that is and can be thought. But while exaggerating to the point of paradox this *negation* and contrast—the only means open to conceptual thought to apprehend the *mysterium*—mysticism at the same time retains the *positive quality* of the "wholly other" as a very living factor in its over-brimming religious emotion (p. 29).

By "wholly other" Otto referred to the nothingness that mystics actually experience as a positive reality (compare: p. 39).

What cannot be discussed, the total negation of the *via negativa*, entered Otto's discussion only when he went on to describe the second category of numinous experience: "the Dionysiac element in the numen" (p. 31) the *fascinans*. Here Otto introduced a separate term that deserves to be as widely famed as *the wholly other*. He referred to "the living 'something more' of the *fascinans*" (p. 35). Experience of the *fascinans* implies but does not disclose Something More. In other words, the *fascinans* is a manifest phenomenon whose experience implies the ulteriority of Something More and, by so doing, discloses itself as a mediating agency. To offer an example, in classical biblical prophecy, experiences of verbal inspirations implied a Revealer who was not manifest but who was responsible for the manifest inspirations. The phenomenology of the *fascinans* includes the implication of Something More; it is only Something More "*in-itself*," supposing there to be— or not to be—such, that is beyond immediate religious experience.

Otto's (1950) well-known claim that "a definitely 'numinous' state of mind . . . is perfectly *sui generis* and irreducible to any other" (p. 7) referred explicitly to a state of mind. He did not make a metaphysical truth-claim concerning the numinous as an objective reality; he made a psychological claim concerning the numinous as a phenomenal experience.

Otto derived a corollary from his initial observation. He concluded that the occurrence of numinous experiences proves the reality of "a unique 'numinous' category of value" (ibid.). With this assertion, he claimed that the numinous, like the beautiful and the moral, is a category of value-judgments and has an aspect or dimension that can only be understood on its own terms as a judgment of value. The numinous can certainly be approached and at least partially explained from sociological and psychoanalytic points of view, but the latter do not exhaust its study. Just as it is both possible and meaningful to discuss beauty as beauty and morality as morality, it is appropriate to discuss numinosity as numinosity.

Numinosity does not exist in the abstract. It is an aspect or quality that phenomena have. Numinosity might be said either to be embodied by numinous phenomena or to manifest through them, but it is never experienced apart from phenomena that are numinous. It is also very much in the eye of the beholder. Not everyone experiences numinous phenomena, and among those who do, some people are more sensitive or responsive than others. Anything and everything can be numinous, but nothing is numinous necessarily. Again, some things are numinous to some people, but not to others; and a person may experience a phenomenon as numinous on some occasions, but not on others. In all, numinosity is a "category of value" that the psyche or soul has the capacity to endow to certain of its experiences (Merkur, 1996).

Enlarging on Otto's concept of the element of mystery within the numinous, the historian of religions Gerardus van der Leeuw (1938) noted its pertinence to the intrinsic limitations of thought.

> The religious significance of things, therefore, is that on which no wider nor deeper meaning whatever can follow. It is the meaning of the whole; it is the last word. But this meaning is never understood, this last word is never spoken; always they remain superior, the ultimate meaning being a secret which reveals itself repeatedly, only nevertheless to remain eternally concealed. It implies an advance to the farthest boundary, where only one sole fact is understood:— that all comprehension is "beyond"; and thus the ultimate meaning is at the same moment the limit of meaning (p. 680).

Van der Leeuw insisted that the ultimacy of religion is both subjective and objective. It is not ultimate only from a subjective perspective; it is also an objective limit. The cosmos is so constituted that every worldview includes limit situations, which are present to thought as inexplicable or insoluble problems.

For example, existence is an insoluble puzzle, an intrinsic mystery that precludes understanding. How can anything exist? Yet it does. And since it does exist, how can it ever not exist? Yet it changes. If existence came into existence, how can it have done so? And from what? And so on and so forth.

How people identify cognitive limit situations, how they attempt partial solutions to the mysteries by recourse to metaphysical speculations, and how they behave in consequence, are all culturally and historically variable. Whether the accommodations to the "beyond" are called "religious" is a further incidental variable. It is the need to conceptualize limit situations that is a cross-cultural constant.

In clarifying Otto's ideas, van der Leeuw unwittingly falsified Otto's claim that the awe, urgency, majesty, mystery, and fascination of the numinous are "nonrational." When van der Leeuw suggested that these affects are responses to the "one sole fact . . . that all comprehension is 'beyond,'" he predicated the nonrational elements of the numinous on an element of rational self-understanding. The "beyond" cannot be known, but the knowledge that it is beyond knowing is a rational cognition.

Paul Pruyser (1983) followed van der Leeuw in staking a claim for the intrinsically religious character of "limit situations" that involve "*transcendence* and *mystery*." More explicitly than van der Leeuw, Pruyser emphasized the rational character of "limit experiences." They are "charged with cognitive, ontological, epistemological, and emotional implications" (pp. 155–56).

The Rational Component in Unitive Experiences

Having defined numinosity as a value-judgment that pertains to limit situations, we may recognize that unitive experiences are intrinsically and inalienably numinous. Less than unity cannot exist. Unity is inherently and necessarily a limit situation. Consider the following self-report of an experience of the solitary self.

> It is an experience which occurred when I was perhaps sixteen or seventeen years old. I no longer remember where it took place, except that it was a summer day on an American beach. I seem to remember that it was early morning, and that I must have been standing on the sand for some time alone, for even now I distinctly remember that this experience was preceded by a sense of utter aloneness. Not loneliness, but a sort of intense solitariness.
>
> I remember that it was a cool, clean, fresh, calm, blue, radiant day, and that I stood by the shore, my feet not in the waves. And now—as then—I find it difficult to explain what did happen. I expect that the easiest thing is to say that

suddenly SOMETHING WAS. My whole soul was cleft clean by it, as a silk veil slit by a shining sword. And I *knew*. I do not know now what I knew. I remember, I didn't know even then. That is, I didn't *know* with any "faculty." It was not in my mind or heart or blood stream. But whatever it was I knew, it was something that made ENORMOUS SENSE. And it was final. And yet that word could not be used, for it meant *end*, and there was no end to *this* finality. Then joy abounded in all of me. Or rather, I abounded in joy. I seemed to have no nature, and yet my whole nature was adrift in this immense joy, as a speck of dust is seen to dance in a great golden shaft of sunlight.

I don't know how long this experience lasted. It was, I should think, closer to a second than to an hour—though it might have been either. The memory of it possessed me for several months afterward (O'Brien, 1949, pp. 223–24).

Because the human mind is capable of forming abstract symbols, so that any signifier can symbolize or signify any signified, human reasoning reaches a lower limit-situation with the conclusion that everything can mean anything; or, to put the same observation another way, that all is one. If any signifier can signify any signified, all signifiers can signify one specific signified, reaching a lower limit-situation. Carefully considered, the formulation "all is one" is accurate for the claims of physicists who reduce all existence to the one substance, mass-energy. Mystics generally mean something different. What mystics mean when they say "all is one" is most frequently that all things are manifestations or symbols that signify the One. The mystical limit-situation proceeds at the level of signification, but not necessarily at the level of concrete sense perceptions.

The potential, inherent in the nature of abstract symbolization, to reduce all to one, is a necessary condition of unitive thinking; but it is not a sufficient one. The potential can manifest as a trivial curiosity of human mental function, as, for example, unitive ideas may appear to nonmystics. The ideas are comprehensible, but they are not felt to be important. What transforms the potential, inherent in the nature of sign-formation or symbolization, into the actuality of unitive thinking is, I suggest, the powerful motivation of the mother-infant relationship. It is infants' love for their mothers that directs symbol-formation to pursue mother-infant fusion fantasies and the sublimation of the latter into unitive thinking.

Granting that unity is a limit situation, why are limit situations numinous? A numinous quality arises, I suggest, when and because consciousness of a limit situation includes the idea of its transcendence. This contention may be considered a logical corollary of W. Ronald D. Fairbairn's (1941) single most important contribution to psychoanalytic object relations theory. A consensus today holds that the internalization of object relations depends on the internalization of complete object relationships, and not object representations alone. Fairbairn (1941) proposed that what is internalized includes, in Kernberg's (1966) words, "a self-image component, an object-image component, and both of these components linked with an early affect" (p. 25) (see also: Modell, 1958; Sandler & Rosenblatt, 1962; Sutherland, 1963; Loewald, 1973; Dorpat, 1981; Sandler, 1981; Arlow, in Boesky, 1983; Boesky, 1983; Settlage, 1993). R. D. Laing (1967) emphasized that the internalizations consist of interpersonal dynamics.

> What is "internalized" are *relations between* persons, things, part-objects, part-persons, not the persons or objects in isolation. . . . What is internalized are not objects as such but *patterns of relationship between human presences*. The more constant patterns of such relationships are what we call family structure. That is to say, the individual does not simply internalize or introject persons, parts of persons, objects or part objects, good or bad breast, penis, mother or father, but the individual incarnates a *group structure*. . . . It is *relations not objects* that are internalized (pp. 111, 114, 118).

Fairbairn's theory means that no memory, and no idea derived by abstraction from a memory, concerns another person alone. Every memory and every idea of another person also concerns the self. Here I would like to emphasize the converse, which is a generally accepted principle in social psychology. The experience of the self is created out of interaction with others and/or the impersonal environment. There is no self without the mirror function of object relations. Every memory of the self includes memory of the nonself. Every idea of the self implies the idea of the nonself.

Accordingly, there can be no unitive experience whose exclusive concern is with the self. The self is never solitary. An experience whose *manifest* content is limited to the self is inextricably associated *unconsciously* with memories and ideas of the nonself. In particular, knowledge of the mother as a discrete person is always a contributing component of fantasies of mother-infant fusion, including those that undergo sublimation into unitive experiences.

Just as the idea of the self undergoes sublimation into the idea of all-being, the idea of the mother undergoes sublimation into the concept of a loved object who transcends the limitations of all-being—the everywhere present, all-encompassing, ever-providing womb and source of All, greater than whom cannot exist. In my view, it is not the mere ultimacy of a limit situation, as suggested by Paul W. Pruyser, but its capacity to evoke the idea of the transcendent—a Something More—that arouses the feeling of numinosity.

The unconscious association of the self and the nonself is observable in the shift in the following self-reports from the idea of infinite being to a concept of the transcendent.

> Often when out alone at night, when the sky is cloudless, I cannot help gazing at the universe beyond our tiny sphere. It provokes in me a great feeling of wonder and makes me realise how relatively worthless we are when considered

side by side with all the work of the great Creator. I cannot help trying to think of a solution as to how space can stop, the mere thought of it going on endlessly almost giving me a brainstorm. I am filled with utmost awe by the spectacle (Paffard, 1973, p. 174).

When I was thirteen . . . my family took a summer trip. . . . One afternoon we were on a leisurely drive. The weather was somewhat humid. My brother and sister were dozing . . . and my parents were talking quietly. . . . As I gazed out the window, I suddenly saw a wide river opening up into a seemingly infinite bay or ocean.

The scene's grandeur overwhelmed me. The surprising and dramatic expanse of water reminded me of infinity, of the universe, and of God. . . . I felt a special connection to God.

It was an intense and unforgettable moment, but I also experienced a sense of insignificance as a human. I was attracted to the scene by its awesome beauty and simplicity: the simplicity of eternity (E. Hoffman, 1992, pp. 26–27).

The endlessness of the universe and the seeming infinity of the ocean led to ideas of God. The association is coherent in terms of psychoanalytic object relations theory. Because babies have mothers, to contemplate all-being is always also to invoke the transcendent—unconsciously, if not also unconsciously. The unconscious association manifests consciously, however, because reality-testing approves it. It is impossible to think logically about an infinite being. The concept of infinite is attained by negating the concept of finitude. Every effort to endow the negation with positive content results in paradox and arrives at a limit-situation. Once the limitation is reached consciously, reality-testing falsifies the concept of infinitude by manifesting the unconscious idea of the nonself as the idea of the transcendent. The concept of the transcendent falsifies the concept of infinitude, because infinitude does not include it.

Unitive experiences are inherently numinous, I suggest, because they invariably include the idea of the transcendent. In experiences of the solitary self, the concept of the All, which can be derived through generalization from the evidence of sense perception, is condensed with the concept of the transcendent. The result is an experience of an all that is itself transcendent: boundless, timeless, self-sustaining. Also condensed into the unitive experience is the concept of the self-alone, which becomes an idea of transcendent-self-alone, that is, the solitary self-schema.

The schema of the solitary self may be treated as the foundational unitive schema. It is the simplest cognitively and presumably the earliest attained developmentally. The schema is nevertheless constructed out of prior ideas of the self, the perceptible environment, and transcendence. Because people are finite, mortal, and intensely social animals, the further unitive schemas correct the irrationality of the foundational schema in various ways. All reintroduce the rational distinction between the self and other.

Rejecting the idea of the transcendent, some unitive schemas elaborate ideas of physicalist unity. Science is based on the premise that being is unified but abides by the evidence of sense perception that being is perceptible, impersonal, and differentiated. Morality proceeds instead from the premise that being is perceptible, personal, and unified, but concedes to reality-testing that beings are differentiated and that only some of them are personal. I suggest, however, that no matter how unitive ideas may be elaborated, their ultimate unconscious foundation in the schema of the solitary self imparts to them a quality of numinosity. The transcendent concerns and numinous character of science and morality may not always be manifest, but they are always present unconsciously. It is because scientific and moral ideas are always unconsciously mystical that they may come to consciousness as manifestly mystical moments.

The lines of unitive development that elaborate the idea of the transcendent are those, I suggest, which are conventionally described as religious, metaphysical, mystical, or spiritual. Many of the world's religious traditions do not subscribe to the concept of a transcendent, creative power. Careful investigation will disclose, however, that the concept of the transcendent is among the topics with which religions regularly contend, whether to accept or to reject. In Christianity, the *via negativa*, "way of negation," is an approach to God by excluding all perceptible, conceivable, and imaginable affirmations. The philosophical defense of the way of negation is epistemological. Every affirmation of God is a product of the human psyche and, as such, inaccurate. God is not present but ulterior, transcendent, unknown, and unknowable. Within the way of negation, God is described metaphysically, in neo-Platonic idiom, as superessential or "beyond being." The term *superessential* is best known through the *Mystical Theology* of pseudo-Dionysius the Areopagite (1987), a pseudonymous fifth-century Christian neo-Platonist. By "superessential" God is not described as nothing, as though nothingness were a state in which some Being or Essence exists. Rather, God is named as a total contrary to existence, a not-existing rather than a nonexistence.

In addition to the Christian tradition, the transcendent was the *Yahweh*, "he causes existing," of Jeremiah and Deutero-Isaiah. It is God, as distinct from the Immanence (*shekhinah*) of God, as these terms have been used in rabbinical Judaism (Abelson, 1912); and it is the *'Ain Sof*, "Infinite," of the kabbalah. The Christian *via negativa* combined the Hebrew heritage with pagan Platonism. The transcendent was the One, distinct from Being, of Speusippus, the nephew and successor of Plato as the head of the academy; and, according to Speusippus, Plato had meant no other by "the Good" (Dillon, 1977, p. 12).

Platonism also influenced Islam. The transcendent was the "God beyond Being" of the Isma'ili (Madelung, 1977); and the Isma'ili philosopher al-Nasafi went so far as to define God as beyond both Being (*al-shay'*) and "non-thing-ness" (*al-lashay'*) (Netton, 1989, pp. 210–14). On the other hand, Muslim neo-Aristotelian philosophers considered but rejected the concept of the "absolute non-existence" of God (Tufail, 1982, p. 32).

The Hindu *Talavakara (Kena) Upanisad* referred to the transcendent:

> He by whom it is not thought,
> by him it is thought;
> he by whom it is thought, knows it not" (Muller, 1879, I, p. 149).

Nagarjuna described the nirvana of Mahayana Buddhism as transcendent:

> Neither as Being nor as a non-Being
> Nirvana therefore is conceived
>
> . . . .
> Indeed both Being and non-Being
> Are dependent on causation
>
> . . . .
> No one can really understand this doctrine which proclaims at once
> Negation of them both together" (Burtt, 1955, pp. 173–74).

The *Tao Te Ching* discussed the transcendent as the cosmic origin:

> The Tao that can be named is not an eternal Name.
> The Nameless [nonbeing] is the origin of heaven and earth;
> the Nameable [being] is the mother of all things" (Lin, 1977, p. 3).

In the Taoist idiom of Wang Pi, the term *nonbeing* conveyed the transcendent (Yu-Lau, 1953, pp. 180–83), since it connoted "no thing" rather than "nothingness."

Concepts of the transcendent are more difficult to show in cultures that lack the vocabulary of philosophical discourse and instead express abstract religious concepts in vivid and concrete images. A careful reexamination of alleged Supreme Beings (Schmidt, 1931) will be warranted before final conclusions may be reached.

My point, however, is neither a theological claim that the concept of the transcendent is veridical, nor a historical one that all cultures venerate such a concept. My contention is psychoanalytic. The human mental capacity to negate, that is, to entertain the concept of "no," the negative, permits the concept of the all to be negated, resulting in the concept of "not-the-all," of differing from any and all of the all, of transcending the all. The concept of transcendence has its basis in negation of the idea of the perceptible environment. It undergoes development into the concept of the transcendent under the unconscious influence of object relations.

When mother-infant fusion fantasies are sublimated into mystical moments of the solitary self, the equation of self and all entails the unconscious
corollary that the mother, who is not-self, is also not-the-all, the transcendent.
As this basic or foundational unitive schema is reality-tested and accommodated
to reality, the unconscious concept of the transcendent may emerge in conscious thought as an explicit idea of a transcendent person, a personal being
who is the transcendent. Let me underscore this point. I am arguing on the
basis of Fairbairn's theory of the object-relational nature of all ideas of self and
others, that the conventional contrast between theism and unitive mysticism is
fallacious. Theistic thinking is, I suggest, one of the developmental lines of unitive thinking. A concept of transcendence is unconscious or implicit in unitive
thinking from its foundational schema. Its refinement and conscious manifestation as a theistic concept of the transcendent arises through a series of accommodations of reality.

The Sense of Transcendence

To account for the varieties of mystical experiences, the transpersonal psychologist Ken Wilber (1977) arranged them in a hierarchical sequence. The
more a mystic advanced along the hierarchy, the closer to absolute metaphysical
truth had been attained, and the more psychological maturity had been
achieved. In keeping with the *philosophia perennis*, Wilber identified the ultimate
mystical experience as an experience of pure consciousness.

Wilber's concept of pure consciousness was used by Arthur J. Deikman
(1982) in a limited version of the common core hypothesis that all mystical experiences are one and the same. Deikman advanced the lesser claim that one variety of mystical experiences must everywhere be one and the same because its
sense of transcendence is absolute. It transcends all personal and cultural media-
tions of experience, because it is a direct experience of pure consciousness.
Deikman's position has since been maintained in several academic defenses of
the common core hypothesis (Smart, 1983; Forman, 1990, 1996).

For purposes of discussion, I term the experience *mystical nothingness*
(Merkur, 1993a, pp. 23–27). It was traditionally privileged as the climactic mystical experience of the *via negativa* by such Christian writers as pseudo-Dionysius the Areopagite (1987); the *Cloud of Unknowing* author (Wolters, 1978); and
the Rhineland mystics Meister Eckhart (1941), Henry Suso (1953), and Johann
Tauler (1961). Mystical nothingness is not manifestly unitive. However, because
nothingness cannot logically vary or otherwise be plural, postexperiential reflection on the logical significance of mystical nothingness has regularly led mystics
to ideas of ultimate unity.

Mystical nothingness is not a philosophical postulation that no one is known actually to have experienced, as Eckhart's *Ungrund* and Buddhist *nirodh* have sometimes been alleged to be. Mystics have actual experiences that they say are experiences of nothing. Experiences of mystical nothingness have also been produced experimentally through hetero-hypnotic work with very deep trance states. Unity may be experienced on the way to nothingness. Just before the climactic experience of nothing, there may be a passage through experiences of the cosmic self and the solitary self. One may feel oneself to contain all, before one feels oneself alone to exist; and only then may nothingness be reached (Tart, 1970, 1979; Sherman, 1972). The return to normal waking consciousness may reverse the sequence by progressing through the different orders of union.

In an experience of mystical nothingness, the element of nothingness has a semantic value. Consider, for example, the following account of the Swedish mystic Hjalmar Ekström (1885–1962), based on a text that was written down "by a younger friend immediately after Ekström's own account" (Geels, 1982, p. 38).

> He went wandering in the woods alone. The path led up a hill. Then it was as if the entire world fissured. It was as if God's eternal love and God's eternal wrath had met in one place like a bolt of lightning, "which flamed down and to the sides like a cross, filling all the heavens and the whole earth, consuming everything." At the same time, he heard a voice which said: "Hereafter the path becomes pathless." And he was cast out into nothingness, a resounding, empty nothingness. Heaven was empty and the earth was empty and Hell as well.— In the first moments he hardly knew whether he saw or heard even with his outer senses. He dimly recalled that it was as if the day of judgment had arrived. But he came to his senses again and continued on his way, tremblingly (ibid.).

Ekström's moments of nothingness had metaphoric significance in their narrative context within the manifest content of his experience. Nothingness was manifestly symbolic of pathlessness. The significance of pathlessness was not stated, but may readily be inferred. The transformation of Ekström's path into nothingness presumably symbolized that his path was not foredetermined. His necessity to make conscious choices was also expressed by the feeling that "the day of judgment had arrived." Ekström's unconscious used the motif of mystical nothingness as a symbol with which to assert his freedom of will, to accept or reject his mystical calling.

Not only may mystical nothingness be a semantic element in what may amount to a waking dream state, but the personal meaning of nothingness within any one mystical moment generally proceeds within a constructed cultural tradition. Consider, for example, the Hasidic attainment of 'ayin, "nothingness" (Matt, 1990; Merkur, 1991a). The following instructions were attributed in *Keter Shem Tov* (1794–95) to the founder of East European Hasidism, Rabbi Israel Baal Shem Tov (d. 1760). Although the attribution cannot be authenticated, it is possibly reliable.

> During prayer it is necessary [for a person] to place all his strength on the spoken [words]. And he should go in this way from letter to letter, until he forgets everything physical and thinks how the letters combine and unite with one another. This is a great pleasure. For if there is pleasure in physicality, it is all the more so in spirituality. And this is the world of formation (*yesirah*). Afterward let him come to the letters of thought, and he will not hear what he speaks [in prayer]. In this way he enters the world of creation (*beri'ah*). After that he can reach the degree of nothingness (*'ayin*), where all his physical powers are suspended. This is the world of emanation (*'asilut*), the degree of wisdom (*Keter Shem Tov*, Part 2, p. 31, col. 4; or Part 2, p. 17, col. 3).

The four kabbalistic worlds (Scholem, 1974, pp. 118–19) are here four realms of thought. They name four distinct topics of meditation that the mystic is to contemplate in sequence.

1. The mystic is to recite prayers aloud, while paying attention to the meanings of the words. This is the physical world of *'asiah*, "making" or "doing."

2. Attention is next devoted to the letters that compose the words spoken in prayer. It is the letters and their combinations into words that provide the words with meanings. Once this level of meditation has been attained, there has been a shift from the physical to the spiritual—a shift from spoken words to meanings or significances. The mystic may now combine and recombine letters, attaining new thoughts. This is *yesirah*, "formation."

3. The mystic must next recognize that the world of formation presupposes the existence of meaning as such. The "letters of thought," which have been contemplated in *yesirah*, can be combined to form meanings only because meaningfulness exists. In other words, *yesirah* presupposes (and so implies) a causation or creation of meaningfulness. Having attained the concept of causation, the mystic's meditations have entered *beri'ah*, the realm of creation.

4. The Creator, who causes both the existence and the meaningful combination of letters, necessarily transcends the realm of creation. He is not a letter, not a meaning, not a thought—but beyond all thought. And so the mystic comes to meditate on what is not a thought, on *'ayin*, on something that is nothing.

When these four ideas, or groups of ideas, are considered in sequence during normal waking sobriety, they constitute a version of the cosmological argument for the existence of God. The Hasidic teaching is quite clear, however, that the meditations are to culminate in *'asilut*, which denotes "emanation" from God. In this instance, then, the cosmological argument does not culminate in a philosophical postulation; it culminates in divine revelation. Sense can be put to the detail, I suggest, if we assume that the Hasidic teaching omits one rather obvious stipulation for purposes of esotericism. The teaching takes for granted that a mystic will enter a trance state before he begins to conduct the four orders of meditation. When the meditations are entertained in sequence during a trance, they have the capacity to induce an experience of mystical nothingness.

The psychological principles are straightforward. Trance involves a successive restriction of the normal functions of consciousness that permits ideas to replace will as the initiators of behavior. During a trance, each new idea functions as an autosuggestion that leaves consciousness only to return to it in the form of an "automatic thought." The automatism of thought is fully as compulsive and commanding of belief as automatic writing and automatic speech. A concomitant of the process of automatism is the repression of all other ideas from consciousness. One idea or group of ideas are automatically maintained in consciousness, while all other ideas are excluded (Shor, 1959; Merkur, 1984). The mystical practice depends on this last feature. For the purpose of achieving mystical nothingness, it may not be terribly important that *'asiah* is completely forgotten once *yesirah* is attained. A different initial sequence might be satisfactory. It is crucial, however, that *beri'ah* is repressed once *'ayin* is attained. The mystic who has successively restricted his thought, eliminating all thought of physicality when entering *yesirah*, all thought of language when entering *beri'ah*, and all thought of nonverbal concepts when entering *'ayin*, arrives at a contemplation of nothing whatever.

Within the kabbalah there are differences of opinion whether mystics directly encounter God when they contemplate *'ayin* (Idel, 1988, p. 137). In *Sefer Ha-Bahir*, the twelfth-century foundation text of the kabbalah, the experience was already attributed to *Keter*, "Crown," the first of ten *sefirot* or "hypostases." Keter was identified with the silent letter *'alef* (Par. 15–18, 26) in expression of the doctrine that experience of mystical nothingness is a linguistic event—or, as we should today say, a semiotic event. Mystical *'ayin* remains within the created order of existence and does not attain to the status of the Creator, who is infinite (*'ain sof*) and ineffable. Even kabbalists who deify the *sefirot* continue to locate the experience of *'ayin* with Keter, rather than with the 'Ain Sof (Matt, 1990).

Whatever may be the theological claims of some religious devotees, confusion of logical categories is not permissible to an academic student of religion. Contemplation of *'ayin* is an engagement with an idea. It is a contemplation of the concept intended by the term. The act of contemplation does not make contact with a reality, external to the mind, which happens to be designated by the term. One does not become wet by contemplating water. Neither does one experience God by contemplating nothingness.

The psychological principles governing trance states similarly underlie Buddhist *samatha* ("calming-down") meditation on the eight *jhanas*. Each meditation leads on to the next, culminating in an effort to achieve "neither perception nor nonperception."

The first stage:
"Detached from sense—desires, detached (also from the other four) unwholesome states, he dwells in the attainment of the first jhana, which is accompanied by applied and discursive thinking, born of detachment, rapturous and joyful. . . .

The second stage:
"From the appeasing of applied and discursive thinking, he dwells in the attainment of the second jhana, where the inward heart is serene and uniquely exalted, and which is devoid of applied and discursive thinking, born of concentration, rapturous and joyful. . . .

The third stage:
"Through distaste for rapture, he dwells evenmindedly, mindful and clearly conscious; he experiences with this body that joy of which the Ariyans declare, 'joyful lives he who is evenminded and mindful.' It is thus that he dwells in the attainment of the third jhana.

The fourth stage:
"From the forsaking of joy, from the forsaking of pain, from the going to rest of his former gladness and sadness, he dwells in the attainment of the fourth jhana, which is neither painful nor pleasurable,—in utter purity of evenmindedness and mindfulness."

The fifth stage:
"By passing quite beyond all perceptions of form, by the going to rest of the perceptions of impact, by not attending to the perception of manifoldness, on thinking 'Endless Space,' he dwells in the attainment of the station of endless space.

The sixth stage:
"By passing quite beyond the station of endless space, on thinking 'endless consciousness,' he dwells in the attainment of the station of unlimited consciousness."

The seventh stage:
"By passing quite beyond the station of unlimited consciousness, on thinking 'There is not anything,' he dwells in the attainment of the station of nothing whatever."

The eighth stage:
"By passing quite beyond the field of nothing whatever, he dwells in the attainment of the station of neither perception nor non-perception" (Conze, 1956, pp. 113, 116, 117–18; compare: Kalupahana, 1987, pp. 63–68).

Is it meaningful to claim that the Hasidic experience of the nothingness of the divine Creator is equivalent to the Buddhist experience of a not-self that is "neither perception nor nonperception"? When Buddhist nirvana is not a richly emotional experience of "bliss-unspeakable" (R. Otto, 1950) it may be a sort of nothingness, as is Hasidic *'ayin*. However, it is not the same sort (Abe, 1985, pp. 130–131; Werblowsky, 1990). The one is achieved through an acosmist denial of phenomenal existence, the other as the end product of a cosmological argument for the creative transcendence of God. An acosmist void is not to be confused with a creative one. Suso's Ungrund and Patanjali's Unmanifested differ yet again. Their unconscious associations, their feeling-tone, their implications, all differ.

Mystics who pursue the *via negativa* by systematically excluding item after item from their consciousness typically arrive at whatever experiences they have not previously negated. St. John of the Cross (1973) was willing to negate everything except an experience of fiery love. For Jan van Ruysbroek (1953) it was sunlight. By negating everything that can be thought, it is also possible to induce unconsciousness. The experience of nothingness occurs short of unconsciousness.

The question before us is whether different personal and cultural constructions of nothingness are somehow rendered uniform in a manner that justifies their cross-cultural study as a single category of mystical experiences. Katz (1978) argues that mystical experiences are no exception to the rule that there are no unmediated experiences. However, Katz has been misunderstood by critics (e.g., Forman, 1990), who think him to be claiming that the entirety of all experiences are constructions of the mind. To argue that the mind mediates the perception of the sky is not, however, the same as to argue that the mind constructs an imagination that it mistakes for a perception of the sky. What then of mystical nothingness? Is it a mediated perception of something real that is common cross-culturally? Or is it an illusion?

In a classic paper that introduced the concept of ego-feelings, Paul Federn (1926) suggested that what is experienced at the moment of mystical nothingness is the "mental ego alone" (p. 437). Federn's hypothesis is untenable, however, because it is an instance of the methodological fallacy that is technically termed a *homunculus*. The idea that consciousness consists of something that is conscious of something else, namely, the contents of consciousness, implies that consciousness occurs to the first something alone. This first something, which alone is conscious, is implicitly imagined as though it were a homunculus, a little person, within the sensorium of the mind. Moreover, the consciousness of the homunculus would, in turn, have to be subdivided into a consciousness and into the contents of that consciousness. Accordingly, to postulate a homunculus is implicitly to postulate an infinite series of homunculi, each within the last.

Deikman (1982), who is both a psychoanalyst and a practicing mystic, devoted a book-length study to mystical nothingness. Like Federn, Deikman identified the sense of self with the observer function (see: Miller, Isaacs, & Haggard, 1965). "The body, the self-image, and the self-concept are all constructs that we *observe*. But our core sense of personal existence—the "I"—is located in awareness itself, not in its content" (p. 10). Unlike Federn, Deikman avoided the homunculus fallacy, but at the cost of abandoning psychoanalysis for Wilber's metaphysics.

> The observing self is not part of the object world formed by our thoughts and sensory perception because, literally, it has no limits; everything else does. Thus, everyday consciousness contains a transcendent element that we seldom notice because that element is the very ground of our experience. The word *transcendent* is justified because if subjective consciousness—the observing self—cannot itself be observed but remains forever apart from the contents of consciousness, it is likely to be of a different order from everything else. Its fundamentally different nature becomes evident when we realize that the observing self is featureless; it cannot be affected by the world any more than a mirror can be affected by the images it reflects (p. 95).

For Deikman, the observing self is an infinite transcendent element that manifests as personal consciousness when it occurs within the finitude of human beings. It is a universal consciousness that undergoes mediation and subdivides into discrete human consciousnesses when and because it is focused within individual human bodies. People are all somehow the very consciousness of the Creator, trapped and fragmented within finite material bodies.

Deikman contradicted himself, however, when he asserted that "the principal aim of meditation is to enhance the observing self until its reality is without question and the meditator totally identifies with it. This permits the emergence of an entirely new form of consciousness called enlightenment, nirvana, awakening, and so forth" (p. 138). If a meditator has the opportunity and need to identify with the observing self, it necessarily differs from the ego's observing function. If the meditator can unite with the observing self, the meditator's ego cannot be the observing self, but must differ from it.

Moreover, mystical nothingness is attained, as we have seen, through the laborious construction of a concept of the transcendent, together with an implicit effort to achieve its perspective as one's own. What is cross-cultural in the experience is (a) the concept of the transcendent and (b) unconscious infant-mother fusion fantasies that elaborate the concept as an experience of being the transcendent. It is an experience of union with the idea of the transcendent, which assimilates the concept to unconscious infant-mother fusion fantasies. The unitive experience retreats from the logical clarity of the idea of the transcendent, under the unconscious pressure of infant-mother fusion fantasies.

In this context, it may be useful to examine some self-reports of the experience of self-transcendence. In these cases, a sense of transcendence coincides with ongoing sense perception of the self that is being transcended.

In the loveliness of the morning, and the beauty of the hills and valleys, I soon lost my sense of sadness and regret. For nearly an hour I walked along the road. . . . On the way back, suddenly, without warning, I felt that I was in Heaven—an inward state of peace and joy and assurance indescribably intense, accompanied with a sense of being bathed in a warm glow of light, as though this external condition had brought about the internal effect—a feeling of having passed beyond the body, though the scene around me stood out more clearly, and as if nearer to me than before, by reason of the illumination in the midst of which I seemed to be placed. This deep emotion lasted, though with decreasing strength, until I reached home, and for some time after, only gradually passing away (Trevor, 1897, p. 268).

I looked round me at the moor stretching for seemingly endless miles. Stretch after stretch of purple and brown until the end of the moor was lost in the beginning of the sky. I looked and felt exhilarated, alive, and in that moment I knew that life was indeed worth living and, in the realisation of this, all earthly attachments vanished. I felt as though I only existed spiritually; my body was no use (Paffard, 1973, pp. 179–80).

Mystical nothingness is, I suggest, this same phenomenon of imagining a transcendent perspective when it occurs in a trance so deep that the contents of the ego have been repressed from consciousness. In the anesthetic condition of deep trance, there may be no experience of the perceptible world. The fantasy of being transcendent may be experienced in the absence of any frame of reference by which the fantasy may be identified as a fantasy. Under these conditions, the resultant self-reports would be limited to such statements as "a feeling of having passed beyond the body" and "I felt as though I only existed spiritually; my body was no use." There would be a sense of a self that is engaged in transcending, but unconsciousness of all that has been transcended.

Ecstatic Death

The idea of the transcendent is also relevant to the understanding of the variety of mystical experiences that have been described in historical studies as "ecstatic," "mystic," or "initiatory death" (Corbin, 1954, pp. 156–57, 1971, p. 79; Eliade, 1958; Scholem, 1965, p. 15; Chernus, 1982, pp. 33–73; Merkur, 1993a, pp. 34–35, 56–57, 71, 138–41, 161–66, 224, 234). Well documented among shamans (Christiansen, 1953; Eliade, 1964; Elkin, 1977; Merkur, 1992a) as well as among mystics, ecstatic death consists of a panic attack that coincides with a vision of immediately impending death. When the emotional state stops, so too does the vision, and the individual discovers that death has been withstood or survived (Alnaes, 1964; Merkur, 1992a, pp. 244–64).

Consider, for example, the following accounts of ecstatic death from an Inuit shaman and a contemporary American LSD-taker.

> Next year I went inland to *Tasiusak*. Here I cast a stone into the water, which was thereby thrown into great commotion, like a storm at sea. As the billows dashed together, their crests flattened out on top, and as they opened, a huge bear was disclosed.

> He had a very great, black snout, and, swimming ashore, he rested his chin upon the land; and, when he then laid one of his paws upon the beach, the land gave way under his weight. He went up in land and circled round me, bit me in the loins, and then ate me. At first it hurt, but afterwards feeling passed from me; but as long as my heart had not been eaten, I retained consciousness. But, when it bit me in the heart, I lost consciousness, and was dead.

> When I came to myself again, the bear was away, and I lay wearied out and stark naked at the same place by the lake (Holm, 1912, pp. 299–300).

> When we were on the bus, it started to thunder and rain and the weather was very hot and humid. It felt as though I was on a continent in the midst of earthquakes and tidal waves, in complete chaos and destruction. Gradually the feeling that I was going to die along with everyone else started to prevail, which strangely enough had a sort of profound beauty in it. The bus started to drive over a bridge and, for some reason, I felt that death would come when the bus reached the middle of the bridge. It seemed that there was no way out of the situation and it would be too risky to panic openly on the bus and cause a big scene. Somehow, I still knew I had taken LSD and that it all could be due to that, although it did not seem in any way separate from reality. I remember just giving up and letting go to the experience whether or not I was going to die, for at that point I was not sure. Pictures of the bridge falling and the bus sinking to the bottom of the river started to spring up in my mind and I saw my body drown and my soul rise from it. At that point the bus reached the other side of the bridge and miraculously the rain stopped and the sun came out; everything seemed to be clean and glistening from the rain. I felt reborn and in a sense was, since this experience has had a profound effect on my consciousness and direction in life (Grof & Halifax, 1978, pp. 178–79).

A few instances of ecstatic death are more informative. In the Syriac Christian Church, mystics of the late seventh century cultivated ecstatic death through visionary practices that they termed *the mystery of the cross* (Widengren, 1961). Dadisho Katraya (1934), who died about 690 c.e., recommended elaborate genuflection, prayer, embrace, and kissing of the crucifix. Taking a Platonic ontology for granted, Katraya imagined these actions to accomplish a direct embrace and kissing of Jesus.

As your sight perceives the light of the Crucifix and your lips feel also its heat when the sun shines on it and you pray to it and kiss it, although the sun itself is in the sky and the Crucifix is on the wall, so also, and in a greater measure, although the man of our Lord Christ in the flesh sits in Heaven on the throne of majesty, according to the preaching of the blessed Paul, yet His power, His glory, His working and His dominion are in the Cross; and you kiss our Lord Himself and embrace Him with love (p. 136).

Following this cultivation of a sense of Jesus' presence, further devotions were made to the crucifix, before the monk returned to his cell. A visionary experience was then cultivated. Katraya's instructions are incomplete, but the portion that was transmitted orally may be inferred from the writings of his contemporaries, Joseph Hazzaya and Isaac of Ninevah. Hazzaya (1934) wrote: "Continual prayer is the perfection of all the commandments, and the intelligible Cross of which our Lord said that anyone who takes it up and follows Him will inherit eternal life with Him" (p. 182). Isaac of Nineveh (1923) stated: "Thou . . . who art victorious, taste the suffering of Christ in thy person, that thou also mayest be deemed worthy of tasting His glory. For if we suffer with Him, we shall also be glorified with Him (p. 150). He also wrote: "I gaze at Thee by the compulsion of the bonds of the cross . . . which is the crucifixion of the mind" (p. 151). Apparently the monk was to visualize himself as Jesus crucified. In his vision, he was to experience himself, as Jesus, dying and resurrecting.

Katraya specified that the monk was to visualize a good angel to his right, and an evil angel or demon to his left. Presumably the angel and demon were visualized as being crucified on crosses to the left and right of the cross on which Jesus was hanged. Katraya (1934) wrote:

Look also in your mind at the angel who is at your right hand and at the demon who is standing at your left hand, and so think spiritually of the meaning of every word that comes out of your mouth, and do not allow distraction to prevail upon you (pp. 139–140).

In order to produce a sense of identification with Jesus, the monk was to move rapidly in his thoughts between Jesus and himself. He was also to maintain the visualization of the two angels.

In reciting the Psalm: "O God, deliver me out of the hand of the wicked and out of the hand of the unrighteous and cruel man," when you say "O God," look towards our Lord on the Cross; when you say "deliver me" look at yourself and towards the holy angel who is standing at your right hand, and through whom you are being delivered; and when you say "out of the hand of the wicked and of the unrighteous and cruel man," look in your thought at the wicked demon who is standing at your left hand and who hates you and fights

against you. Furthermore, when you recite "Let them be ashamed and brought
to confusion together that rejoice at mine hurt, and let them be clothed with
shame that magnify themselves against me," turn your sight towards the demon
(p. 140).

As his prayers continued, the monk could expect his active efforts of visualization to be rewarded by the onset of a vision in which various events would
occur spontaneously. However, the image of Jesus crucified was to be maintained.

> When you recite "let them shout for joy and be glad that favour my victory"
> look in your thought at the holy angel who helps you, and at his holy brother-
> angels who often repair to him in order to honour him and to express their joy
> in your exercises. And when you recite "Let them say continually that the Lord
> is great who had pleasure in the peace of His servant, look also in your mind at
> our Lord on the Cross (ibid.).

Visualization of demons formed an integral part of the mystical practice,
because panic attacks were attributed to the demon. Faith in Jesus would suffice,
however, to cause the fear to subside. Joy would then follow.

> And when you recite "Let the demons be cursed, but mayest Thou, O Lord, be
> blessed, and may I, Thy servant, rejoice in Thee," in saying "Let them be
> cursed" look at the demons; in saying "mayest Thou be blessed" look at our
> Lord; and in saying "Thy servant" think of yourself and of your angel. And if
> the demon waxes wrathful and terrifies you with his visions and frightens you
> with his temptations, be not afraid, excited and disturbed, but look at our Lord
> on the Cross, and have trust and confidence in the holy angel who is standing
> at your right hand to help you and guard you. In this way your fear will im-
> mediately vanish and you will be filled with joy. Act in this way when you pray
> at the end of each Doxology (ibid.).

A monk was to proceed in a similar fashion with every prayer, accompany-
ing the pronunciation of the different words with visualizations of himself, Jesus,
the good angel, and the demon.

> When you cry to our Lord in your prayer, "Help me, O God, our Saviour, so
> that I may love Thee and keep Thy commandments; purge away my sins and
> deliver me from mine enemies for Thy name's sake," in pronouncing "Help
> me, O God," look at our Lord; in pronouncing "purge away my sins and de-
> liver me," at yourself; in pronouncing "from mine enemies," at the demon who
> is standing at your left hand; and in pronouncing "by the prayers of the holy
> angel who guards me," at your guardian angel who is standing at your right

hand. Apply to yourself every word or Psalm in which there is mention of sorrow or penitence; and pray, implore, grieve and ask for mercy, as if it were you who had sinned. In reciting the Psalms and praying in this way, sleep will not overcome you, nor will distraction harass you; the demon will not frighten you, and the Devil will not overpower you (pp. 140–141).

The mystical practice culminated in a "joy" whose intensity "has no parallel in creation." The euphoria coincided with a visionary state of "the revelation of the Light."

> And during your prayer and your recitation of the Psalms, your intelligence will be illuminated with understanding and strengthened by hope, and will shed sweet tears mingled with joy and love. At the end of your service you will rejoice in God with a joy that has no parallel in creation, like a man possessing the treasure of life in his soul, and through your joy, in your vigils, your recitation of the Psalms and your prayer, the labour of the canonical Hours of the day will be lightened for you. In this way, through the continual and daily labours which you experience in your solitude, you will dwell in the mighty refuge of Christ, which leads to the House of God.

> Side by side with the labours which you experience in your body, learn also little by little the labours of the mind through which you attain the purity of heart which sees God in the revelation of the Light (p. 141).

As a fourth example of ecstatic death, I offer the following self-report. For many years I have been in the habit, when alone and thinking in the privacy of my thoughts, of reflecting on divine omniscience and God's knowledge of whatever I am thinking. I will then often think thoughts in address of God, as though I were communicating with Him. Sometimes I experience thoughts in reply.

On one occasion, I recall vividly, I had been thinking mostly to myself, but in consciousness that God knows whatever I may think, when suddenly I experienced the verbal thought, "You are going to die!" The words were expressed with a vehemence and certainty. Wordlessly, I responded with a nod, as if to say, "Yes, I know." My mood was one of acceptance of the inevitable. Inspiration continued, but more gently, with the funerary formula, "Ashes to ashes, dust to dust." As the words manifested in my mind, I found myself experiencing a visual fantasy that was superimposed spatially on my sense perception of my body—I was seated, with my elbows resting on my knees. My fantasy consisted of a visual impression of empty darkness, like a dark night or a black TV or movie screen, in which there were tiny dots of monochrome brightness. Coinciding with this image was the idea that I—my body—consists mostly of empty space, since the atomic nuclei and electrons occupy only a tiny portion of my body's volume. This initial image and idea can have lasted only a moment, during the inspiration of the phrase "dust to dust."

Immediately following the last word my vision began to change in a fashion not unlike the beginning of some cinema films. The unmoving monochrome image became a moving color image of stars moving slowly about the center of a galaxy. As soon as I recognized what it was that I was seeing superimposed on my sense perception of my body, a further thought came to consciousness. "Cosmic dust," was the wording of the inspiration. The tone was one of explanation. The idea pertained simultaneously to the funereal phrase "dust to dust," to the vision of subatomic particles, and to the vision of stars in the sky. At that moment I knew that I am mortal, that I am constituted of atomic matter that knows life and will die, and that I am one with the very substance of the cosmos. It is because I am one with the cosmos that I am mortal. I marveled in wonderment at the cosmos and at the existence of life.

I have had other experiences of ecstatic death. My early experiences involved a great deal of panicky fear at the prospect of dying. Over time, my spontaneous and involuntary fear has increasingly diminished, and the most recent experiences have generally been calm and comforting. The experience that I have described is the only instance, however, when I experienced ecstatic death as a manifestly unitive experience.

In his work using psychedelic drugs as an adjunct to verbal psychotherapy, Stanislav Grof (1975, pp. 138–49) found that the cognitive contents of "the death-rebirth experience" would typically recur until they ceased to be greeted with panic. Over the course of a number of separate drug experiences, a drug-taker would gradually learn to be unafraid when confronted with vivid fantasies of dying immediately. East Greenland shamans, whose practices depended on a combination of sensory deprivation and visualization techniques, similarly reported that their ecstatic deaths gradually changed character through repeated experience. Where they were initially killed upon the attacks of hostile spirits, they came in the end to acquire the spirits as helpers (Merkur, 1992a, pp. 190–92, 194).

The following self-report concerns a modern American psilocybin experience.

> I found myself grunting in agreement or mumbling, "Of course it has always been this way" over and over again as the panorama of my life seemed to be swept up by this unifying and eternal principle. . . . I seemed to relinquish my life in "layers:" the more I let go, the greater sense of oneness I received. As I approached what I firmly believed to be the point of death, I experienced an ever greater sense of an eternal dimension to life (Pahnke & Richards, 1966, p. 71).

I would like to suggest that ecstatic death is an unconsciously unitive experience. I suggest that when a sense of the solitary self undergoes reality-testing, and the sense of boundless timeless being is recognized as erroneous, one of the logical options, that is, one line of unitive development, is to elaborate the idea of finite, temporal, nontranscendence. It is a negation of a prior union. It retains a concern with the singular; but like scientific thinking, it abides by the evidence of sense perception. As it is corrected through reality-testing, the unconscious idea of the solitary self manifests as a vivid fantasy that death is impending. *Ex hypothesi* it is only because the schema of the solitary self condenses the idea of the transcendent that its negation entails the idea of nontranscendence, which is death. The knowledge of death is a limit situation of the self-representation.

The idea of dying is fearful. During the process of its manifestation to consciousness, before reality-testing has the opportunity to analyze the idea, the fantasy of dying is experienced uncritically, and it is fearful. Much as might be the case in a dream of natural sleep, a fantasy of dying arouses terror as long as reality-testing delays or fails to identify the fantasy as fantasy. Once commenced, the panic may prove traumatic and inhibit the work of reality-testing.

When panic at the idea of impending death subsides, self-observation provides the insight that the idea of dying had been treated as though it were as frightening as the actuality of dying. Knowledge of the absurdity of the error permits the idea of dying to be considered more objectively. Death, a cessation of bodily experience, is not fearful. Moreover, because the reality of the living person transcends the limit-situation of the self-representation, an element of transcendence enters into the experience, and a sense of numinosity is aroused. With repetition of the experience, the trauma is mastered, panic ceases to occur, and unitive development is able to progress toward more advanced reflections on the nature of death.

Summary

My argument that infant-mother fusion fantasies undergo sublimation into unitive thinking entails the corollary that a nonsexual reality is being assigned a psychosexual value through the process of sublimation. This nonsexual reality I have argued to be the concept of the transcendent. Called "Something More" by Otto and "Beyond" by van der Leeuw, the transcendent is a speculative idea, but its attainment is an unconscious universal of human psychology. The unconscious psyche extrapolates from its knowledge of infant-mother relations in order to understand the relation of all-being and the transcendent. Just as the idea of self is developed into the unitive schema of the solitary self, the idea of the mother is developed into the idea of the transcendent. Theistic thinking is consequently to be regarded as a developmental acquisition arising from unitive thinking.

Experiences of mystical nothingness arise when the idea of the transcendent is taken up as the manifest content of infant–mother fusion fantasies. Union with the transcendent is experienced as the perspective of the transcendent. The same schema is operative in conjunction with sense perception of the environment, in experiences of self-transcendence.

Also related to the idea of the transcendent is another variety of mystical experience, the phenomenon of ecstatic death. When the schema of the solitary self is reality-tested and falsified, several different accommodations to reality are possible. The schema of incorporation is a compromise with reality that remains fantastic. Other accommodations are more successful. Although the idea of the transcendent is a speculative postulate, there is nothing illogical or falsifiable about it. Another accommodation of the solitary self proceeds by falsifying its element of timeless infinity, rather than its element of self identity. The result is an idea of mortal finitude, which arouses the panic of an ecstatic death.

FIVE

Unity as
Metaphor

Whether its topic is scientific, moral, or religious, unitive thinking varies from grossly irrational fantasies to highly intelligent speculations. The variable factor is presumably the proportion of assimilation to accommodation. Does the irrational fusion fantasy dominate the unitive thinking, or do the rational components? Under what circumstances is the tendency to irrationality increased and decreased?

The Sense of Presence as a *Fascinans*

I have emphasized the Romantic dualism to which Otto alluded by referring to the *fascinans* as Dionysiac, because the Romantic categories reflected a psychological distinction that warrants scientific attention. Otto implied that religious experiences may in general be subdivided into two classes, depending on whether their numinosity manifests as a *fascinans* or as a *mysterium tremendum*. In this chapter I shall argue that in the former event, the religious speculations are tenable; in the latter, they are logically untenable, reified, and delusions.

Let us consider, for example, experiences of the sense of a divine presence, to which William James (1902) devoted a well-known chapter. Although the sense of presence is conventionally treated as a theistic experience, I have argued in chapter 2 that it is reasonably seen as a unitive experience. It is one of a series of unitive experiences that pertain to metaphysical powers. Because the metaphysical power happens to be love, it manifests an element of unity in the bond between lover and beloved that love constitutes. In the last chapter, I have further argued that theistic thinking in general is derivative of the schema of the solitary self and, as such, is a developmental line of unitive thinking, comparable to scientific and moral thinking. For these reasons, I see no obstacle to the discussion of the sense of presence as a schema of unitive thinking.

James emphasized that experiences of the sense of presence pertained to a presence that was invisible. The following self-report is from James's collection.

> I stood alone with Him who made me, and all the beauty of the world, and love, and sorrow, and even temptation. I did not seek Him, but felt the perfect unison of my spirit with His. The ordinary sense of things around me faded. For the moment nothing but an ineffable joy and exaltation remained. It is impossible fully to describe the experience. It was like the effect of some great orchestra when all the separate notes have melted into one swelling harmony that leaves the listener conscious of nothing save that his soul is being wafted upwards, and almost bursting with its own emotion. The perfect stillness of the night was thrilled by a more solemn silence. The darkness held a presence that was all the more felt because it was not seen. I could not any more have doubted that He was there than that I was. Indeed, I felt myself to be, if possible, the less real of the two.
>
> My highest faith in God and truest idea of him were then born to me. I have stood upon the Mount of Vision since, and felt the Eternal round about me. But never since has there come quite the same stirring of the heart. Then, if ever, I believe, I stood face to face with God, and was born anew of his spirit. There was, as I recall it, no sudden change of thought or of belief, except that my early crude conception had, as it were, burst into flower. There was no destruction of the old, but a rapid, wonderful unfolding (pp. 67–68).

The experience consisted of a vivid waking imagination. Although the imagination presumably drew its concept of a presence from childhood memories of parents, the experience was not a fantasy about the presence of the father or the mother. The imaginative experience conveyed the concept of a very different sort of presence.

The language of the report was somewhat paradoxical. Part of the experience was evidently consistent with a positive theology. The report uses language such as "Him who made me," "the Eternal round about me," and "face to face with God." Other phrases indicate, however, that these affirmations required important qualifications. It was "a presence that was all the more felt because it was not seen." No presence was actually sense perceived—whether as tangible, visible, or otherwise. Rather, there was a sense, a subjective response, *as to* a presence; but no being was objectively present to evoke the subjective response. What was present was accordingly designated as God's "spirit," and the report's phrasing unwittingly indicates a distinction between God and his spirit: "the perfect unison of my spirit with His"; and "I stood face to face with God, and was born anew of his spirit." These linguistic subtleties indicate, I suggest, that the presence was *experienced as a metaphor*. The manifest content of the experience utilized a concrete sense of presence in order to convey the abstract concept of the wholly spiritual character of divine omnipresence. It was, I suggest, its self-evidence as metaphor that permitted the manifest presence to imply the transcendence of Something More.

When the sense of presence is experienced as a *fascinans*, verbal paradoxes that are indicative of metaphoric experiences may regularly be noted in the self-reports.

> I had a revelation last Friday evening. I was at Mary's, and happening to say something of the presence of spirits (of whom, I said, I was often dimly aware), Mr. Putnam entered into an argument with me on spiritual matters. As I was speaking, the whole system rose up before me like a vague destiny looming from the Abyss. I never before so clearly felt the Spirit of God in me and around me. The whole room seemed to me full of God. The air seemed to waver to and fro with the presence of Something I knew not what. I spoke with the calmness and clearness of a prophet. I cannot tell you what this revelation was. I have not yet studied it enough. But I shall perfect it one day, and then you shall hear it and acknowledge its grandeur (James, 1902, p. 67).

> I went out one afternoon for a walk alone. I was in the empty unthinking state in which one saunters along country lanes, simply yielding oneself to the casual sights around which give a town-bred lad with country yearnings such intense delight. Suddenly I became conscious of the presence of some one else. I cannot describe it, but I felt that I had as direct a perception of the being of God all round about me as I have of you when we are together. It was no longer a matter of inference, it was an immediate act of spiritual (or whatever adjective you like to employ) apprehension. It came unsought, absolutely unexpectedly. I remember the wonderful transfiguration of the far-off woods and hills as they seemed to blend in the infinite being with which I was thus brought into relation (Herford, 1929, pp. 9–10).

The first report emphasized the abstract concept generated by the sense of presence. There was a clear subjective distinction between the "Something I knew not what" and between "the Spirit of God" that was immediately present. The Spirit was a *fascinans*, whose immediate experience implied a mysterious Something More.

The second report instead emphasized the concrete metaphor. The "spiritual . . . apprehension" of God could not be described. What could be described was "the wonderful transfiguration of the far-off woods and hills as they seemed to blend in the infinite being with which I was thus brought into relation." The seemingly endless distance apparently inspired the metaphoric concept of an infinite being.

Both reports attest to the individuals' powerful emotional involvement with the manifest content of the experiences. The intensity of affect loaned credibility to the imagination of a presence. The metaphoric character of the presence was self-evident, but it was not necessarily known self-consciously. The individuals responded to their senses of presence as though the manifest contents were metaphors, but there is no evidence that they self-consciously recognized that they were doing so. Both the sense of presence and its metaphoric implication of Something More seem to have manifested in consciousness, without conscious reflection on the fact that the concept of Something More had been generated by a metaphor. In both cases, however, God's omnipresence was self-evidently *supra*natural, a beyond-nature that did not contravene the perceptible world, but instead transcended it. The speculations were properly bounded; they could be neither proved nor falsified.

The *fascinans* experiences may all be described as imaginations, as distinct from fantasies, according to the technical distinction suggested by Hanna Segal (1991). Fantasies are irrational flights from reality. Imaginations similarly utilize images, but they adapt rationally to reality by conceptualizing possible realities. Imaginations are speculative, but they are tenable.

Otto recognized that experiences of the *fascinans* are invariably instances of negative theology. I add that their interior logic also conforms with the structure of the so-called cosmological argument (Merkur, 1996), the argument for the existence of deity by inference from the manifest existence of the god's creative activities (Rowe, 1975). Insofar as the *fascinans* implies Something More, its experiences share the logical structure of the cosmological argument, which maintains that the order and lawfulness of the cosmos cannot be accidental, but attest to the activity of a Cause or Creator—Something More than the cosmos. For cross-cultural purposes, the ethnocentric aspects of the philosophical argument must of course be abandoned, but its concern with causality may be retained. In Western theologies, the cosmological argument is ordinarily an argument for the existence of God, but the internal logic of the cosmological argument can be used in reference to one spirit among others, to an impersonal concept, and so forth. *Fascinans* experiences may attain the concept of Something More by reasoning from a particular work of creation—for example, a presence, or a revelation— rather than from the cosmos as a whole. In all cases, however, an argument from an effect to its transcendent creator is integral to *fascinans* experiences.

The Sense of Presence as a *Mysterium Tremendum*

When the sense of presence manifests instead as an experience of a *mysterium tremendum*, a series of features differ systematically. The following self-reports are again from James's (1902) collection.

> Whenever I practice automatic writing, what makes me feel that it is not due to a subconscious self is the feeling I always have of a foreign presence, external

to my body. It is sometimes so definitely characterized that I could point to its exact position. This impression of presence is impossible to describe. It varies in intensity and clearness according to the personality from whom the writing professes to come. If it is someone whom I love, I feel it immediately, before any writing has come. My heart seems to recognize it (p. 64).

I had read some twenty minutes or so, was thoroughly absorbed in the book, my mind was perfectly quiet, and for the time being my friends were quite forgotten, when suddenly without a moment's warning my whole being seemed roused to the highest state of tension or aliveness, and I was aware, with an intenseness not easily imagined by those who have never experienced it, that another being or presence was not only in the room, but quite close to me. I put the book down, and although my excitement was great, I felt quite collected, and not conscious of any sense of fear. Without changing my position, and looking straight at the fire, I knew somehow that my friend. A. H. was standing at my left elbow, but so far behind me as to be hidden by the armchair in which I was leaning back. Moving my eyes round slightly without otherwise changing my position, the lower portion of one leg became visible, and I instantly recognized the gray-blue material of trousers he often wore, but the stuff appeared semi-transparent, reminding me of tobacco smoke in consistency [—and hereupon the visual hallucinations came] (pp. 63–64; bracketed words by James).

Sometimes as I go to church, I sit down, join in the service, and before I go out I feel as if God was with me, right side of me, singing and reading the Psalms with me. . . . And then I feel as if I could sit beside him, and put my arms around him, kiss him, etc. When I am taking Holy Communion at the altar, I try to get with him and generally feel his presence (p. 71).

In the first report, the production of automatic writing manifested both the urgency and the majesty of the *tremendum*. The second report asserted "that my whole being seemed roused to the highest state of tension or aliveness." The third testified to an impulse to embrace and kiss the presence. In all three reports, the presences were palpable. Although the presences were not touched, they were felt to be tangible in nature. They were located in finite places in space: in an "exact position" "external to my body"; "not only in the room, but quite close to me . . . at my left elbow, but so far behind me as to be hidden"; or on the "right side of me" and "so very palpable that it could have been, but was not, embraced and kissed." The arousal of a distinct sense of tangibility in the absence of actual sense perception by touching was paradoxical: a *mysterium*, at once familiar and Wholly Other.

Otto's (1950) subtitle described the numinous as a "nonrational factor in the idea of the divine" because he regarded its element of mystery as an emotional response to an absence of cognitive content. The evidence of numinous experiences instead establishes that a *mysterium tremendum* arouses a sense of mystery in response to a logical paradox. The paradox of a *mysterium* is invariably *preter*natural, an explicit contravention of nature. The presences were not physical, yet they were tangible and located finitely in space. Whether the presence was a personality responsible for automatic writing, or a friend presently found semitransparent, or God, was a variable feature. In all cases, the presences were instances not of illusions, but of illusions that had lost their proper boundaries and become irrational.

In being both palpable and Wholly Other, the presences maintained no distinction between the manifest and the transcendent. The two categories were instead blended in a paradoxical sense that the manifest somehow partook of the transcendent, as though it could be transcendent, but happened then not to be. The presences were not bound by physical limitations, yet they seemed palpable and localized in space. From a doctrinal perspective, experiences of the *mysterium tremendum* may be considered instances of the ontological argument, which maintains that what is ultimate or supreme is necessarily a perfect and real Being (Merkur, 1996). With a *mysterium tremendum*, there is no Something More to impart numinosity to a manifest experience. The paradoxical self-reference of a Wholly Other always accords numinosity to its very being.

James (1902) noted that the sense of a presence sometimes arouses not positive emotions, but feelings of fear, dread, discomfort, or abhorrence. Negative experiences of presence are invariably instances of *mysterium tremendum*.

> Quite early in the night I was awakened. . . . I felt as if I had been aroused intentionally, and at first thought some one was breaking into the house. . . . I then turned on my side to go to sleep again, and immediately felt a consciousness of a presence in the room, and singular to state, it was not the consciousness of a live person, but of a spiritual presence. . . . I felt also at the same time a strong feeling of superstitious dread, as if something strange and fearful were about to happen (p. 64).

The presence was sufficiently palpable and localized to give the impression that "some one was breaking into the house."

A negatively experienced sense of presence may have a distinctly moral character. The presence is felt to be evil as well as distressing. The following self-reports are from Sir Alister Hardy's (1979) collection.

> It was our custom to say Mass every day and meditate for about half an hour afterwards. . . . There came a day when *I felt beset by an evil power like a gray cloud of evil*. After about ten minutes I could stand it no longer. I arose from my knees and went home. The second day it happened again. I got up and moved to the nave and prayed there without distraction. The third day I went back to my stall for meditation but was restless. Then my curate got up and went into the nave and knelt there, as if he was conscious of "something" he didn't like. The next day he

came to see me. He said: "Have you been noticing anything in the Church after Mass lately?" I asked him what he meant. He said: "The spirit of Evil. For several days I haven't been able to pray because *I felt this evil around me.*" I was very relieved to hear this, and told him of my own experience. The whole thing cleared up after a few days. Of course, in the West Indies there is a good deal of "Obeah", Black Magic, and we were constantly having to deal with it. But on this occasion we could not relate it to any person or special happening (p. 78).

[While asleep] Suddenly I became aware of a sense of the uttermost evil, so much so that I became awake. I could feel this sense of evil enveloping me. I had the terrifying impression that this evil force of presence was bent upon taking possession of me. How does one describe evil? I only knew that I was enveloped by this revolting force, so vile and rotting I could almost taste the evil. I was in terror, so much so I could not call out or move. A part of my mind told me I must at all costs act or I would be lost. I recall that I managed by a great effort to stretch out my right hand and with my index finger I traced the shape of the Cross in the air. Immediately on my doing this the evil enveloping me fell away completely, and I felt a wonderful sense of peace and safety (p. 63).

The moral significance of these presences indicates a contribution by conscience to the content of the imaginative experiences.

James's discussion of the sense of presence was consistent with its traditional regard in Western Christianity as a variety of intellectual vision. In the fifth century, St. Augustine of Hippo (1982) categorized visions as corporeal, imaginative, and intellectual, on the premise that spiritual beings and phenomena might appear, respectively, to the bodily senses, the imagination, and the intellect. Augustine accepted the traditional view of Aristotelian psychology that imagination combines memory images but is incapable of generating an innovative idea. For imagination to be creative, its image-forming had to occur in the service of the intellect or reason. As a consequence, religious visions whose mental images depicted Jesus, an angel, saint, or demon, were classified as intellectual visions, rather than as imaginative ones. Because the metaphysical entities had never been sense perceived, Augustine maintained that the visions could not be derived by imagination from sensible memories, but had instead to be inspired by the spiritual perceptions of the intellect. Medieval authors consequently postulated the existence of interior senses of the soul (H. A. Wolfson, 1935; Harvey, 1975).

In contrast with James, I adhere to a modern conception of imagination and emphasize that the sense of presence does not conform with Aristotelian categories, but instead cuts across them. Some presences seem to appear to the imagination, and others are purely conceptual. Others again seem external and perceptible to the senses (Merkur, 1996). For example, the following report concerns a sense of presence that occurred in the form of a corporeal vision that was seemingly apparent to sense perception.

Some years before . . . she had gone through a certain spiritual crisis. Without any definite cause she felt herself to be bad, common, outcast, and she prayed eagerly to God for certainty and for the forgiveness of sins, after which the inner pressure gradually eased. Then on one occasion it happened that while she was in Stockholm she saw, at the corner of Drottninggatan and Fredsgatan, thus in the centre of the city, the Saviour walking at her left side. It was He Himself in an indescribable light, "as it were a spiritual light." This vision assumed great importance for her inner development. "It came livingly to her from Him: 'The blood of Jesus Christ, God's Son, cleanses you from your sins—, if His blood does not cleanse, what then can cleanse us?" (Arbman, 1963, pp. 16–17).

Not necessarily tangible, but visible and finitely located in space, the presence of Jesus in this report was paradoxically contained within "a spiritual light." It was an instance of the *mysterium tremendum*. *Fascinans* presences are metaphoric in character; but experiences of the *mysterium tremendum* have features—tangibility and localization in space—that warrant their classification, in Freudian terms, as *concrete ideas*. They contain both "mental imagery" and the equivalent mental representations that correspond to the other senses: mental sounds, mental smells, and so forth.

Reflections on Reification

The vicissitudes of the sense of presence furnish evidence for a variety of psychoanalytic reflections. Perhaps the most surprising is the function of the sense of presence, as it manifests in *fascinans* experiences, as the latent content of the *mysterium tremendum* experiences. The elements of tangibility, visibility, and localization in space, which occur in *mysterium tremendum* presences, are *symbols* of the idea of presence, which have been introduced within the experiences through the well-known "dream-work" processes (Freud, 1900) of unconscious symbol-formation. It is as though unconsciously generated religious metaphors underwent reification in the course of their conscious manifestations. Consciousness could not distinguish the manifest contents of the metaphors from their abstract conceptual meaning, but instead confused the two. The idea of the transcendence of Something More is able to manifest, but only as it is equated with what would otherwise have been a metaphoric imagination. Due to the equation, the experience manifests not as a *fascinans* that refers to a nonmanifest Something More, but as a paradoxically self-referring Wholly Other. The compromise is presumably necessitated by resistance, which limits the idea of Something More to only partial manifestation. Since similar compromise formations are regular consequences of resistance in clinical situations, it is presumably resistance that converts a *fascinans* experience into an experience of a *mysterium tremendum*.

The conversion of the *fascinans* into the *mysterium tremendum* through resistance and symbol-formation is simultaneously responsible for transforming what would otherwise be a tenable imagination that is not inconsistent with natural reality, into an improperly bounded, preternatural experience that directly contravenes reality. The indifference to reality by the manifest content of a *mysterium tremendum* is further evidence of unconscious resistance.

These conclusions are consistent with the fact that meditation on the cosmological argument during states of trance does not induce experience of the *fascinans*, but rather of the *mysterium tremendum*. In Hasidism, for example, meditations in sequence on (1) the words of prayer, (2) the meanings of the words, (3) the composition of meanings by letters, (4) the phenomenon of meaningfulness, and finally (5) the Creator of meaningfulness, precipitate mystical union with *'ayin*, the "nothingness" of God (Merkur, 1991a; see also: chapter 4). Ronald E. Shor (1959) suggested that the trance state replaces the general orientation to reality with a special orientation that treats the contents of trance experiences as reality.

> The world of outer consensual reality . . . is replaced by the world of inner sensation, which *seems* to be the real world. The sense of reality is usually transferred from the outside inward with the permission of an indulgent ego which, to a certain extent, foregoes strict reality testing (Committee on Psychiatry and Religion, 1976, p. 778; see also: Merkur, 1984).

The reification is apparently accomplished through the repression of memories of the ordinary sense of reality. With its data base unavailable, the process of negation cannot function in its ordinary manner as a reality-testing process. It has no criteria by which to falsify unrealistic ideas.

Generalizing from these observations, I suggest that the *mysterium tremendum* is reducible to the *fascinans*, as it manifests with imperfect clarity under the constraints imposed by psychological factors consistent with states of trance, that is, by resistance. When an experience of the *fascinans* attempts to manifest despite resistance, it undergoes symbolization. Due to the suspension of reality testing, the symbols cannot be recognized as metaphors and are consequently treated as realities. The numinous element in the experience then becomes self-referring, and the cosmological implication of Something More collapses into an ontological paradox of the Wholly Other.

Resistance to the *fascinans*, which causes it to undergo compromise-formation as the *mysterium tremendum*, may arise from any of several causes. Extensive psychoanalytic findings have established that infantile fixations limit and shape religious beliefs. Resistance may also be induced through simple disbelief, fatigue, various psychoactive drugs, and both meditative and hypnotic techniques for the induction of trance states.

Although the concept of a Something More does not manifest in *mysterium tremendum* experiences, it clearly undergoes symbolization and must be regarded as part of the latent content of the experience. Freud's (1910) argument, which would treat the Something More as a *symbol* of the father, cannot be correct; neither is the Something More a symbol of the mother. The Something More is not the manifest content of a symbol that displaces other ideas. Something More is a latent content that itself undergoes displacement. Religiosity is not the manifest content of something unconscious that is secular. Religiosity is, as Viktor E. Frankl (1975) appreciated, itself capable of being unconscious.

Moreover, if numinous experiences are the defining characteristic of religion, and experiences of the *mysterium tremendum* derive, through symbol-formation, from *fascinans* experiences, unconscious religiosity must, at core, be considered rational. *Fascinans* experiences arise through rational concerns with limit situations that generate the idea of Something More as their logical solution. The solutions are speculative but tenable; they can neither be proved nor falsified. Nevertheless, they are products of rational problem-solving. Unconscious religiosity is not a question only of images (Rizzuto, 1974, 1979), but also of discursive theological reasoning.

Regressive and Adaptive Symbolism

The idea of a metaphysical presence serves, I have argued, as a metaphor indicating Something More. In *fascinans* experiences, the metaphor is experienced consciously. In *mysterium tremendum* experiences, the metaphor is instead reified. The latter circumstance is consistent with Freud's (1900) theory of symbol-formation; the former is not.

The relevant contribution to the puzzle of religious symbolism was made by Herbert Silberer (1912), who distinguished between two types of symbol-formation. In the type discussed by Freud (1900), symbols express ideas that can be expressed more effectively by existing, linguistically expressed ideas. Because the symbols were formed, according to Freud, through a regression from verbal concepts into concrete representations, I have suggested that they may technically be termed *regressive symbols* (Merkur, 1988a).

In the other type of symbol-formation, Silberer maintained that the symbols express abstract ideas for which no corresponding linguistic abstractions have yet been attained. In such cases, there is an advance from concrete pattern perceptions into a figurative use of concrete ideas in both thought and speech. For example, the alchemical concept of sublimation, which refers to the repeated distillation by which floral juices are successively transformed into colognes, perfumes, and essences, has metaphoric use in psychoanalysis to name an imperfectly understood process that adapts human sexuality to nonsexual realities. The symbols are efforts to adapt inadequate images to serve as symbols for abstract ideas, because appropriate verbal abstractions have not as yet been invented or learned. I have suggested that the term *adaptive symbol* aptly describes the function of these symbols.

In a notable effort to blend psychoanalysis and behaviorism, the psychologist J. Cyril Flower (1927) advanced a closely similar theory of symbolism for the explanation of religion.

> Religious behavior originates in the discrimination of a situation in relation to which existing [mental] equipment, in the form of original or acquired tendencies, is inadequate, and may be said to break down . . . what happens [next] is the initiation of fantasies and images around the situation which has the "beyond" character, and these are projected upon the situation in two main ways: (1) a projection which employs the fantasy and image as means through which practical control is gained, and (2) a projection which is in the nature of a partial substitution, the situation not being actually or fully brought under control, and thus the fantastic or imaginal compound is itself responded to in place of the situation . . . this means that the unfamiliar is now incorporated, by the aid of thought, in the system of that universe to which there is adequate practical adaptation, and (b) the situation remains in actuality out of range even after fantasy and image work, and consequently it is mainly to the fantasy and image that the overt response takes place (pp. 31–32).

In Flower's presentation, images are applied to phenomena to which they are inappropriate. In doing so, they acquire valid use in an extended or metaphoric sense. Science and religion consequently differ in degree but not in kind. In science, fantasy is adequate to the explanation of reality. Where explanation is unavailable, mystery remains, and the label "religion" is applied to the fantasies.

As examples of regressive and adaptive symbols, consider the following passage by Deutero-Isaiah, which prophesied the ingathering of the Jews from the Babylonian captivity. The prophet had Yahweh's state:

> For a long time I have held my peace,
>   I have kept still and restrained myself;
> Now I will cry out like a woman in travail,
>   I will grasp and pant.
> I will lay waste mountains and hills,
>   and dry up all their herbage;
> I will turn the rivers into islands,
>   and dry up the pools.
> And I will lead the blind
>   in a way that they know not,
> in paths that they have not known
>   I will give them.

I will turn the darkness before them
   into light,
the rough places into level ground (Is 42:14–16).

The likening of Yahweh's innovation of a new activity to a woman giving birth was an instance of regressive symbolization. The image of birth allegorized the abstract concept of novelty, which the poet was able to express verbally, but did not do. However, the likening of a woman's body in labor to a devastation of the earth introduced the first of a series of adaptive symbols that together expressed the concept of a removal of obstacles from the routes that the Jews would have to travel in order to return to Zion. The metaphoric significance of the earth's devastation was expressed by the juxtaposition of the further images. Since the blind cannot benefit from light, the images of leading the blind along unknown ways and turning darkness into light do not form a meaningful sequence when they are treated literally. The pairing of the images urges their interpretation as metaphors, and so creates a metaphoric sensibility before the poetry returns to its initial image of an earthquake, which is now more optimistically described as turning rough places into level ground. The images of guidance, light, and level ground together made clear that Deutero-Isaiah had all along been prophesying the abstract concept of a removal of obstacles, and was not to be interpreted as having referred literally to an eschatological earthquake. Deutero-Isaiah did not formulate the concept of Yahweh's expediting the return to Zion in equivalently abstract terminology. His poetry relied exclusively on images, because images were what he had used to attain the concept.

Deutero-Isaiah's use of images as adaptive symbols may be used to illustrate an important point of psychoanalytic theory. Freud (1900) followed Aristotle's account of the imaginative faculty when he limited the unconscious—later, the id—to the "dream-work" of translating ideas into images.

> The dream-work is not simply more careless, more irrational, more forgetful and more incomplete than waking thought; it is completely different from it qualitatively and for that reason not immediately comparable with it. It does not think, calculate or judge in any way at all; it restricts itself to giving things a new form (p. 507).

Freud's assignment of all intelligent reasoning to consciousness—later, the ego, is inconsistent, however, with the biblical evidence. It can be argued that regressive symbols depend on intelligence that is exclusively conscious. They can be formed by reverting mechanically from verbally expressed ideas to the mental images that they name. However, adaptive symbols differ. They cannot be back-formed from verbal thoughts that themselves remain latent. Adaptive symbols serve to express ideas that have never previously been verbalized. Their formulations require images to be juxtaposed, condensed, and/or displaced. The coherence that adaptive symbols display must be attributed to the very processes of condensing and/or displacing images.

This circumstance is consistent with a series of persuasive studies on dreams by Thomas M. French (1937, 1939, 1952, 1954, 1957; French & Fromm, 1964; French & Whitman, 1969). French and his coworkers demonstrated that the dream-work, which converts latent ideas into manifest dream images, must be attributed to a psychic agency that is rational as well as unconscious. The dream-work's choice of imagery invariably serves the purpose of conveying latent ideas to consciousness. The condensation and displacement of symbols not only conceal objectionable ideas. The two aspects of symbolization serve simultaneously to reveal them. The unconscious process of symbol-formation is not, as Freud (1900) proposed, an irrational consequence of freely associating psychic energies. It is rational and intelligent. More recently, Robert J. Langs (1988, 1991, 1994) has further explored the idea that dreams are intrapsychic communications that convey "deep unconscious wisdom" to consciousness.

The distinction between regressive and adaptive symbolism is important to the vicissitudes of the sense of presence. When the presence manifests as a metaphoric *fascinans*, it is an adaptive symbol that seeks to convey the idea of Something More. Should the adaptive symbol encounter resistance, it secondarily undergoes a regressive symbol-formation that fantasizes the additional features of its tangibility and finite location in space. Regressive too is the displacement that equates the manifest with the transcendent, producing the paradox of the Wholly Other.

Silberer's contention that there are two types of unconscious symbol-formations won general acceptance among psychoanalysts (Rank & Sachs, 1916; Jones, 1916; Fenichel, 1945). The clinical value of the concept of adaptive symbols was established in the 1920s through the introduction of the play therapy of children. In the symbols of their play, children can express both feelings and concepts that they do not know how to articulate verbally. Religious symbols may be employed similarly. Oskar Pfister (1932) argued that psychotherapy can be accomplished successfully by addressing unconscious dynamics through appropriate manipulations of religious symbolism. He suggested that religious healing can constitute an "instinctive psychoanalysis," if its manipulation of religious symbolism conveys the appropriate insights in symbolic form. "The inner reconciliation as a result of symbolic understanding takes place in a much more effective manner than if a rational explanation were suddenly given, for such hasty explanation would quicken all the insidious resistances connected with rendering the material conscious" (pp. 251–52). Discussing recent clinical work by Ana-Maria Rizzuto (1979) and W. W. Meissner (1984), Jacob A. Arlow suggested that because God functions as "a transferential figure," analysis of the health of a person's relation with God can function as an analysis of transference (in L. Grossman, 1993). In the last several years, the general utility of metaphors in psychotherapy has begun to be recognized and developed into clinical techniques (Siegelman, 1990; Kopp, 1995).

Metaphoric thought is not restricted to the realm of poetry, play, and religion. It also plays a prominent role in scientific discovery and scientific reasoning (Hesse, 1970; Barbour, 1974; Leatherdale, 1974; MacCormac, 1976; Leary, 1990). Prosaic verbal formulation of a discovery generally follows its initial attainment (Langer, 1957, p. 102). Indeed, a major problem with psychoanalytic theory arises from the failure to move beyond heurisms. Most psychoanalysts have retreated into the reification of Freud's metaphors of apparatuses, energies, structures, and mechanisms (Holt, 1989). Similar problems surround the inherently metaphoric internal objects or imagoes of Kleinian object relations theory.

Silberer advanced his theory of symbolism in the explanation of the nature of myths. He suggested that the world's myths are narratives that are constructed out of adaptive symbols. Theodor Reik (1959, 1960, 1961) and David Bakan (1979) analyzed biblical legends in parallel; and I have elsewhere interpreted the two dozen principle myths of the Inuit (Merkur, 1988a, 1991b) in keeping with Silberer's theory. Arlow (1961) suggested that myths furnish imagery that children's psyches use in instinctually meaningful ways that are phase-specific developmentally. The imagery may be used either adaptively, to facilitate development, or neurotically, as symptoms of neurosis. L. Bryce Boyer (1979) added that all cultural symbols serve the same functions as myths.

The difference between regressive and adaptive symbolism imposes an important qualification on Freud's (1910) assertion that "a personal God is, psychologically, nothing other than an exalted father" (p. 123; see also: 1913, p. 147; 1930, p. 74). Freud assumed that God was a regressive symbol. Only a regressive symbol would mean nothing more than the latent idea that it displaces.

Freud's assumption was conclusively refuted by Rizzuto (1979), whose psychoanalytic case studies persuasively demonstrated that "the God representation changes along with us and our primary objects in the lifelong context of other relevant beings" (p. 52). Rizzuto's clinical findings (see also: McDargh, 1983; J. W. Jones, 1991; Finn & Gartner, 1992) conclusively refuted the implication that an infantile attitude to the father must be fixated, if it is to persist unconsciously and undergo displacement to become the idea of God. Rizzuto (1974) wrote:

> People's dealings with their God are no more, and no less, complex than their dealings with other people—either in early childhood or in any other age; i.e. they are imperfect, ambiguous, dynamic and, by their very nature, have potential for both integrating and fragmenting their overall psychic experience (p. 88).

If God representations were fixated, that is, if religion were tantamount to group neurosis, clinical evidence would not disclose the richness, versatility, and regular change and growth that occurs within people's relations to God.

Treating God representations as adaptive symbols has markedly different implications than Freud imagined. Psychoanalysis may address unconscious motives influencing the choice of *manifest* religious *symbolism*, but adaptive symbols have an unstated, *implicit meaning* that remains conscious and doctrinal (Merkur, 1988a). For example, unconscious attitudes to human fathers inform the symbolization of God as a father; but the raison d'être of the symbol remains the metaphysical postulation of a transcendent Something More. Bakan (1966a) remarked that "Freud failed to see . . . that the projection of fatherhood on God must also be interpreted as mankind projecting its own fatherhood" (p. 200). For God to be an exalted father, as Freud claimed, does not mean that a religious person is in the position of a child. Quite to the contrary, a religious person must be in the position of a father, or fatherhood would never be projected onto the transcendent. In speaking of the transcendent as a *father*, people do not intend the term literally. Whether God's fatherhood refers to God's relation to humanity, or to the relation of the first and second persons of the Christian Trinity, God is not thought to engage in biological reproduction, nor in reproduction of any kind. God is discussed under the symbol of a father, as a metaphoric means by which to speak of the transcendent. The image of the metaphor arises out of human biology; but because the image is used as a metaphor, its latent meaning remains a metaphysical assertion. It is an error in psychoanalytic method, a category mistake in diagnosis, to confound metaphors known as such with symbols whose symbolic character is unconscious. Metaphors do not have to be similes—for example, God does not have to be said to be expressly *like* a father—for a religious symbol to have rational function and meaning.

Summary

When the sense of presence is experienced as a *fascinans*, its manifestly illogical or paradoxical contents are experienced as metaphors. The metaphors imply "Something More"—a rational, albeit speculative postulate.

When the sense of presence is instead experienced as a *mysterium tremendum*, its manifestly illogical or paradoxical contents are both increased in number and seemingly nonmetaphoric. The experiences are preternatural; they contravene nature. Their psychoanalysis indicates, however, that the illogical or paradoxical features are *symbols* that have been reified. Because their symbolic nature and meaning is unconscious, they are manifestly irrational. However, their latent meanings are consistent with *fascinans* experiences—rational, albeit speculative in character.

The metaphoric character of *fascinans* experiences is inconsistent with Freud's (1900) theory of regressive symbol-formation, but coherent in terms of

Silberer's (1912) theory of symbols that express abstract ideas for which no corresponding linguistic abstractions have yet been attained. Silberer's theory has not attained the celebrity that it deserves but is necessary to psychoanalytic discussions of religious imagery. Regressive symbols are irrational; but regressive symbols are reifications of religious metaphors that may themselves be entirely rational.

This argument brings to a close my efforts to show that mystical moments sublimate infant-mother fusion fantasies, as metaphors for the expression of speculations. Whether the speculations are scientific, moral, or metaphysical in content, they are efforts to press fantasies into the service of understanding reality. In keeping with expectable vicissitudes in cognitive development, individual speculations vary from absurd errors to tenable possibilities. Cognitive development is not unilinear, but proceeds by trial and error in many directions.

SIX

Euphoria and Desolation

Freud (1910) maintained that "a personal God is, psychologically, nothing other than an exalted father" (p. 123; see also: 1913, p. 147; 1930, p. 74). After 1923, when Freud introduced his theory of the superego, his position was understood to mean that the image of God symbolizes the exalted father that was internalized in or as the superego (Weiss, 1932). My distinction between imagery pertaining to the mother and its application as a metaphor for the transcendent adds a further qualification to Freud's theory, but remains within his psychoanalytic paradigm. So too did Helene Deutsch's (1927) explanation of theistic mystical experiences as a fusion of the ego and the superego.

> In the ecstatic experience the self fades away and God moves into its place, but this God is neither a loving nor a punishing personality but is the experience itself, the attainment of a new consciousness, that of one's own divinity through disappearance of the frontier between the self and God. In the state of ecstasy the idea of God that was projected outside is taken back into the ego again, but there is no conflict between ego and superego or between self and God, because self and God are both self (p. 719; compare: Kris, 1934; Hopkins, 1940; Flugel, 1945; Brierley, 1951; Lewin, 1951).

Responding to Deutsch's ideas without criticizing her by name, Freud (1930) asserted that he imagined "that the oceanic feeling became connected with religion later on" (p. 72). Freud's view that the sense of "oneness with the universe" might exist apart from its association with the idea of God was consistent with unitive experiences that were not theistic. Mystical unions that included the additional element of divinization might be explained, he suggested, as secondary developments of the oceanic feeling.

Richard Sterba (1968) resolved the issue when he suggested "that there will be a great variety of mystic experiences according to . . . the extent to which the mystic enlarges his Ego boundaries to include part or the whole of the outside world" (p. 81). This enlargement of the self sets mystical experiences apart from other fusion states.

There seems to be one condition which makes such a fusion a *mystic* experience. The outside object with which the Self fuses in the *unio mystica* has to be larger, more powerful, much higher in the evaluation of the person who experiences the mystic state. It is this participation in the *superior*, through the act of fusion, which endows the mystic with the feeling of bliss, which often amounts to ecstasy. It also gives the person the feeling of experiencing the ultimate truth, the conviction that the emotional and cognitive material experienced during the mystic state is of a higher kind of reality beyond all reasoning (p. 83).

Sterba observed that unitive experiences regularly portray a self that is superior to the self's reality. Whether it is a solitary self that is imagined to be timeless and boundless, or an extrovertive union that portrays the self extended to the external world in one manner or another, or the mortal self of ecstatic death, the ideas of the self that are portrayed in unitive experiences are invariably ideas of an ideal self or, in Freud's phrase, "ego ideals."

Because the formulation and maintenance of ego ideals is one of the functions that Freud (1914, 1921, 1933) ascribed to the superego, I suggest that *unitive schemas as a group may reasonably be considered ideals that are produced by the superego.*

Attributing unitive experiences to the superego provides a further corrective to the mistaken theory of mysticism as regression. Following Freud's lead, psychoanalysts traditionally conceptualized unitive experiences as regressions to narcissistic grandiosity. But is mystical euphoria rightly considered narcissistic? Narcissism is a reaction-formation in which grandiosity is maintained consciously in order to continuously deny and suppress a preconscious deficit of self-esteem. Federn (1932) consequently objected that "we always find the narcis[sis]tic comprehension of the universe to be very uncertain," whereas "religious feeling . . . makes man's attitude towards the world peaceful and secure" (p. 133). Federn noted that rather than a narcissistic investment of the ego, the oceanic feeling "appears when the normal limits of the ego are extended to the human, earthly and cosmic surrounding world" (p. 133). Due to its extension to the universe, the ego feels a "pleasurable relaxation" that "may give rise to high mental raptures" (pp. 133–34). As well, the oceanic feeling is not preoccupied with the self, but instead "has the character of love for many people" (p. 134).

Might it not be preferable to interpret mystical euphoria straightforwardly as a powerful enhancement of self-esteem? Reporting psychoanalytic treatment of a Buddhist meditator, Jeffrey Rubin (1992) remarked:

In offering an image of, and a vehicle for, self-perfection, Buddhist meditation afforded him a substitute set of missing ideals and values, thus strengthening a dimension of himself that he needed to fortify to feel good about himself.

These ideals were restitutive and restrictive. . . .

> But it [meditation] also became an agent of self-condemnation and self-inhibition. . . .
>
> We feel better when we achieve our ideals. We feel badly when we do not attain our ideals (p. 104).

Freud (1933, p. 117; 1940, p. 206) attributed the production of pride and self-esteem to the superego's approval of the ego. Otto Fenichel (1945) explained the origin of self-esteem as an internalization of mother's love within the superego. "The first supply of satisfaction from the external world, the supply of nourishment, is simultaneously the first regulator of self-esteem" (p. 40). Unconscious mother-infant fusions may be integral to the superego's action. Winnicott (1958) argued that the capacity to be alone presupposes an internal object relation that replicates the mother-child interaction. Mahler (with Furer, 1968, p. 222) expressed the same idea less metaphorically. She asserted that a child cannot generate self-esteem until it can maintain a constant sense of being loved by its mother (see also: Joffe & Sandler, 1965; Spitz, with Cobliner, 1965; Kohut, 1971; Tolpin, 1971; McDevitt, 1979).

The short-term regulation of self-esteem in response to individual mental and physical actions is ordinarily discussed as the function of conscience. Although momentary self-esteem may commence as early as the initial formation of the body-image, the superego's regulation of self-esteem with respect to long-term achievements and intentions permit more or less continuous experiences of self-regard, constituting a basic mood (Jacobson, 1954b, p. 121; 1957, p. 83; 1964, pp. 29, 133; Eisnitz, 1980, p. 379; Settlage, 1993, p. 478). The basic mood is interrupted from time to time by all manners of emotion, including judgments of conscience that pertain to specific intentions; but long-term self-regard provides an emotional baseline.

The euphoric character of unitive experiences may, I suggest, be interpreted in parallel, as expressions of positive self-regard in response to the ego ideals whose attainment form the cognitive contents of unitive experiences. Self-esteem is maximized when and because a unitive ideal is momentarily integrated within the self.

Winnicott (1958) raised the question "whether there can be a value in thinking of *ecstasy* as an ego orgasm" and brought unitive experiences into relation with theatrical catharsis and the play experiences of children. He suggested that unitive experiences belong to a class of experiences whose occurrence from childhood through adulthood is entirely normal, and that differ from the pathological symptoms known to psychoanalysis.

> In the normal person a highly satisfactory experience such as may be obtained at a concert or at the theatre or in a friendship may deserve a term such as ego orgasm, which draws attention to the climax and the importance of the climax.

> It may be thought unwise that the word orgasm should be used in this context;
> I think that even so there is room for a discussion of the climax that may occur
> in satisfactory ego-relatedness. . . .
>
> The so-called normal child is able to play, to get excited while playing, and to
> feel satisfied with the game, without feeling threatened by a physical orgasm of
> local excitement. . . . Whatever the unconscious symbolism, the quantity of ac-
> tual physical excitement is minimal in the one type of experience and maximal
> in the other" (p. 35).

Winnicott's metaphor of an "ego orgasm" may be connected to an observation by Freud. Discussing the historical attainment of the abstract idea of God,
which Freud (1939) considered a "triumph of intellectuality over sensuality" (p.
119), Freud remarked that "all such advances in intellectuality have as their consequence that the individual's self-esteem is increased" (p. 115). Euphoria, due
to heightened self-esteem, may reasonably be expected to attend the creative attainment of any similarly intellectual idea.

Some practical consequences of mystical euphoria were noted by Ross
(1968), who remarked that mystical experiences are "often, but by no means always associated with a capacity for relatively mature object relations" (p. 271).
He suggested that mystical experiences provide a basis for object-relations of increased maturity.

> Although I would not equate the contemplatives, the religious mystics, the
> mescaline cultists, the Yogi, the Zen Buddhists as identical. . . . It is my guess
> that . . . [unitive experiences] satisfy so deeply . . . that they leave such individ-
> uals free to experience object relations of a higher order, although this is by no
> means either an outcome of the ability to have mystical experiences, or a nec-
> essary accompaniment of it (p. 273).

Self-esteem is necessary not only to the capacity to be alone, but also to the capacity to relate healthfully to others.

Freud's "Disturbance of Memory"

My contention that unitive experiences are positive superego manifestations is consistent with Freud's treatment of "A disturbance of memory on the
Acropolis" (1936) as an instance of guilt, or tension between the ego and superego. When Freud was invited to offer a tribute on the occasion of Romain Rolland's seventieth birthday, he penned an open letter that reports and analyzes an
experience that Freud had had in 1904, when he had visited the Acropolis in
Athens while vacationing with his brother Alexander.

The occasion of Freud's essay implies that he believed that his experience was pertinent to the "oceanic feeling" of Romain Rolland (Werman, 1977; Masson & Masson, 1978; Harrison, 1979). In a letter to Freud, dated 5 December 1927, Rolland had included a fragmentary self-report of a mystical experience. The letter referred to

> the simple and direct *sensation of the eternal* . . . subjective in character . . . without . . . in any way harming my critical faculties and my freedom to exercise them— even if against the immediacy of this internal experience. . . . I add that this "oceanic" feeling has nothing to do with my personal aspirations. . . . But the sensation that I feel is thrust upon me as a fact. It is a *contact* (Fisher, 1976, pp. 20–22).

Freud (1930) discussed Rolland's experience in the first chapter of "Civilization and Its Discontents." Why, six years later, did Freud associate his "disturbance of memory" with Rolland's mystical experience?

Freud (1936) and his brother decided to visit the island of Corfu. After making their way to Trieste, a business acquaintance there strongly advised them against proceeding to Corfu. He instead suggested that they travel to Athens. Freud wrote:

> As we walked away from this visit, we were both in remarkably depressed spirits. We discussed the plan that had been proposed, agreed that it was quite impracticable and saw nothing but difficulties in the way of carrying it out; we assumed, moreover, that we should not be allowed to land in Greece without passports. We spent the hours that elapsed before the Lloyd offices opened in wandering about the town in a discontented and irresolute frame of mind. But when the time came, we went up to the counter and booked our passage for Athens as though it were a matter of course, without bothering in the least about the supposed difficulties and indeed without having discussed with one another the reasons for our decision. Such behavior, it must be confessed, was most strange. Later on we recognized that we had accepted the suggestion that we should go to Athens instead of Corfu instantly and most readily. But, if so, why had we spent the interval before the offices opened in such a gloomy state and foreseen nothing but obstacles and difficulties?
>
> When, finally, on the afternoon after our arrival, I stood upon the Acropolis and cast my eyes around upon the landscape, a surprising thought suddenly entered my mind: "So all this really *does* exist, just as we learnt at school!" To describe the situation more accurately, the person who gave expression to the remark was divided, far more sharply than was usually noticeable, from another person who took cognizance of the remark; and both were astonished, though not by the same thing. The first behaved as though he were obliged, under the impact of an unequivocal observation, to believe in something the reality of which had hitherto seemed doubtful. If I may make a slight exaggeration, it was as if someone, walking beside Loch Ness, suddenly caught sight of the form of the famous Monster stranded upon the shore and found himself driven to the admission: "So it really *does* exist—the sea-serpent we've never believed

in!" The second person, on the other hand, was justifiably astonished, because he had been unaware that the real existence of Athens, the Acropolis, and the landscape around it had ever been objects of doubt. What he had been expecting was rather some expression of delight or admiration (pp. 239–41).

In his analysis of his experience, Freud remarked that "the depression at Trieste and the idea on the Acropolis were intimately connected" (p. 241). He further observed that an internal frustration had been projected onto external events, which caused a conscious feeling that external events ought to be frustrating even when they did not prove so. "The Fate which we expect to treat us so badly is a materialization of our conscience, of the severe super-ego within us, itself a residue of the punitive agency of our childhood" (p. 243). Freud cited three manners in which the projection of frustration may take form. Of the three, *derealization*, which occurred to Freud on the Acropolis, is the feeling that "a piece of reality . . . is strange" (p. 245).

When Freud attempted to specify against what his disturbance on the Acropolis had been a defense, he neatly and all but invisibly subverted his argument.

> It must be that a sense of guilt was attached to the satisfaction in having gone such a long way: there was something about it that was wrong, that from earliest times had been forbidden. It was something to do with a child's criticism of his father, with the undervaluation of earlier childhood. It seems as though the essence of success was to have got further than one's father, and as though to excel one's father was still something forbidden. . . . Thus what interfered with our enjoyment of the journey to Athens was a feeling of *filial piety* (pp. 247–48).

No one has previously remarked that the logic of Freud's theorizing was defective in this passage. Freud claimed that filial piety forbade him to enjoy an achievement greater than his father. With the word "piety" he alluded to religious sentiment and so implied that his experience on the Acropolis was relevant to Rolland's oceanic feeling. Freud also alluded to his general theory of religion as a devotion to symbols of the father (1910, 1913, 1927). The reference to "filial piety" was misleading, however, because Freud did not have a religious experience. What he experienced was depression.

Comparison with religion would be appropriate not for Freud, but for an experience that he did not have, the "expression of delight or admiration" (p. 241) that another individual might have had in his place. Consider, for example, the experience of the historian Edward Gibbon (1932) on the occasion of his first visit to Rome.

> My temper is not very susceptible of enthusiasm, and the enthusiasm which I do not feel I have ever scorned to affect. But at the distance of twenty-five years I can neither forget nor express the strong emotions which agitated my mind as I first approached and entered the *eternal city*. After a sleepless night, I trod, with a lofty step, the ruins of the Forum; each memorable spot where Romu-

lus *stood*, or Tully spoke, or Caesar fell, was at once present to my eye; and the several days of intoxication were lost or enjoyed before I could descend to a cool and minute investigation. . . . It was at Rome, on the 15th of October 1794, as I sat musing amidst the ruins of the Capitol, while the barefooted friars were singing vespers in the temple of Jupiter, that the idea of writing the decline and fall of the city first started to my mind (pp. 122–24).

The ancient history of Rome gave meaning to Gibbon's experience of the city of 1794 because it provided ideas through which he could articulate his excitement and euphoria. Gibbon's peak experience was a unitive one. The history or temporal existence of Rome was collapsed into the one existential moment of Gibbon's ecstatic experience.

Freud's depression may be brought into comparison with Gibbon's ecstasy, as Freud implied, but only if we assume that he unconsciously resisted an enthusiasm that Gibbon permitted himself.

A Comparison of Desolation and Unitive Experiences

Freud's depression on the Acropolis may usefully be considered an instance of the class of extraordinary experiences that Marghanita Laski (1962) and Michael Paffard (1973) termed *desolation* experiences. The experiences manifest a variety of depressive affects. In some, the dominant emotion is a helpless, passive, horrifying desolation. In others, it is a fear or terror that motivates active flight or escape. I suggest, however, that desolation experiences deserve as a group to be brought into relation with unitive experiences.

Desolation experiences frequently involve a sense of loneliness and insignificance with respect to the universe. The attendant emotions may be "melancholy," "dread," feeling "desolate" (Paffard, 1973, pp. 196, 175, 193) or, as in the following self-report, "horribly aware of terror."

> I think I would associate this feeling with something that happened while camping. It was the first time I'd ever really *seen* a dandelion flower, not just a yellow bobble on a green stalk reproduced thousands of times over, but the sheer beauty of the pattern and the actual formation of the flower. For some reason I then became horribly aware of what I can only describe as the terror of the universe—the, for me, impossible problem of trying to gain some concept of the size of infinity,—and our own insignificance of it all (p. 137).

The dandelion's "sheer beauty" served as a symbol of the infinity of the universe and occasioned terror. The report can be seen as a precise contrary to unitive experiences of the oceanic feeling. Rather than delicious serenity at a sense of inclusion within a boundless, timeless cosmos, there was desolation at loneliness. The oceanic feeling of infinite unity was presupposed as a standard of value against which the sense of insignificance was measured. Note also the il-logicality of finding "sheer beauty" in a single dandelion flower, but one's own equally limited existence insignificant.

Another subgroup of desolation reveries again involves a sense of intense loneliness. The emotion may be "most terrifying," "a feeling of being dwarfed" (Paffard, 1973, pp. 175, 197) or, as in the following self-report, a "hateful feeling."

> The coming of night always terrifies me and makes me uneasy in some way. In a town this feeling can be subdued because the area seen is limited, and there are always some lights and signs of life around. In the country where there is a wide view of the surrounding land—e.g. from the terrace, one cannot escape it. The grey oppressiveness settles down more and more heavily over the ground—slowly because it need not hurry, being outside time and space, yet relentlessly; and even the breeze seems to die at the moment when the birds become silent. Even if there has been a magnificent sunset, the feeling is still there. The sunset may be triumphant but only heralds the last few minutes be-fore the grey silence spreads—and may be as a shriek of anguish before it. This is not like the death of a day, or anything else. It is something more than and passing beyond that, something inexplicable. The silent, breathlessly waiting dusk, the pivot point when movement is stopped for a moment before day slides down into night and relief, is a time when I need to be doing something practical and material, or be engulfed in the hateful feeling of being outside the relevancies of the world and what is beyond it (p. 194).

The phrasing, "being outside the relevancies of the world and what is be-yond it," suggests that a customary or unquestioned religious faith was momen-tarily insupportable during the desolation. The involuntary denial of religiosity was consistent, I suggest, with the relation of the desolation experience to uni-tive experiences. The sense of lonely isolation in the desolation is precisely con-trary to a type of unitive experience that I discussed in chapter 2 as a sense of relatedness. Consider the following example.

> I . . . frequently go for long walks alone to get away from the reality of life and mankind. On the lower marshy fells I sit alone and watch the ants, bees etc., and feel company. Then I continue my walk to the bleak heather covered fells and lie on my belly. I listen to the lonely curlew and the quietness that only Mother Nature can grant. Whether fine or rainy I feel as though I have a com-panion; this companion is as peaceful, as sacredly quite as nature, and under-standing; words are superfluous, thought unnecessary; the peaceful solitude reaches the inner most depth of my soul and I am completely satisfied (p. 189).

In unitive experiences of relatedness, the unitive ideas are of being related to an All. The corresponding desolation experience is of not being related to an All, of being lonely and isolated in an all-encompassing manner.

In other cases, desolation experiences are not occasioned by a sense of lonely isolation.

> One particularly vivid experience was while I was walking along the sea shore. After walking along the sand I climbed up to the cliffs and walked along them to the end of the point where the cliff is crumbling. There are great boulders and huge crannies. It was early evening and a particularly wild night. The sky was full of dark cloud[s] and there was no moon to be seen. The sea was extremely rough and the huge waves were thundering against the rocks and sucking in and out the crannies sending huge sheets of foam up, occasionally splashing me. It was an exhilarating experience at first: everything seemed still and eerie except for the wind and waves. At first I dodged back as I saw a huge wave to avoid the spray and then as I became more fascinated listening to the wind and sea and watching the waves beneath, I just stood at the cliff edge fascinated. I gradually began to get wet by the spray; at first I was oblivious of it being so fascinated by the wildness of the scene below me. Then suddenly a huge wave came and the spray drenched me. Suddenly I was terrified and I had a horrible feeling I was being sucked in and out of the crannies by the waves and thrown against the rocks. So I turned and ran all the way back to the road (pp. 184–85).

The experience of the "wildness of the scene below me" was initially "exhilarating" and fascinating. Abruptly the mood changed into terror and horror of death on the rocks below. Being drenched with spray suggested a fantasy of "being sucked in and out of the crannies by the waves and thrown against the rocks." Acting-out in response to the terror, the person "turned and ran all the way back to the road."

The references to wildness in the self-report, in the phrases "a particularly wild night" and "the wildness of the scene below me," suggest that the desolation might usefully be contrasted with the type of unitive experiences that I have termed *propriety*, because the peak experiences consist of an ecstatic sense that everything is proper, right, functional, harmonious, perfect, beautiful, and good.

> Vauxhall Station on a murky November Saturday evening is not the setting one would choose for a revelation of God! I was a young theological student aged nineteen, being sent from Richmond Theological College (London University) to take the services somewhere—I cannot remember where—for some minister in a Greater London church who had fallen ill. The third-class compartment was full. I cannot remember any particular thought processes which may have led up to the great moment. . . .
>
> For a few seconds only, I suppose, the whole compartment was filled with light. This is the only way I know in which to describe the moment, for there was nothing to *see* at all. I felt caught up into some tremendous sense of being

within a loving, triumphant and shining purpose. I never felt more humble. I
never felt more exalted. A most curious but overwhelming sense possessed me
and filled me with ecstasy. I felt that all was well for mankind. . . . All men were
shining and glorious beings who in the end would enter incredible joy. Beauty,
music, joy, love immeasurable and a glory unspeakable, all this they would inherit. Of this they were heirs. My puny message, if I passed my exams and
qualified as a minister, would contribute only an infinitesimal drop to the
ocean of love and truth which God wanted men to enjoy, but my message was
of the same *nature* as that ocean. I was right to want to be a minister. I had
wanted to be a doctor and the conflict had been intense, but in that hour I
knew the ministry was the right path for me. For me it was right, right, right.
. . . An indescribable joy possessed me (Hardy, 1979. p. 53).

Where, in the unitive experience, everything great and small is wonderfully
right, in the desolation, nothing is right. Everything is horribly, deadly wrong.

Desolation experiences also include a variant of the type of religious experience that James (1902) termed a *sense of presence*. In the following self-report, a
sense of a mysterious, supernatural presence is initially met with delight, but the
ecstasy presently transforms into a bad fright that the individual attempted to
conceal from the presence.

In my childhood, I used to have a fear of trees in the moonlight. This was only
if I was alone. I sometimes used to feel the presence of something there. It was
just as though the supernatural was round me. I would at first delight in daring
to enter the mysterious. Then, after a time, I would make the mystery seem
even deeper than it was, and I would walk quickly, trying to conceal my fright
from that which had frightened me (Paffard, 1973, p. 176).

The close affinity of desolation and unitive experiences is further indicated
by the occasional termination of a desolation through a sudden change within
the alternate psychic state that transforms it into an ecstasy.

I was one Saturday evening at a dance and I didn't feel like dancing. I sat
watching the people enjoying themselves and felt I did not belong. I was overcome by a feeling of frustration both physical and mental and a realisation of
apparent futility in this life. Oppressed by the sight of these people deceiving
themselves, I went out into the cold, starry night. After walking under the trees
I began to pray and tears came to my eyes. The vastness of the sky served at first
only to increase the feeling of futility and insignificance but as I became aware
of the Divine, I was comforted by thoughts of God (p. 196)

The report concerns a desolation at the unattainability of unitive inclusion,
which was followed by a sense of relatedness to God.

In another instance, a unitive experience of inclusion turned into a deso-
lating loneliness. The lasting effect of the experience was nevertheless unitive.

One afternoon while I was at home, just relaxing, I started thinking about the universe, how big it must be, perhaps never ending. I was wondering about that. How could something never end? Suddenly, it was as if a funnel was in the top of my head and my consciousness went out into it, spreading wider and wider as it went. This went on for quite some time until I suddenly realized that I was conscious of everything that is, and that I was part of it all. Then I became aware of it from a different aspect. I was everything that is. It seemed curious at first, but then turned into a feeling of being very much alone. I thought surely there must be something or somebody outside of me, but I searched and searched and could find nothing that was not a part of me. Desperately, I wanted someone to share my existence. Finally, the loneliness became overwhelming and I snapped back into my usual self. This was experienced almost twenty years ago but I have never forgotten it. It changed my life, giving me a strong feeling of empathy for all the people around me and even all those I have never met. We are all in the same boat (Maxwell & Tschudin, 1990, pp. 171–72).

These examples indicate that a desolation may follow upon, or be followed by, a euphoric unitive experience; but the moments of desolation never coincide with the moments of euphoria. Different desolation experiences nonetheless share the underlying structure of several varieties of unitive experiences. The cognitive elements that are experienced positively and euphorically in the unitive experiences are instead attended by fear, terror, horror, despair, or desolation in the desolation experiences. The desolation experiences are negative in terms of both their affects and cognitions of unity. The ideas of unity, inclusion, relation, and propriety that are greeted ecstatically in the unitive experiences are instead mourned and feared as absences, as nonoccurrences or unattainables, in the desolation experiences.

Desolation experiences may reasonably be brought into relation with unitive experiences. Desolation experiences are depressive rather than ecstatic, but they presuppose unconscious ideas of union. Without an unconsciously unitive aspect to desolation experiences, there would be nothing to be denied nor, through its loss, to support terror, horror, or desolation.

Resistance and Desolation

Freud explained his "disturbance of memory" as a manifestation of a guilty conscience. Gibbon's ecstasy could be interpreted in parallel as a manifestation of an innocent conscience. Should these theories be extended as generalizations governing unitive and desolation experiences in general? Are unions and desolations to be understood as inspirations of conscience?

The theoretical question may be phrased more precisely by avoiding the methodological error of anthropomorphizing mental processes. "Conscience" and the "superego" are metaphors that permit a group of information processes to be discussed as though they were an actor on the interior stage of the mind. When we avoid anthropomorphizing conscience as "innocent" and "guilty," we may state that Freud resisted unitive inspirations whose conscious manifestation Gibbon enjoyed. Working with Freud's theory of resistance, we should not think in terms of a guilty conscience or a severe superego. When the information process of "conscience" identifies a discrepancy between the self and its standard of values, it concludes its reasoning process with the idea of an opportunity for self-improvement. It is only when the desire for self-improvement is refused and resisted that anxiety, shame, guilt, and other negative emotions may arise. Accordingly, the theory of resistance obliges us to subdivide the anthropomorphic metaphor of a severe superego into two information processes. On the one side are fixated repressions. On the other is unconscious unitive thinking. Due to the unconscious association of the fixations with the unitive thinking, the repression of the former inhibits the manifestation of the latter. The inhibition generates anxiety that manifests as a distortion or skewing of the unitive experiences and transforms euphoria into desolation.

Such an interpretation would be consistent with a formulation by Arnold H. Modell. Because he assumed that unitive experiences have the unconscious significance of merger with the mother, Modell (1968) emphasized that merger states are so varied that diagnoses must proceed on an individual basis.

> The merging with a "good" object can be experienced as a state of religious mysticism, sexual ecstasy, or a manic denial. . . . Conversely, when there is an intense fear of merging with a "bad" object the subject may fear a loss of identity, a dread of being influenced, and ultimately may fear complete annihilation (p. 37).

In some cases, unconscious fears of the mother permit unitive experiences to occur, but causes them to assume distressing forms. In other cases, unconscious fears may be responsible for preventing the very occurrence of unitive experiences (Ross, 1968).

Modell's theory seems to be supported by what we know of Freud's "disturbance of memory." Freud interpreted his depression at Trieste and Athens in terms of guilt and piety, but his self-diagnosis was a self-deceiving rationalization. The logic of his argument was inconsistent with the evidence that he presented. Freud did not experience pious wonderment. Neither did he direct guilt and atonement toward the Acropolis. (Arguably, Gibbon did; his desire to chronicle the decline and fall of the Roman empire can be treated as an act of reparation or restitution.) For Freud, the derealization of the Acropolis avoided the very occasion for piety. He did not have to be pious when and because he doubted Athens's very existence. Freud credited himself with unconscious piety, but the internal logic of his theories instead requires the contrary conclusion that his unconscious was impious.

Freud's claim of filial piety is doubly misleading because there is reason to doubt that his depression on the Acropolis was motivated by unconscious feelings toward his father Josef. A growing body of psychoanalytic opinion refers instead to Freud's unconscious conflicts regarding his mother Amalie (Abraham, 1982; Lehman, 1983; Hardin, 1987, 1988a, 1988b; Holt, 1992). Several writers have noted that Freud made no reference to his mother in his essay about the Acropolis. He also failed to mention both the virgin-goddess Athena, the patron of Athens, and her temple the Parthenon, which dominates the Acropolis. Because a statuette of Athena was Freud's single most favorite item in his collection of antiquities, Athena is conspicuous by her absence from the essay. There is evidence, however, of the return of the repressed. The snake that Athena trod underfoot, in her classical portraits, appeared in Freud's essay in the displaced form of the Loch Ness monster; and an anecdote about Napoleon's coronation, which occurred at Milan, was mistakenly located in the essay at Notre Dame (Kanzer, 1969; Abbott, 1969; Niederland, 1969; Slochower, 1970; Harrison, 1979). Abbott (1969) explained Freud's depression as "an unconsciously frightening reaction to his own castrated and castratively threatening mother" (p. 39). If these observations and interpretations are valid, Freud apparently repressed his conflicts with his mother at a cost of disproportionate circumspection in his references to her. His unconscious aggression toward her was displaced onto his father, whom he consequently maligned (Abraham, 1982).

Freud's denial of Athena suggests that his discussions of religion were skewed (Merkur, 1992b) by the same biographical sources that distorted his theories of female psychology. It was due to unresolved conflicts concerning his mother that Freud was temperamentally incapable not only of the oceanic feeling, but also of ecstatic enthusiasm over his visit to Athens and the temple of its ancient goddess.

Summary

Reverting to the concern with superego theory in chapter 2, I suggest that unitive experiences manifest ego ideals. When the ideals are welcomed, the mystical moments are euphoric. When the ideals are instead resisted, the mystical moments take form as desolation experiences. Recognizing the discrepancy between its unitive ideals and the standards that the ego maintains and rationalizes, the ego's reality-testing function generates anxiety in the form of a depressive affect. Both the euphoria and desolation are reactions by the ego to its ego ideals.

SEVEN

The Integration
of Spirituality

Many religions talk about what, for cross-cultural purposes, we may term *spiritual transformation*; but spiritual transformations are of many types. Anthropological studies of rites of passage have most frequently discussed "initiations" as nothing more than ritual changes in social status (Gennep, 1960; Allen, 1967; Turner, 1969). Certainly it would be difficult to point to Jewish circumcision and Christian baptism as spiritually meaningful to the infants who undergo the rites. In many other cases, spiritual transformations are primarily ideological, a question of acquiring new information in which to believe. Adequate explanatory models can then be developed by reference to learning theory. On the other hand, actual personality change has been demonstrated in the tribal initiations of boys in highland New Guinea, where gender identity was traditionally consolidated through highly brutal and traumatic ordeals (Whiting, Kluckhohn, & Anthony, 1958; Herdt, 1982; Lidz & Lidz, 1989; Herdt & Stoller, 1990). As with thought reform or "brainwashing" (Lifton, 1956, 1961; Schein, 1956, 1959), trauma was inflicted precisely in order to repress existing ego ideals, so that a new set of values might be inculcated as fixations.

Historians of religion augmented but did not significantly alter or challenge the general understanding of initiation that anthropologists and sociologists developed. Goblet D'Alviella (1914) acknowledged two basic types of initiation: the tribal initiations and secret societies that are social institutions; and initiations, such as those of magicians and shamans, which grant personal power (Bogoras, 1928; Christiansen, 1953; Eliade, 1964; Halifax, 1980; Peters, 1982; Merkur, 1992a). Other initiations into personal power include the ancient Egyptian priesthood (Bleeker, 1965), Israelite prophetism (Merkur, 1988b), the Hellenistic mysteries (Burkert, 1987), gnosticism (Merkur, 1993a), Western alchemy (Eliade, 1962; Merkur, 1993a), early Buddhism (Levy, 1957), Hindu and Buddhist tantra (Levy, 1957, pp. 44–45; Hoens, 1965; Bharati, 1980), and Japanese magic (Blacker, 1965). Most and perhaps all of these instances of initiatory empowerment involve habitual and/or professional practices of ecstatic religious experiences.

Agehananda Bharati (1976) and David P. Brown and Jack Engler (1984) emphasized, however, that mystics set out to acquire a skill set. They seek to become proficient at a religious use of one or more alternate psychic states. For example, several Jewish and Christian apocalypses narrate that upon ascension to Heaven, the seer acquired the priestly garments and function of an angel, standing in the angelic choir and singing the praises of God (Himmelfarb, 1993, pp. 29–46). It has not been demonstrated, however, that the achievement involved anything more than an apocalyptist learning to control his vision by directing his visionary state to portray desired contents. Similar cautions attend the evaluation of such visionary exercises as those outlined in Tibetan tantra (Kongtrul, 1996). Brown and Engler (1984) noted that one living Buddhist master was more mindful and creative than less accomplished meditators; but they offered no evidence to suggest that mastery of the Buddhist skill-set promotes personality integration. It may be a question of a predisposing talent. Better personality integration may facilitate mastery of a mystical-skill set, precisely as it facilitates so very much else in life. The emotional component of shamanic initiation or training as a mystic may be analogous to the strain endured during graduate school (see: Loewenberg, 1985, pp. 48–66).

Carl G. Jung (1968, 1970a, 1970b) used the terms *transformation* and *initiation* in reference to any psychotherapeutic process that involved symbolism that is found in alchemic initiations (see also: Mahdi, Foster, & Little, 1987). For Jung, it was immaterial whether the unconscious psyche manifested in waking fantasies, in nocturnal dreams, in active imagination, or in any other context. Mircea Eliade (1962) remonstrated: "The uninitiated person who has alchemical dreams and comes close to a psychic integration, also goes through the ordeal of an 'initiation': however, the result of this initiation is not the same as that of a ritual or mystic initiation, although, functionally, they are akin" (p. 224). Jung took for granted that a change in the content of symbolism implies a transformation of the unconscious personality; but he never earned the premise. It is absurd to suppose that the manifestation of a symbol in a healthy context is equivalent to its manifestation in morbidity. It is equally untenable that a symbol's manifestation in a profoundly meaningful context is equivalent to its manifestation in a trivial or casual context.

To my general conclusion that the history of research has not established whether and, if so, which mystical paths accomplish positive personality changes, there is one exception. Working with *The Spiritual Exercises* of St. Ignatius Loyola (1991), Howard L. Sacks (1979) found a measurable change in participants of a thirty-day retreat. Judgments of conscience were done prior to the retreat partly in conformance with social demands and partly out of independent conscience. However, following the retreat, there was a measurable shift toward independent conscience. Sacks concluded that "the spiritual exercises have an overall effect of raising the integrative capabilities of individuals, thereby increasing the individual's ability to assimilate various conflicting expectations"

(p. 49). This finding is consistent with the argument to be made in this chapter. Not only do mystical moments consist of positive manifestations of conscience, but they have the potential to promote the self's increased accommodation or integration of its ego ideals and conscience.

The claim that spiritual transformation entails genuine personality change remains central to contemporary transpersonal psychology (Merkur, 1995–96). It was also of interest to the founders of the psychology of religion, Edwin Diller Starbuck and William James, who treated spiritual progress as their central topic. In Starbuck's (1911) opinion, the spiritual path begins with conversion but culminates in "sanctification . . . the step, usually after much striving and discontent, by which the personality is finally identified with the spiritual life which at conversion existed merely as a hazy possibility" (p. 384). Sanctification involves an extinction of evil habits, together with a growth in altruism, which permit a sense of freedom from temptation and sin, of having been cleansed, and of complete union with one's spiritual ideals.

James (1902) expanded Starbuck's model. According to James, "healthy-minded religion" develops straightforwardly, without dramatic processes. The healthy-minded "are not distressed by their own imperfections" (F. W. Newman, 1852, p. 89; as cited in James, 1902, p. 78). The healthy-minded consequently feel no need to undergo spiritual development in any meaningful sense of the term (L. Nixon, personal communication, 1996). It is only the sick soul that must be twice-born in order to attain its natural inner unity and peace. The divided self gains unity through conversion. Some conversions occur during mystical moments. Others do not. When conversion is not followed by backsliding but is permanent, the individual achieves saintliness—a quality that is characterized by asceticism, strength of soul, purity, and charity. James's treatment of asceticism implied that the twice-born remain somewhat morbid, no matter how saintly they become. James suggested that "subliminal influences play the decisive part in these abrupt changes of heart, just as they do in hypnotism" but he left "the *process* of transformation . . . a good deal of a psychological or theological mystery" (pp. 214–15).

Following these notable beginnings, the topic of spiritual transformation was replaced on the scholarly agenda by a debate about conversion. *Sanctification* is a theological term, which Starbuck was able to use in a psychological sense only because he limited its definition to Wesleyan usage. The term is used differently in Roman Catholic, Lutheran, and Pentecostal teachings (Alexander, 1989). Conversion too is a theological category that does not translate neatly into any one scientific category (see: Rambo, 1993). The term is applied variously to spiritual awakenings, to dramatic intensifications of already existent religiosity, and/or to changes of allegiance from one institutional religion to another.

The spiritual progress that Starbuck and James described can be discussed from a psychoanalytic perspective as an initial manifestation of religious ideals, followed by a period of their conscious consideration, prior to their integration within the sense of self (Merkur, 1995–96). It is my contention that the manifestation of ego ideals—that is, positive superego materials—and their integration within the sense of self is analogous to the psychoanalytic processes of acquiring insight and working it through. Enlightenment begins as a momentary and passive experience, but it must be actively accepted and put into effect in order to gain permanence.

Integration of the Self and Its Ideals

Ideals manifest and are integrated within the sense of self in a great many different ways. Not only do the ideals differ among themselves, but they may or may not be resisted. Resistance may take many forms as well. Consider the following self-report by a woman whose son was near death with active tuberculosis. Although not previously religious, she prayed intensely for her son's recovery. A unitive experience then accomplished a spiritual awakening.

> Then I had a profound experience. I knew that a veil was lifted. I was as God. I was everywhere and everything. The only two things I now remember being was a tree and a squirrel. I thought how odd it was that anyone had difficulty accepting that God *was* everywhere and everything. *I* was, and it seemed so natural and obvious. Also I saw millions of jigsaw pieces all floating into their correct position. All was well. All was completed. As I know now that it is; but within our Earth concept of time and space, we still have the working through of it to accomplish.

> I have no idea how long this state of heightened consciousness lasted, but at some time during it I made the commitment "Thy will (not mine) be done". Because of my state, it was obviously my Higher Self that made the commitment. It was years before my conscious self could repeat it with integrity.

> I was thrown into the deep end, not understanding what it was all about, but I was immediately given guidance in writing, where to start off so that I could begin at A, after experiencing Z.

> From then on I have been guided every step of the way, as everyone is after commitment. Again, as with most people on the path, those steps took me into great darkness and hazardous journeys. Many times I had difficulty in believing in the light at the end of the tunnel, but I learned to have total trust in the process (Maxwell & Tschudin, 1990, pp. 127–28).

The wish for the son's wholeness motivated the woman to pray, and the willingness to pray—better, the lessened resistance to a belief in prayer that apparently already existed—triggered a unitive experience of divine omnipresence. The sense of omnipresence yielded, in its turn, to an awareness of the finite human need to work through "our Earth concept of time and space." With this awareness came the distancing from God and the humbling admission, "Thy will (not mine) be done." This experience of "commitment" articulated a personal ideal so profoundly that it served for many years as a goal, before its achievement was attained.

The ego may resist unconscious mysticism for many reasons, including self-pity and selfishness. Consider the following self-report.

> In 1966 I was one day alone in the house when quite suddenly I became aware of my own attitude to life. I realised that I was wrapped up in deep self pity, that my thoughts were all for myself and my own sorrows, that I had not thought of others. I thought how others in the world suffered too. I was rather shocked at my selfish attitude and was filled with compassion for others; then, as if without thinking, I knelt down in the room and made a vow to God that from then on for the rest of my life I would love and serve mankind. The following morning when I awoke I had a sudden experience, for into my mind poured knowledge (which knowledge has remained with me ever since); I knew that the love and service of mankind was the will of God for mankind. That we are to love all. That we serve God by serving his purpose and by our service of others, that God is manifest in all living things. . . . My whole outlook on life changed from that time. To explain my experience figuratively, it was as if all my life I had been in a darkened room and then I had suddenly walked out of it into the sunlight of day (Hardy, 1979, pp. 56–57).

Here self-observation, which like conscience is a superego function, provided the individual with insight concerning selfishness. A judgment of conscience—"I was rather shocked"—was followed by a wish to make reparation: "compassion" and the prayer to "love and serve mankind." The next morning, these altruistic sentiments provided an opportunity for the manifestation of unitive theistic ideas: "God is manifest in all living things." The increased integration of the ideals within the conscious personality proved permanent.

In the following self-report from Australia, a girl approaching adolescence attended an evangelical meeting for young people, where she heard an uninspiring preacher. The social occasion sufficed, however, to encourage unitive ideas to manifest.

> I had a seat next to a doorway, and as the service was about to end, something impelled me to slip outside. It was a strange church and I did not know where the door led, so was a little bewildered by my act of faith. I have a vague memory of doors in all directions and finally of someone directing me upstairs. I didn't want to go upstairs, but not knowing where else to go, I went. I remember not-

ing the dusty unwelcome appearance of the place as I climbed, until as I neared the top step something inexplicable happened. It was as though I had suddenly pushed up through the mists into a clear beautiful atmosphere. I neither saw nor heard. I just felt an indescribable ecstasy as I was suddenly conscious of an over-whelming love which seemed to encompass all that was and is and will be. It was all-encompassing and personal at the same time and lifted me to superb heights. I can remember feeling exultantly "This is God", and God, after all, was both personal and immense. I wish I had at my command the words which would truly convey the power, the depth, the infinity, the gentleness, the serenity and the intimacy which intermingled then. Somehow one doesn't separate the qual-ities which were evident. One just wants to enjoy the Oneness of it all.

I remember entering a room where were people I knew, but while I acknowl-edged their greeting, I was still lost in my new world. . . . For days it seemed that I lived in that rarer atmosphere. . . .

At the end of about a week while I was talking to my own minister it all sud-denly disappeared. It seemed as though I was suddenly plunged into darkness, and I was in despair. One doesn't easily let such an experience just vanish, so again I began to search, this time knowing what I was seeking. For months I searched and then gradually, very gradually, some of the Love returned (that full Love which is very hard to describe), and some of the understanding, but the ecstasy was gone. However, I found after a while, that if I were alone, preferably right out in the bush, I could sometimes recapture a little of the moment again, and I began to rebuild my life on the scraps which I recovered . . . but always I had that moment to recall and take courage from (Johnson, 1959, pp. 23–24).

An unconscious prompting urged the girl to leave the room through a strange door. Shortly after she opened the door as a proxy for herself, a unitive experience overwhelmed her. The euphoria and ideas of "the Oneness of it all" lasted for "about a week" before disappearing. The girl keenly felt their loss and "searched" to repeat their experience. She gradually recaptured "some of the Love . . . and some of the understanding" as a permanent aspect of her sense of self; but she could recapture "the ecstasy" only if she "were alone, preferably right out in the bush."

The relaxation of resistance to unconscious mysticism may be accom-plished through participation in a culturally endorsed ritual event.

Before going to the meeting I knelt beside my bed and prayed the sincerest prayer I had prayed so far in my life. My whole life was behind that simple prayer: "O Jesus, save me tonight." And he did! A ray of light pierced my dark-ness. Hope sprang up in my heart. I found myself saying, "He's going to do it." I now believe he had done it, but I had been taught that you found him at an altar of prayer. So I felt I must get to the church to an altar of prayer. I found myself running the mile to the church. The eagerness of my soul got into my body. I was like Christian running from the City of Destruction to the Celestial City. I went into the church and took the front seat, a thing I had never done before. But I was all eagerness for the evangelist to stop speaking, so I could get to that altar of prayer. When he did stop, I was the first one there. I had scarcely bent my knees when Heaven broke into my spirit. I was enveloped by assurance, by acceptance, by reconciliation. I grabbed the man next to me by the shoulder and said: "I've got it." "Got it?" What did I mean? I see now it was not an "it": it was a him. I had him—Jesus—and he had me. We had each other. I belonged. My estrangement, my sense of orphanage were gone. I was reconciled. As I rose from my knees, I felt I wanted to put my arms around the world and share this with everybody (E. S. Jones, 1968, pp. 27–28).

The individual experienced the beginning of a religious conversion at home, but resisted the full manifestation of the unconscious materials until the appropriate ritual occasion, which was an altar call during a church service. The unitive experience of relatedness to God manifested as an intense experience of assurance, acceptance, reconciliation, and belonging. Unitive thinking also elaborated an altruistic desire, of wishing to share the sense of belonging with the whole world.

The tendency of emergent spirituality to include both theism and a unitive vision, either of humanity or the world, may also be noted in a further self-report. Here the integration of superego materials within the conscious sense of self was followed by projections that accomplished a thoroughgoing integration of spirituality with the sensible world.

In the midst of a solemn struggle of soul, an impression was made on my mind, as though a voice said to me, "Thy sins are all forgiven thee." Divine light flashed all round me, unspeakable joy sprung up in my soul. I rose to my feet, opened my eyes, and it really seemed as if I was in heaven; the trees, the leaves on them, and every thing seemed, and I really thought were, praising God (Cartwright, 1856, p. 37).

In this report, a sense of forgiveness was expressed verbally by an inner voice, and an "unspeakable joy" followed. The religious experience continued, however, with the illusion that "the trees, the leaves on them, and every thing seemed, and I really thought were, praising God."

These examples of religious integration through a lowering of resistance to unconscious superego materials all happen to be drawn from English-speaking Christianity. Comparable findings may also be expected, however, of both Confucianism and Buddhism, in which alternate states of consciousness have traditionally been cultivated in order to promote personality changes that were simultaneously religious and moral. Confucian practices of meditation seek to produce unitive experiences that transform the moral character of the practitioner by aligning him with the inherently moral nature of the cosmos (Ivanhoe, 1993). In Buddhism, the acquisition of a benevolent or altruistic personality is considered an inevitable by-product of meditations on metaphysical topics (Conze, 1959, p. 72; Lamrimpa, 1992, pp. 113–14).

Partial Integrations Due to Unresolved Conflicts

Mystical moments regularly manifest ego ideals, but their integration within the personality remains an independent variable. Consider, for example, the changes in the religious imagery in the conversion experience reported by the American evangelist Charles Finney (1876).

> As I closed the door and turned around, my heart seemed to be liquid within me. All my feelings seemed to rise and flow out; and the utterance of my heart was, "I want to pour my whole soul out to God." The rising of my soul was so great that I rushed into the room back of the front office, to pray.

> There was no fire, and no light, in the room; nevertheless it appeared to me as if it were perfectly light. As I went in and shut the door after me, it seemed as if I met the Lord Jesus Christ face to face. It did not occur to me then, nor did it for some time afterward, that it was wholly a mental state. On the contrary it seemed to me that I saw him as I would see any other man. He said nothing, but looked at me in such a manner as to break me right down at his feet. I have always since regarded this as a most remarkable state of mind; for it seemed to me a reality, that he stood before me, and I fell down at his feet and poured out my soul to him. I wept aloud like a child, and made such confessions as I could with my choked utterance. It seemed to me that I bathed his feet with my tears; and yet I had no distinct impression that I touched him, that I recollect.

> I must have continued in this state for a good while; but my mind was too much absorbed with the interview to recollect anything that I said. But I know, as soon as my mind became calm enough to break off from the interview, I returned to the front office, and found that the fire that I had made of large wood was nearly burned out. But as I turned and was about to take a seat by the fire, I received a mighty baptism of the Holy Ghost. Without any expectation of it, without ever having the thought in my mind that there was any such thing for me, without any recollection that I had ever heard the thing mentioned by any person in the world, the Holy Spirit descended upon me in a manner that seemed to go through me, body and soul. I could feel the impression, like a wave of electricity, going through and through me. Indeed it seemed to come in waves and waves of liquid love; for I could not express it in any other way. It seemed like the very breath of God. I can recollect distinctly that it seemed to fan me, like immense wings. . . .

> How long I continued in this state, with this baptism continuing to roll over me and go through me, I do not know. But I know it was late in the evening when a member of my choir—for I was the leader of the choir—came into the office to see me. He was a member of the church. He found me in this state of loud weeping, and said to me, "Mr. Finney, what ails you?" I could make him no answer for some time. He then said, "Are you in pain?" I gathered myself up as best I could, and replied, "No, but so happy that I cannot live" (pp. 19–21).

Finney initially experienced a strong desire to pray. He hurried into the back room to pray, and immediately had a vision of Jesus Christ who seemed so real to him that Finney did not recognize it as "a mental state" for some time afterward. Finney made a thorough confession, wept, and presumably cleared his conscience. When he returned to the outer room, he experienced what he termed "a mighty baptism of the Holy Ghost." In keeping with the baptismal image for mystical union, Finney felt an "impression, like a wave of electricity, going through and through me." The water image continued: "waves and waves of liquid love." The water imagery was followed by air symbolism: "the very breath of God . . . it seemed to fan me, like immense wings." The motif was presumably inspired by the idea of the Holy Spirit: Hebrew *ruach*, Greek *pneuma*, and Latin *spiritus* all mean both "wind" and "spirit."

The differences among the four phases of Finney's experience may be interpreted as consequences, among other matters, of a steady lessening of resistance to the conversion experience. The initial and inexplicable desire to pray was, I suggest, a response to an unconscious prompting whose manifestation was being resisted. To circumvent the resistance, the unconscious prompting underwent displacement and manifested as a desire that was more consciously acceptable at the time. Immediately after Finney consented to pray and implicitly entertained a desire that his prayer should be answered, the unconscious materials were able to manifest with greater clarity.

The second phase of Finney's experience was a reified vision of Jesus Christ, to whom Finney responded with confession, tears, and atonement. Finney's submission to Jesus was a voluntary effort to accept his religious ideals without compromise. Finney's willingness to integrate his ideals within his consciousness was the precondition, in turn, for the transformation of his ecstasy from a highly concrete vision of Jesus' presence to a more abstract and unitive conception. God now took form as a wave of electric love, washing through Finney, baptizing him with himself, the Holy Spirit. In the fourth phase, water imagery yielded to wind imagery. The symbolism again consisted of a tangible substance, but the choice of symbolism continued to be increasingly abstract.

Resistance to newly formed unitive ideas is responsible, I suggest, for the somatizations that cause many mystical experiences to resemble hysterical spells (Moxon, 1920). The somatizations are compromises between the unitive materials and the resistance. Consider, for example, the following North American self-report of a Hindu kundalini experience.

> I had been studying and in a very intense state of concentration for most of the day. . . .
>
> That evening, after supper, I discovered that I had an intense pressure headache. My friend suggested that he try giving me a head massage to relieve the headache. I sat down in a comfortable position, and he began to massage my scalp.
>
> Suddenly, my whole body started shaking uncontrollably. I felt rushes of energy coursing up my body to my head, and my whole body jerked with the pulses of energy. My back, arms, and legs all jerked repeatedly as the energy pulse raced upwards. I could not stop the shaking. My body was rocked and shaken by these energy pulses from about 9:30 p.m. until 3:30 a.m. I was fully conscious the whole time, and was acutely aware of what was happening in my body.
>
> I was very frightened during the shaking episode. I had no idea what was going on. I could not control my body; I could not stop the jerking movements of my body and limbs. I shouted out to my friend, asking what was happening. He did not know, and he just sat with me to comfort me. I knew it could not be a seizure, because I was fully conscious throughout the whole episode. Later I found it interesting that my headache had disappeared a soon as the energy pulses began. When the energy rushes and body shaking finally stopped, I felt overwhelmingly fatigued, as if I had experienced a tremendous release of some sort. I crawled into bed and went to sleep immediately.
>
> In the morning when I awoke, I felt as if I had been reborn. When I opened my eyes, the world seemed to have become a magical place. I felt as if I were in love with the world, and that the universe and I were making love to each other. It seemed as if the world was filled with light; all the colors and dimensions of objects seemed clearer and more beautiful. Every sensation was enhanced. It was as if I was breathing in the life energy of the universe with each breath. I felt as if my consciousness had expanded to immense proportions, and I felt totally at one with the entire universe. I felt the oneness of all things, and I felt that all was well in the Divine plan of the universe.
>
> As I basked in this blissful state, I started to spontaneously recite scriptures. . . . I started to spontaneously go into yoga postures and do yoga mudras, or hand movements (Kason, with Degler, 1994, pp. 51–52).

The energy that was experienced somatically as a convulsive state was the same "life energy" that was experienced conceptually the next morning. The convulsions subsided around 3:30 A.M., presumably because the unconscious process of sublimation (rather than the resistance) was at an end. Because the night's sleep resolved the resistance, the sublimations ceased to undergo somatization, and simply manifested directly as a unitive experience. The shift of the unitive experience from "the life energy of the universe" to "consciousness . . . expanded to . . . the entire universe" probably represented a further inspiration that originated only in the morning, after the accumulated materials had successfully manifested.

A movement from more opaque to more transparent symbolism is consistent with a decrease in resistance. In other cases, however, religious symbolism is initially plastic but soon arrests in an inflexible manner that is indicative of unresolved resistance. The following self-report by Satomi Myodo of Japan derives from a woman who had abandoned her responsibilities to her parents, husband, and child and become a spirit medium. After many years, she became attracted to Zen Buddhism and to the life of a celibate nun. When she first attempted to meditate, she had the following experience.

> It was the second day of the *sesshin*. I was working very hard with my *hara*, saying, "Mu, Mu," when all of a sudden—"Unh!"—it was as if three people had pulled me over backward. "Oh no!" I thought. I repulsed this with effort, straightened my posture, and resumed, "Mu, Mu." Then again "Unh!"—I was dragged down.

> "This is awful!" I thought. I kept trying to pull myself together, but no matter how many times I tried, it was no use. "What now?" I thought. "I wonder if I'm dozing off." When the walking meditation was over, I thought to myself, "Okay, now!" and sat, hardening my *hara* all the more. As I did so, once again it started. "Very strange," I thought. "I know! It's a possessing spirit! The spirit of a dead person." (In possession by spirits of the dead, one is thrown onto one's back, facing up; in the case of spirits of the living, one is pushed over onto one's face.) "I don't know if it's a good spirit or a bad spirit, but there's more than one of them, anyway! . . . Okay. . . ."

> "Hey! Everybody!" I said silently to the spirits. "Wait a minute, please! When I attain *kensho*, I will without fail perform a memorial service for you. Until then, please be patient and wait quietly on the spirit shelf." With this statement to free me of their presence, I saw with all the more intense effort. After that, I was not dragged over as badly as before, but if my effort slackened even a little, I was instantly pulled down. This continued all day.

> I was dead tied. That evening when I tried to settle down to sleep, the instant I laid my head on the pillow, I saw: "Ah! This out-breath is Mu!" Then: "The in-breath too is Mu!" Next breath, too: Mu! Next breath: Mu, Mu! "Mu, a whole sequence of Mu! Croak, croak; meow, meow—these too are Mu! The bedding, the wall, the column, the sliding door—these too are Mu! This, that and everything is Mu! Ha ha! Ha ha ha ha ha! That Roshi is a rascal! He's always tricking people with his 'Mu, Mu, Mu'! . . . Hmmm. I wonder if, after this, I should rush to Roshi's room for *dokusan*. No, that would be childish. . . ."

> I felt as if a chronic disease of forty years had been cured in an instant. I slept soundly that night. (King, 1993, pp. 105–6).

Satomi Myodo's conflicts over her life choices manifested in the symbolism of her experience. The family whom she had abandoned were symbolized by the spirits whom she had embraced as her family's substitute, and whom she was now attempting to abandon in favor of Buddhism. The achievement of *nibbana*, by contrast, had the significance for her of autonomy. It was impersonal, not familial, solitary, not enmeshed in relationships, and Buddhist, not the traditional Shinto associated with her family. Much as the spirits kept dragging her down and onto her back—a transparent symbol—, union permitted her to transcend the spirits. Once everything was reduced to one, the spirits no longer existed, and Satomi Myodo no longer had reason to manifest psychosomatic guilt over the failed interpersonal relationships in her life. Her achievement of union did not resolve her guilt, but it permitted her to deny the guilt by dismissing the separate existence of other people as an illusion. The unitive experience constituted a compromise that was symptomatic of unresolved conflict. The union was a flight from the many to the one, an abstention that rationalized the life-style of a nun and did not serve as a prelude to greater accommodations to physical and social reality.

Self-Actualization

These self-reports illustrate a theoretical distinction introduced by Marjorie Brierley. Discussing Christian monasticism, Brierley (1951) suggested that the "aim of Christianity tends to appear as the pursuit of ego and super-ego ideal integration, although Christians themselves, particularly mystical Christians, would maintain that it is the pursuit of total integration" (p. 224). She argued that "the spiritual life, sincerely followed, is a way of sublimation and sanctity, a rare but genuine type of integration rather than a disease" (p. 226). Brierley maintained that integration of the ego and superego may be successful even when it involves "total sublimation of genital drives and total surrender of ego-direction to superego control" (p. 228). Sterba (1968) similarly suggested that "every mystic experience of lasting effect is a . . . *tour-de-force* conflict solution" (p. 79). These results are consistent with statistical studies, which found that people reporting mystical experiences scored lower on psychopathology scales and higher on measures of psychological well-being than controls (Hood, 1976, 1977; Caird, 1987; Spanos & Moretti, 1988).

Brierley cautioned, however, that the ego–superego integration that is possible through spiritual progress falls short of the psychoanalytic ideal of human development.

> Even if the unification of the Saints is to be thought of as self-cure rather than disease, the impression remains that the integration of sanctity should, never-

theless, be regarded as a striking variation rather than as the end stage of the main line of human development. The true spiritual vocation is very rare and the findings of psycho-analysis suggest, very definitely, that the high road for the majority does not lead to super-ego autocracy and selective idealization, but to a more inclusive and democratic harmonization of id, ego, and super-ego systems, to the development of more comprehensive reality-sense, and to the more enlightened ego-direction of personal life (p. 229).

Brierley's shift in this passage from the integration of the ego and superego, to that of the id, ego, and superego, warrants emphasis. A similar point was made by the psychologist Abraham H. Maslow (1968) in the following description of self-actualization.

[Self-actualization] may be seen as a fusion of ego, id, super-ego and ego-ideal, of conscious, preconscious and unconscious, of primary and secondary processes, a synthesizing of pleasure principle with reality principle, a healthy regression without fear in the service of the greatest maturity, a true integration of the person at all levels (p. 96).

Maslow associated self-actualization with the cognitive orientation that manifests in "peak experiences," many of which display religious features; but he acknowledged that the instinctual desires of the biologic organism must also be integrated within the personality, if self-actualization is to be achieved.

Summary

Mystical moments typically consist of positive superego materials. When mystical moments function as religious conversions, they invariably integrate at least some positive superego materials within the conscious sense of self. The materials may manifest directly. When they must instead compromise with the ego's resistance, they manifest only as they are displaced into symbolic substitutes. Part of the materials then fails to manifest, and full integration is impossible.

There is no evidence, however, that the integration of repressed fixations is achieved through spiritual development. The self may be integrated with its ideals but, as the case of Satomi Myodo demonstrates, both may proceed in denial of the instincts, rather than in their accommodation. Psychotherapy, in the traditional psychoanalytic sense of the ego's reconciliation to repressed instincts, aims at a different type of transformative integration and may be appropriate as an independent adjunct to spiritual development.

EIGHT

The Meaning
of Miracles

Belief in the miraculous, providential, or magical character of specific everyday events in one's life is popularly said to be mystical. There is much to recommend the popular usage. The frequency with which miracles are experienced following spiritual awakenings or conversions (Grof & Grof, 1990, pp. 175–76; Morse, with Perry, 1992; Sutherland, 1992; Merkur, 1997) suggests that the unitive line of development includes the widespread practice of interpreting coincidental physical events as purposively caused, providential miracles.

Dissenting from Otto's definition of religion in terms of the numinous, Arbman (1939) suggested that religious thought has its basis in a physical event that is "referred to certain fictive wills or forces postulated by faith, in which it is conceived as a potentiality" (p. 27). In keeping with Roman Catholic usage, Arbman referred to physical events that are conceived as products of numinous powers under the term *supernatural event* if they violated no laws of natural science, and *miracle* if they did (pp. 25–26). Seeking, for comparative purposes, to avoid the Christian bias endorsed by Arbman's language, Åke Hultkrantz (1983) refers more simply to miracles: "It is religious belief, and not exceptions from natural laws, that selects the miracle" (p. 240).

A distinction must immediately be made, however, between miracles that people actually experience and the considerably more fabulous events that are reported in myths and legends. The miracles that people actually experience invariably conform with natural laws; and it is they alone that can engender religiosity. The miracles of oral and written tradition may attract faith once faith already exists. However, the experience of a miracle may actually produce a conversion from irreligion to religiosity. Due to the secondary, derivative, and often fictitious character of oral and written traditions about miracles, my further remarks will be limited to the primary phenomena: the experience of miracles, their presuppositions, and consequences.

Whatever may be the temporal origins of religions in both the lives of individuals and in the corporate lives of societies, miracles function as the experiential foundations of living religiosity. As John Bowker (1973) observed:

No matter how "God" is constituted, if there is no feedback at all into the actual situations and experiences of life, plausibility is under maximum strain; if no effect of God can ever be discerned or specified, then in effect God is nowhere. Thus all theistic traditions have at some point suggested discernible (claimed) effects of God . . . there must be sufficient feedback into experience, whether social or individual, for plausibility to be maintained: not an invariable answer to prayer, but some answer; not an invariably correct prediction of the future, but some prediction (p. 84).

Bowker limited his remarks to monotheistic religions, but his case may be extended cross-culturally. Religions retain the adherence of their followers because religious people experience the (seemingly) objective confirmation of their faith. Indeed, people presumably differ in the extent or intensity of their religiosity, due, among other variables, to the quantity of perceived confirmation.

Miracles are not the only experiences in which religious people find confirmation of their faith, but miracles are very possibly the most important. A person may alert or awaken from a vision or a unitive experience only to dismiss the alternate state as a fallacy; but there is no awakening from sense perception of the physical environment. Miracles are the class of religious experiences that are least easy to dismiss. In a functional sense, miracles are the ultimate or foundational religious experiences.

Consider, for example, Knud Rasmussen's (1929) account of the personal religiosity of Padloq, an Inuit shaman of the Iglulik band in the northwestern region of Hudson Bay.

Padloq might be said to be of a humble, religious turn of mind, and it was his firm belief that all the little happenings of everyday life, good or bad, were the outcome of activity on the part of mysterious powers. Human beings were powerless in the grasp of a mighty fate, and only by the most ingenious system of taboo, with propitiatory rites and sacrifices, could the balance of life be maintained. Owing to the ignorance or imprudence of men and women, life was full of contrary happenings, and the intervention of the angakut [shamans] was therefore a necessity (p. 32).

The Inuit experienced miracles that they valued both positively and negatively. Kaj Birket-Smith (1953) reported the following account of a positively valued miracle in the Chugach band in southwestern Alaska.

Once Makari and some others were out hunting in their baidarkas [a type of boat] and saw a sea otter swimming around with its young one, singing: "oho, . . . oho. . . ." They stopped to learn the song. . . . [The] sea otter taught its "song" to Makari. A song of this kind was a deep secret, as the hunter would lose his luck if it was learned by another person (pp. 32, 118).

The religious experience of the physical event depended, of course, on cultural expectations. When the men observed the sea otter's behavior, they did not harpoon the animal for meat but stopped to learn the sea otter's song. The men acted in the implicit belief that they were encountering the numinous power of the Sea Mother, as it was being manifested through the agency of the living sea animal.

Negatively valued miracles are generally easier to demonstrate because the believer's response is usually emphatic. The following report is again taken from Rasmussen's (1929) ethnography of the Iglulik.

> I remember my mother was very distressed about it [the hunting trip] for she did not think the old man, armed as he was only with bows and arrows, would ever get any game. . . . Mother had cooked some ribs of walrus, and was sitting eating, when the bone she held suddenly began to make a noise. She was so frightened, she stopped eating at once, and threw down the bone. I remember her face went quite white; and she burst out: "Something has happened to my son!" And so indeed it was; soon after, Qupanuaq [her husband] returned late one night, and before entering the house, he went round outside to the window and called out: "Dear Little Thing. It is my fault that you no longer have a son!" (p. 50)

The noise made by the walrus rib was experienced as a miracle. The woman's fear was involuntary, irresistible, and unwanted. It imparted the sudden and certain conviction that something had happened to her son. The noise of the walrus rib was experienced as a miracle at the time. Because the woman's terror was subsequently discovered to be valid, her experience was remembered and reported. Had the woman's fears proved vain, she would have dismissed her fright and we should never have learned of it.

When random physical events are interpreted from a secular perspective, they are judged coincidental and pronounced meaningless. They acquire religious significance, that is, they are interpreted as miracles when and because their meaning or significance for their observer(s) is found to be numinous. Coincidences are readily experienced as miracles because they are limit situations. Just as neither of two roads is responsible for their intersection, but the two together give rise synergically to something more than either can produce independently, so the physical causation of the events that happen to coincide in a coincidence never extends to the fact of their coincidence, and every coincidence transcends the limit situations of its constituent events. Due to the transcendent factor, the numinosity of miracles is always of the type that Otto (1950) termed the *fascinans*. Indeed, to paraphrase a Hasidic teaching, a miracle may be defined as a natural, physical coincidence that has the capacity to arouse wonder at its transcendent cause. A miracle is always felt to manifest an intention. It is always taken to imply Something More than its manifest content. Its occurrence implies its deliberate and purposive causation by a nonmanifest cause that is intelligent and that knows the observer's thoughts.

Belief in the occurrence of personal miracles is popularly considered mystical, I suggest, because the experience of a miracle is preconsciously recognized as a form of unitive thinking. In a miracle, self and external physical coincidences attain unity through a sharing of meaning. Miracles are felt to be responses that are mediated to the self by the impersonal environment at the will of a transcendent power.

Contemporary Christian Miracles

Conceptions of the miraculous vary from culture to culture. The paperback Christian literature that has flooded the bookstores in the 1990s exhibits a distinctly Christian conception of miracles. Whether the miracles are attributed to God or his angels, they reflect a conception of God as Savior. Miracles are interpreted when fortuitous events can be seen as benevolent. Consider, for example, the following report.

> Debra dreamed of expanding [her business], but. . . . She couldn't afford more than a $650 monthly rental—too modest for the area she had in mind. And buying a second refrigerator would take all her savings. Was it too risky? Debra talked it over with God. "If You want me to do this," she told Him, "You'll have to figure it out."
>
> Soon Debra found an apartment complex in a perfect location. But the two-bedroom rents were too expensive. She kept looking—and praying—and occasionally checked back with the complex.
>
> "You're in luck," the rental agent told her one day. "Because of renovations, we're lowering rents on all two-bedroom units for the next six months."
>
> "How much will they be?" Debra scarcely dared to ask.
>
> "Six hundred and fifty-two dollars," the agent answered.
>
> Debra was *almost* convinced that this was God's answer. But there was one more thing. "I'm expanding my home business," she told the agent. "I'm going to need an apartment with two refrigerators."
>
> . . . Debra went home, almost afraid to hope. But the next day, the agent phoned. "This is odd, Debra," she began. "Remember I told you we're in the middle of a huge remodeling job?"
>
> Debra remembered.

"Well, we ordered two hundred and twenty new refrigerators. Yesterday they delivered two hundred and twenty-one. It will be cheaper for us to put the extra in your apartment than to send it back."

Debra had no more doubts. Today her business is thriving, thanks to prayers answered at just the right time (Anderson, 1994, pp. 32–33).

Narrow escapes from tragedy may also be attributed to God. Traffic mishaps are a staple of the genre, but natural disasters are also frequently reported. Due perhaps to the missionizing character of the publications, the miracles reported in popular Christian literature are always salvific. They portray God as a benevolent, gratuitous Savior who rescues people from evil. They offer no explanations for the evil's occurrence.

Also to be counted as miracles of salvation are signs from God. A sign does not need to be coherent. It needs only to occur, in order to be interpreted as divinely intended to encourage faith and, through the grace of faith, salvation.

When we were travelling to Oregon for my grandmother's funeral I saw a rainbow that was so unbelievably close it was as if it came right through the car. Physically I felt frightened at first and then enormously elated. I felt very much that it was a sign or a symbol of something. I'm still kind of coming to terms with it (Wuthnow, 1978, pp. 62–63).

Inarticulate though a sign may be, its very occurrence communicates God's positive interest in the recipient. Since God deigns to express an interest in a person, he must presumably be favorably disposed.

Hasidic Miracle-Working

A third cultural variation provides further points of interest. Several of the early Hasidic masters performed what they, no differently than their followers, believed to be miracles; and their adoption of an active role in the occurrence of miracles may again be considered an instance of unitive thinking. Not only did their God engage them by means of his actions in the world; but they engaged him through theirs.

Early Hasidic teachings describe all miracles as natural events, and all of nature as a miracle (Buber, 1947, pp. 71, 92; Aryeh & Dvorkes, 1974, pp. 106–7). There was no difference in principle between a revelation and a miracle. In the one case, there was an act of divine creation directly within the soul; in the other, in the world perceptible to the soul. Both proceeded in nature or, more precisely, in creation. The equivalence of revelations and miracles was particularly obvious in instances when miracles occurred not only in the physical world, but in the involuntary actions of a Hasid's own body.

It is told:

Once Rabbi Elimelekh was eating the sabbath meal with his disciples. The servant set the soup bowl down before him. Rabbi Elimelekh raised it and upset it, so that the soup poured over the table . . .

Some time after this, it became known that on that day an edict directed against the Jews of the whole country had been presented to the emperor for his signature . . . he signed the paper. Then he reached for the sand-container but took the inkwell instead and upset it on the document. Hereupon he tore it up and forbade them to put the edict before him again (Buber, 1947, p. 259).

The equivalence of revelations and miracles also extended to their induction. Just as Hasidim engaged in a variety of techniques that induced the onset of ecstatic states in whose course revelations might be granted, so too they knew procedures that facilitated the occurrence of miracles. Rabbi Elimelech of Lizensk, who achieved particular fame as a wonder-worker, emphasized, however, that miracles are miraculous even to their performer.

The Lizensker commented on the expression: "Show a miracle for yourselves" (Ex. 7:9). He said: "When a magician performs his acts on the stage, they are magical in the eyes of the audience. The magician himself, however, knows them to be merely tricks. But when the man of God is commanded to perform a miracle, he himself is greatly astonished at the wonder. The Lord intended to say: 'Pharaoh will invite you to demonstrate a miracle that will be a marvel even in your own eyes, unlike the magical tricks of his court magicians'" (Berger, 1910, p. 35; as cited in Newman, 1963, pp. 261–62).

The transformation of a passive witnessing of miracles into an active program of wonder-working is little explained in the literature. One Hasid's methods may be inferred, however, from the teachings and biography of Rabbi Nachman of Breslov (1772–1810), a great-grandson of the Baal Shem Tov, and the founder of the Breslover sect of Hasidism. Nachman experienced miracles as divine judgments. He said: "If a man does not judge himself, all things judge him, and all things become messengers of God" (Buber, 1956, p. 39). Whatever good fortune he encountered, he accepted as divine approval. However, he regarded adversity neither as a divine reproof nor as a demonic persecution. Instead, he treated adversity as an obstacle that God created in order to test his faith.

There is no obstacle that one cannot overcome, for the obstacle is only there for the sake of the willing, and in reality there are no obstacles save in the spirit (p. 40).

Nachman's interpretation of adversity as positive opportunities to exercise initiative formed the cornerstone of his theory of wonder-working. Whatever miracles occurred, subsequent to his active initiatives, were divine responses to his actions, which would not have occurred had he not acted to provoke them. In this manner, Nachman conceived of a pilgrimage to the Holy Land in 1798–99 as a prophetic mission that advanced the world's redemption by trail-blazing a path in virtue. Buber explained:

> In Rabbi Nachman's teaching as it has come down to us . . . we meet the "Obstacles" in connection with Palestine again and again. The obstacles have, according to this teaching, a great significance. They are put in the way of the man whose yearning and destiny impel him into the Holy Land, so that he may overcome them. For they excite and exalt his will and make him worthy to receive the holiness of the land. Whoever intends to be truly Jewish, that is to say, to climb from step to step, must "smash" the obstacles. But in order to conquer in this fight, "holy boldness" is needed, the kind in which God delights, for He praises Israel because of the holy boldness and obstinacy of the Israelite man for the sake of which the Torah was given. This struggle is ultimately a spiritual struggle; for the powers of evil increase the obstacles in order to confuse the understanding, and fundamentally it alone is the source of the obstacles. But the greater a man is, the greater are the obstacles before him, for an all the more intense struggle is demanded of him in order to raise him on to a higher level (p. 188).

Implicit in Nachman's biography is the belief that by making certain choices, he was able to engage God in a dialectic of human action and miraculous providence. Because both Nachman and his community saw him as a *tsaddik*, a "righteous one," he did not experience adverse miracles as punishments. He was confident of his virtue, and he discounted the possibility of divine rebuke. He refused to regard adversity as misfortune and instead interpreted it as a divinely intended opportunity.

The theory of wonder-working depended on the assumption that God would continue to provide Nachman with opportunities to progress in virtue as long as he lived. If Nachman met every challenge, exhausting each opportunity that God presented him, God would be obliged to resort to miracles in order to provide further opportunities. Proceeding in this manner to conquer obstacle after unanticipated obstacle, Nachman felt himself led, step by step, to accomplish a prophetic mission.

Miracles and Gods

The gods and spirits of the Inuit are typical of hunter religions as a group. They are theoretical postulates by which people explain the differences among the miracles that they experience. Among the Inuit, for example, the great god Sila was conceived as the power of life that indwells within the very air that we all breathe. All miracles associated with the atmosphere—chiefly frost, storms, and blizzards—were attributed to him. The Sea Mother, who was conceived as the power of the sea herself, was the major source of nourishment in the traditional hunter-fisher economy. All miracles associated with the sea—the waves and currents; the locations and behaviors of fish and sea-animals—were attributed to her. Some Inuit bands attributed the land and land animals to a goddess called the Earth Indweller; others attributed the land animals to the Mother of Caribou and Walrus. Miracles associated with sexuality and fertility were attributed to the Moon Man, whose cyclical power encompassed the tides, death, and rebirth.

The Inuit regarded the forces of nature as gods on the evidence of miracles because the occurrence of miracles proved natural forces to be anthropopsychic, that is, having minds like those of people. Social intercourse with the gods was possible; and appropriate behavior—the cultic behavior of Inuit religion—permitted the Inuit to remain on good terms with their gods. As the forces of nature were envisioned in dreams and in the ecstasies of shamans, they were seen to have anthropomorphic souls; and myths described them sometimes in their physical forms as natural forces, but often in the human forms of their souls.

Unlike the gods, the spirits of the Inuit were metaphysical beings that were unrelated to natural forces. They too wielded powers. Many of the spirits provided aid in hunting. Others provided protection against evil spirits; and, of course, evil spirits visited the Inuit with disease, famine, and other manners of misfortune (Merkur, 1991b).

In the agricultural religions of Africa, East and Southeast Asia, and Oceania, the gods and spirits of nature and the hunt make room for agricultural concerns. The economics and familial emotions involved in the inheritance of arable land tend to coincide with a religious concern for ancestral ghosts. Ghosts receive so-called ancestor worship and are credited with spirit possession and mediumship, because they are the beings to whom miracles are attributed.

Arbman was joined by his student Erland Ehnmark (1935, 1939) and by the classicist Walter Otto (1954) in demonstrating that the Homeric gods of archaic Greece performed miracles by wielding the forces of nature, even though they were conceived anthropomorphically in their assembly on Olympus. The anthropomorphic conception of a divine council was also common to Canaanite and early Israelite religions (Mullen, 1980) and should be connected, so I suggest, with the seasonal pattern of ancient Near Eastern and East Mediterranean theologies (Gaster, 1950). It is not simply that the political organization of early urban societies was projected onto the gods as an assembly or council. Rather, with the emergence in human society of urban life, with its specializations of labor and economic interdependence, there was a comprehension of the interdependence of the gods. Where the religions of hunters and small farm villages generally relate independent myths for each of their gods, the religions of the ancient Near East and East Mediterranean spoke of their gods' dealings with each other—their combats, their loves, their alliances, and their dependencies. Through the symbolism of their narratives, the great myth-cycles chronicled the shifting balances among the forces of nature during the annual round of the seasons. These myths attest to a growing sense of the orderliness of nature and, with it, an increasing limitation of the domain of the miraculous.

The religion of ancient Israel represents a further decisive shift in the comprehension of the miraculous. From its inception, the concept of Yahweh embodied a statesman's concern with history. The religion of Yahweh was founded, legend tells us, by a prince of Egypt who became a prophet, war-leader, and nation builder. Moses was followed by Joshua, a war-leader; and the premonarchic judges of Israel seem all to have been either war-leaders or their spiritual advisers. Israel's first kings, Saul and David, combined in themselves prophets and war-leaders. As late as Elijah and Elisha, two disenfranchised revolutionaries, the calling of a prophet was to politics. "Yahweh is a man of war" (Ex 15:3). It was only in the middle of the eighth century B.C.E., as the northern kingdom of Israel faced imminent absorption within the Assyrian empire, that the prophets Hosea and Amos turned from politics to social criticism and to the preaching of personal morality. Hope for the state could no longer be sustained, so hope came to be placed in the individual.

From the burning bush onward, Yahweh was, as it were, a unified theory of the miraculous. Where Canaanite religion had sought to chart a viable human path amid the seasonal variations of natural forces, Israelite religion took the orderliness of nature for granted. Yahweh alone was responsible for the food supply, health, fertility, and prosperity. The miracles of Yahweh were not limited, however, to these topics of traditional concern. The religion of Yahweh also postulated the unified, coherent, purposive, superordinate, and miraculous governance of human political destiny.

There is, I trust, no need to argue that prayers everywhere seek the occurrence of miracles; that magic attempts to produce miracles on demand; that religious moralities, observances, taboos, and rites hope to manage favorable and unwanted miracles; and that ideas of deities are, at least in part, ideas of the causes of miracles. A very considerable part of all religions may be conceptualized as a body of theory and practice in the management of miracles.

Miracles and Meaningfulness

If we define a miracle as an external physical event that happens by coincidence and nevertheless has meaning for an observer, there is no scientific difference between a miracle and a random coincidence. What transforms a chance event into a miracle is its appreciation by an observer. The observer has a subjective experience of the event's meaningfulness.

A miraculous event happens by coincidence, but its apparent meaning is sufficiently compelling that its observer does not dismiss the meaning as a subjective fantasy. The observer instead postulates the purposive causality of the event's meaning. Consciously and/or unconsciously, the observer believes that the event was caused to happen in order to be meaningful, that is, in order to convey its meaning to the observer. A miracle is, as it were, a species of revelation that employs sense perception of the physical world as its medium of communication.

Jung (1960), who discussed miracles as "acausal phenomena" or "synchronous events," also described them as "meaningful coincidences" (p. 114). By the expression, Jung sometimes referred to events that happened by coincidence to have coherent or intelligible meaning or significance. However, he also referred to random events that were meaningful in a statistical sense. This slippage from subjective to objective concepts of meaning permitted Jung to discuss miracles together with clairvoyance and foreknowledge. Jung (1960) wrote:

> The phenomena . . . can be grouped under three categories:
>
> 1. The coincidence of a psychic state in the observer with a simultaneous, objective, external event that corresponds to the psychic state or content . . . where there is no evidence of a causal connection between the psychic state and the external event, and where . . . such a connection is not even conceivable.
>
> 2. The coincidence of a psychic state with a corresponding (more or less simultaneous) external event taking place outside the observer's field of perception, i.e., at a distance, and only verifiable afterward. . . .
>
> 3. The coincidence of a psychic state with a corresponding not yet existent future event that is distant in time and can likewise only be verified afterward (p. 110).

Although I endorse Jung's treatment of clairvoyance and foreknowledge together with miracles as a single psychological problem, I stress that for psychoanalytic purposes, clairvoyance and foreknowledge are adequately described as instances of coincidental knowledge. The experiences consist of imaginations that accurately present facts or events that should logically be unknown to the subject. The imagined knowledge may pertain to events of the past, present, or future—although, by definition, neither to the past of the subject, nor to his or her presently perceptible environment. The fit between the imagined knowledge and the objectively real events is coincidental. For psychoanalytic purposes it is not significant whether the coincidence is to be explained by reference to random chance, parapsychology, metaphysics, divine revelation, or any other explanatory theory. These ideological considerations have preoccupied most previous researchers but lie outside the province of psychoanalysis. What psychoanalysis is competent to address is the subjective experience that coincidental knowledge is not random and meaningless, but is instead meaningful and purposive. Why do people generally speak not of lucky fantasies, but of clairvoyance and foreknowledge?

In parallel fashion, miracles may be said to entail the discovery of meaning in coincidental occurrences of external events. The occurrence of events in the person's physical environment seemingly embodies meaningful knowledge that is addressed to the observer.

Philosophically, there is no categorical difference between clairvoyance and foreknowledge, on the one side, and miracles on the other. Meaning is imputed to coincidental events in all cases. In the former, the coincidental events are the imaginations that transpire within the nervous system; but in the latter, the coincidences are located in the world external to the body.

Volney P. Gay (1989) considered the psychology of miracles from a psychoanalytic perspective as "occult experiences." By the occult, Freud referred to telepathy, and psychoanalysts have since referred to phenomena that are conventionally described as parapsychological (Gay, 1989, pp. 4, 145). For Gay, occult experiences involve hidden connections between mental events and the external world (pp. 4–5). So defined, the "occult" includes the same range of phenomena that Jung termed "synchronicity" (p. 148).

Most research on the occult questions whether the experiences are true (Devereux, 1953; Fodor, 1959; von Franz, 1980; Aziz, 1990; Combs, 1990). Gay left open the question of veridicality and instead addressed the psychological conditions under which a person may have an occult experience. To examine the problem, Gay applied the psychoanalytic self-psychology of Heinz Kohut.

In his seminal research on narcissistic disorders, Kohut (1971, 1977, 1978, 1984) argued that an infant consolidates a sense of the self on the basis of the mirror or reflection of the self that is contained in the responses of the mother and other people. During this early phase of development, when self is still fragmentary and undergoing consolidation, the infant experiences other people in a paradoxical manner as *self-objects*. Others are both external beings and part of the infant's internal psychic reality. Kohut also suggested that everyone treats everyone as selfobjects to some extent. We are social beings, and our senses of self and identity depend partly on the responses of others. Kohut further maintained that everyone occasionally experiences narcissistic wounding that results in "fragmentation anxiety" concerning the self. This anxiety may manifest as narcissistic rage. It may instead precipitate a regressive state that is characterized by unusually intense treatment of other people as selfobjects.

Noting that occult experiences like selfobjects are always both internal and external, Gay (1989) suggested that "in the face of . . . [fragmentation] anxiety . . . the person creates an external experience—the occult moment—which provides a momentary sense of self-repair and self-coherence" (p. 17). Occult experiences are creative solutions to "failures in self and selfobject relationships" (p. 107) that answer to "internal needs" (p. 105). "A perceived failure in the self-object dimension of a relationship causes one to scan one's emotional environment searching for a clue or sign from a transcendent power. That transcendent power is given the task of reorganizing the self and repairing the breach in it caused by the failure of the selfobject" (p. 145). However, Kohut's notion of the self is problematic and controversial (Kernberg, 1982); and Gay's theory can be expressed in more traditional Freudian terms (compare: Josephs, 1989).

Let us begin with the general observation that the experience of a miracle is a form of unitive thinking. To experience a coincidental event as a miracle, a person must appreciate the event empathically, that is, as an embodiment of attitude, ideas, and purposes belonging to a transcendent being. In some cases, empathic imagination of oneself as from the perspective of a transcendent being enhances self-esteem. The transcendent being approves and rewards, or takes interest, or provides opportunity. In other cases, the exercise of empathy imagines disapproval of the self. In every case, a miracle is a judgment on the self, mediated by a coincidental event, which is attributed to a transcendent power. In other words, miracles are experienced when judgments of conscience are projected externally onto coincidental events. The superego's interpretation of a coincidence as a judgment on the self causes the event to be experienced as a miracle.

The judgment is not discounted as a fantasy because the physical coincidence exists objectively in the perceptible world. Its meaningfulness is logically consistent with meaning in general. Either a sunset, a child's birth, or the successful completion of a difficult task have no meaning, because their meanings are all fantasies that are projected onto objectively existing physical events, or coincidences may logically be treated as miracles. What alone is illogical is to impose a double standard, with the miraculous significance of coincidences being excluded from the domain of consensually recognized meaning.

It is similarly the superego's function as conscience that causes coincidental imaginations to be experienced as revelations. When one imagines events at a distance or events in the future, and the imaginations prove accurate or true, the agreement of imagination and external physical events proceeds by coincidence. The projection of meaning onto the coincidence causes the imagination to be appreciated as a revelation and implies that a miracle has happened in the human mind.

The speculations that transform coincidental events into miracles and coincidental imaginations into revelations conceptualize the physical world as a medium for object relations with a transcendent Something More. In normal waking sobriety, the physical world is not ordinarily so perceived. As long as consciousness is occupied with causal relations among physical realities, scientific thinking is active and religious speculations do not manifest. However, events that are coincidental, and so have no meaning in terms of physical causality, oblige the ego to suspend thinking about physical causality. Sublimation, the assignment of instinctual meanings or values, cannot then be continued through thinking about physical causality and shifts instead to another line of thought. There are both ego and id contributions. The lacuna in (ego) meaning provides an opportunity for the entertainment of a speculative (superego) explanation, and instinctual (id) desire provides a motive. The speculative invention of meaning proceeds unconsciously and manifests through the external projection of meanings. The projections empathetically imagine the meaning that the event has for a transcendent being.

Experiences of miracles may occur as responses to anxiety, as Gay suggested; but it is a mistake to endorse psychological theories of religious development that neglect the normative character of the experience of miracles (e.g., Fowler, 1981). Statistically it is significant that most people who undergo spiritual awakenings or conversions commence, from that time forward, to experience miracles (Grof & Grof, 1990, pp. 175–76; Morse, with Perry, 1992; Sutherland, 1992). It is as though the integration of the self and spirituality must be achieved, at least in part, before the schema can grow to accommodate external reality, through its development into a unitive schema that integrates self, spirituality, and the perceptible world.

Since coincidences can be experienced as meaningful, that is, as miracles, it is philosophically incoherent to claim that events are objectively meaningless because they are coincidences. The logical status of coincidences is consistent with the status of the class of intelligible phenomena that medieval philosophers termed universals. For example, red, yellow, blue, and green exist, but color is a concept that has no physical reality. Similarly, the separate events that coincide to form a coincidence each has a necessary chain of physical causality, but the coincidence itself has none. A coincidence is an intelligible phenomenon, an interpretation or abstract conception; yet it is fully as real and objective as the intelligible phenomenon of color. Like the beautiful, the moral, and the holy, the miraculous is a judgment of value that exists "in the eye of the beholder." It is no less real for being so. The cosmos is so structured that material signifiers are able to support intelligible signifieds that exceed their material limitations.

Because the physical circumstances of the cosmos include coincidences in time and space that are not governed by physical causality, speculations regarding transcendent causality are forever free from falsification through reality-testing.

As long as a coincidence is genuine, and it is attributed to a cause that is transcendent, its interpretation as a miracle cannot logically be refuted. Of course, many events that are interpreted as miracles have physical causes that happen to be unknown to the religious devotees. However, insofar as physical events are genuinely coincidental, their interpretation as miracles and revelations cannot be falsified, and the religious speculations are logically tenable.

Summary

The interpretation of coincidental events as miracles, acts of providence, acts of magic, and so forth, is a normative religious practice cross-culturally. Gods and spirits may be regarded, in part, as theoretical explanations of the occurrence of miracles. Prayers everywhere seek the occurrence of miracles. Magic attempts to produce miracles on demand. Religious moralities, observances, taboos, and rites hope to manage favorable and unwanted miracles.

Interpretations of coincidental events as miracles differ from culture to culture, as the examples of Inuit hunter religion, popular American Christianity, and early Hasidism show. In all cases, however, miracles project judgments of conscience externally onto coincidental events. The superego's interpretation of a coincidence as a judgment on the self causes the event to be experienced as a miracle.

Because speculations regarding the meanings of coincidences cannot be falsified, interpretations of coincidences as miracles are consistent with reality-testing and are logically tenable.

NINE

A Theory
of Revelation

In this book, I have argued, so far as possible, that a broad range of religious experiences are consciously and/or unconsciously unitive, and that unitive thinking is a natural line of psychological development. I have repeatedly stressed that some religious ideas and beliefs are logically tenable speculations that can be neither proved nor falsified; but my account of unitive thinking has made no appeal to revelation or to grace. I have consistently excluded the metaphysical from my explanations. All has been argued to be natural and normative, *ex hypothesi* cross-culturally.

In this final chapter, I wish now to shift roles and to speak theologically; for my concern throughout has been to expand psychoanalytic theory until it becomes serviceable for the purposes of spiritual development.

Aristotle's First Theory of Motion

Whether coincidental events and imaginations should or should not be found meaningful and, if meaningful, according to what system(s) of interpretation, are not questions for psychoanalysis to decide. The questions deserve, however, to be addressed.

Philosophically, it is logically necessary to maintain that there is and can be nothing random in the cosmos. The classical form of the argument was the first of all the many theories of motion that Aristotle discussed in book 6 of his *Physics*. The argument resolved the classical Greek conundrum of Being and Becoming. It also advanced a compelling proof of the omnipotence of God. Interestingly, Aristotle did not state whether he endorsed or rejected the theory. He merely stated it and then went on to review others. However, it was generally held in late antiquity that Aristotle's writings sometimes contained a secret or esoteric level of intended meaning (Galston, 1990, pp. 27–35). Aristotle possibly concealed some of his views out of fear of religious persecution (Strauss, 1952). We know, for example, that he fled Athens at the end of his life, as he said, "lest Athens sin a second time against philosophy." At any rate, because Aristotle (1984) placed this theory first, and because it alone is a logically satisfactory theory, I advance it in his name.

> [Either] magnitude . . . time, and . . . motion . . . are composed of indivisibles and are divisible into indivisibles, or none. This may be made clear as follows.
>
> If a magnitude is composed of indivisibles, the motion over that magnitude must be composed of corresponding indivisible motions: e.g. if the magnitude ABC is composed of the indivisibles A, B, C, each corresponding part of the motion DEF of Z over ABC is indivisible. Therefore, since where there is motion there must be something that is in motion, and where there is something in motion there must be motion, therefore the being-moved will also be composed of indivisibles. So Z traversed A when its motion was D, B when its motion was E, and C similarly when its motion was F. Now a thing that is in motion from one place to another cannot at the moment when it was in motion both be in motion and at the same time have completed its motion at the place to which it was in motion (e.g. if a man is walking to Thebes, he cannot be walking to Thebes and at the same time have completed his walk to Thebes). . . . And if a thing is in motion over the whole ABC and its motion is DEF, and if it is not in motion at all over the partless section A but has completed its motion over it, then the motion will consist not of motions but of movings, and will take place by a thing's having completed a motion without being in motion; for on this assumption it has completed its passage through A without passing through it. So it will be possible for a thing to have completed a walk without ever walking; for on this assumption it has completed a walk over a particular distance without walking over that distance. Since, then, everything must be either at rest or in motion, and it is therefore at rest in each of A, B, and C, it follows that a thing can be at the same time continuously at rest and in motion; for, as we saw, it is in motion over the whole ABC and at rest in any part (and consequently in the whole) of it (*Physics*, VI, 1; pp. 391–92).

Aristotle here addressed the classical puzzle of Becoming and Being. Heracleitus of Ephesus (fl. c. 500 B.C.E.) had maintained that change was constant. "It is not possible to step twice in the same river" (Freeman, 1978, p. 31). "Cold things grow hot, hot things grow cold, the wet dries, the parched is moistened" (p. 33). "Fire lives the death of earth, and air lives the death of fire; water lives the death of air, earth that of water." "War is general (*universal*) and jurisdiction is strife, and everything comes about by way of strife and necessity" (p. 30). To account for the constancy of change, Heracleitus maintained that the cosmos is composed exclusively of fire. "This ordered universe (*cosmos*), which is the same for all, was not created by any one of the gods or of mankind, but was ever and is and shall be ever-living Fire, kindled in measure and quenched in measure" (p. 26). "The thunder-bolt (*i.e. Fire*) steers the universe" (p. 29).

Parmenides of Elea (fl. c. 475 B.C.E.) instead argued "that Being Is; for To Be is possible, and Nothing is not possible." From this premise, he reasoned that Being "never Was, nor Will Be, because it Is now, a Whole all together, One, continuous." It cannot have sprung "from Not-Being; for it is neither express-ible nor thinkable that What-Is-Not Is." By the same token, Being cannot in fu-ture become Not-Being. Parmenides concluded that Being "is motionless in the limits of might bonds, without beginning, without cease, since Becoming and Destruction have been driven very far away." He also maintained that "Being shall not be without boundary." It is spatially finite (pp. 43–44).

Aristotle expressed these concepts in mathematical idioms. He wrote of in-divisible and divisible rather than finite and infinite, and he used the examples of points and lines to clarify his reasoning. Agreeing with Heracleitus, Aristotle maintained that whatever is indivisible, that is, finite, must always be at one point in space, or another, but can never be at an indefinite location between points. Since what is at a point, and neither approaching nor departing it, is motionless, and everything must always be at one point or another, motion cannot exist. At the same time, Aristotle accepted the evidence of sense perception that motion manifestly occurs. What was unacceptable was the logical consequence of Her-acleitus' position. Anything in motion can never be at a particular place in space. It must always be in motion *through;* it can never be *at.* It must consequently be indefinite or infinite.

Aristotle resolved the dilemma by treating time as an independent factor. At any point in time, he proposed, all things must be at one point in space or an-other. However, there is no necessity that at two successive points in time, things must be in the same place. At no time is anything in motion, indefinite, or infi-nite. But over the course of the continuum of time, the successive finite place-ments of things in space generate an illusion of motion.

Aristotle's first theory of motion describes the principle of motion that today underlies motion pictures. A series of still positions, rapidly juxtaposed, generate an optical illusion of motion.

Aristotle's theory of motion entails a theological corollary. The cosmos can-not be self-subsisting, as both Parmenides and Heracleitus claimed, but must in-stead owe its motion to a transcendent Projector. For motion to be an optical illusion, an Unmoved Mover, outside time and space, must be responsible for repositioning all things each and every moment.

From these considerations, it follows that the Unmoved Mover must pos-sess universal knowledge and perfect omnipotence. There is and can be nothing truly random.

Randomness is nonetheless a valuable heurism. Randomness is an agnostic way of talking about what, in reality, is a free choice by the Creator.

A Theory of Random Symbol-Formation

With the understanding that the existence of randomness is a heuristic fiction and that the apparent meanings of coincidences are intelligible realities that are causally created by God, it becomes possible to develop a model of the psychology of revelation. Because good theory is built from the bottom up, and not from the top down, I shall revert to methodological agnosticism to continue my argument.

What I postulate in discussing coincidentally meaningful imaginations is that a distinctive function of unconscious thought is constituted in such a fashion that it serves as a vehicle or medium of random imagination. Like a deck of cards in parapsychology laboratories, the unconscious mental function permits the occurrence of a high number of random neurochemical events. Occurring at molecular levels within the brain/mind, the random processes produce fantasies or imaginations which, through coincidence, happen to correspond to external reality.

The circumstances necessary for random imaginative activity must be expected of the mental process that is responsible for unconscious symbol-formation, in which any mental element can be used to symbolize any other mental element. The arbitrary relation of signifiers to the signified proves that symbol formation is at least sometimes a randomly acting process. Semiotic thought could not exist unless an element of randomness were built into the physicochemistry of the nervous system. We know that symbol-formation may be driven by instinctual desire, or by a rational need to solve a problem. When the same mental processes are more or less idle, their more or less random combinations may be expected to make possible the high number of coincidences necessary to produce complex imaginations that correspond to events at a distance or in the future. Such a theory of the brain's random activity would be consistent with the well-known fact that clairvoyance and foreknowledge occur most frequently during hypnagogic states (Mavromatis, 1987), as the mind shifts from waking to sleeping and is momentarily engaged in neither.

If we postulate that a naturally occurring human thought process is so constituted as to readily produce randomly meaningful imaginations, we can conceptualize the induction of ostensibly paranormal or revelatory experience. Meditation, visualization, prayer, psychoactive drug use, sensory deprivation, and so forth, all cause the natural activity of the imaginative process to shift its momentary organization in a direction that increases the likelihood of random activity. In other words, sobriety may be compared with sorting a deck of cards, but spiritual induction techniques with shuffling. No shuffle, no randomness, no coincidental imaginations of meaning—no revelation.

Mystical Moments as Revelations

My theory of revelation implies that revelation is accomplished through the random, coincidental reassembly or reorganization of existing mental contents into new and meaningful patterns. The mental contents—the ideas and affects, the percepts and memories, mental images, fantasies, somatizations, instincts, and so forth—are all natural. Revelation is accomplished, when it is accomplished, through their random combination in novel and meaningful ways. Unitive thinking is no exception to this general rule. The unconscious elaboration and disclosure to consciousness of unitive thinking may occur naturally, but when it occurs at random, it may instead be revelatory.

The difficulty of discerning natural attainments from revelations is unimportant for practical purposes. Whether natural or revelatory, religious experiences articulate ideals toward which one may aspire. It is not religious experiences, but the aspiration and endeavor to fulfill the ideals that they articulate, which is the substance of a religious life.

BOOKS CITED

Abe, Masao. (1985), *Zen and Western Thought*. Ed. William R. La Fleur. London: Macmillan.

Abell, Arthur M. (1955), *Talks with Great Composers*. New York: Philosophical Library.

Abbott, John A. (1969), Freud's repressed feelings about Athena on the Acropolis. *American Imago* 26(4):355–63.

Abelson, J. (1912), *The Immanence of God: In Rabbinical Literature*. Rpt. New York: Hermon, 1969.

Abraham, Ruth. (1982), Freud's mother conflict and the formulation of the oedipal father. *Psychoanalytic Review* 69:441–53.

Adamson, Sophia (Ed.). (1985), *Through the Gateway of the Heart: Accounts of Experiences with MDMA and other Empathogenic Substances*. San Francisco: Four Trees.

Alexander, Donald L. (Ed). (1989), *Christian Spirituality: Five Views of Sanctification*. Downers Grove, IL: InterVarsity.

Allen, Michael R. (1967), *Male Cults and Secret Initiations in Melanesia*. Melbourne, Australia: Melbourne University Press.

Almond, Philip C. (1982), *Mystical Experience and Religious Doctrine: An Investigation of the Study of Mysticism in World Religions*. Berlin & New York: Mouton.

Alnaes, Randolf. (1964), Therapeutic application of the change in consciousness produced by psycholytica (LSD, psilocybin, etc.): The psychedelic experience in the treatment of neurosis. *Acta Psychiatrica Scandinavica*, Supplementum 180, 397–409.

Amsterdam, Beulah Kramer & Levitt, Morton. (1980), Consciousness of self and painful self-consciousness. *Psychoanalytic Study of the Child* 35:67–83.

Anderson, Joan Webster. (1994), *Where Miracles Happen: True Stories of Heavenly Encounters*. New York: Ballantine.

Angela of Foligno. (1966), *The Book of Divine Consolation of the Blessed Angela of Foligno*. Trans. Mary G. Steegmann. New York: Cooper Square.

Aranya, Swami Hariharananda. (1981), *Yoga Philosophy of Patanjali: Containing His Yoga Aphorisms with Vyasa's Commentary in Sanskrit and a Translation with Annotations Including Many Suggestions for the Practice of Yoga*. Trans. Paresh Nath Mukerji, 3rd ed. Calcutta: Calcutta University Press; rpt. Albany: State University of New York Press, 1983.

Arbman, Ernst. (1939), Mythic and religious thought. In: *Dragma: Martin P. Nilsson . . . Dedicatum*. Lund.

———. (1963–1968–1970), *Ecstasy or Religious Trance: In the Experience of the Ecstatics and from the Scientific Point of View*, 3 vols. Stockholm: Svenska Bokforlaget.

159

Aristotle. (1984), *The Complete Works of Aristotle: The Revised Oxford Translation*, 2 vols. Ed. Jonathan Barnes. Princeton, NJ: Princeton University Press.

Arlow, Jacob A. (1961), Ego psychology and the study of mythology. *Journal of the American Psychoanalytic Association* 9:371–93.

―――. (1995), Bisexuality in Jewish Mysticism. In: Mortimer Ostow (Ed.), *Ultimate Intimacy: The Psychodynamics of Jewish Mysticism*. Madison, CT: International Universities Press, pp. 245–53.

Aryeh, Isaiah & Dvorkes, Joseph (Eds.). (1974), *The Baal Shem Tov on Pirkey Avoth*. Trans. Charles Wengrov. Jerusalem: Jerusalem Academy.

Augustine, St. (1982), *The Literal Meaning of Genesis*, 2 vols. Trans. John Hammond Taylor. New York: Newman.

Aziz, Robert. (1990), *C. G. Jung's Psychology of Religion and Synchronicity*. Albany: State University of New York Press.

Bakan, David. (1966a), *The Duality of Human Existence: Isolation and Communion in Western Man*. Boston: Beacon.

―――. (1966b), Science, mysticism and psychoanalysis. *Catholic Psychological Record* 4:1–9.

―――. (1979), *And They Took Themselves Wives: The Emergence of Patriarchy in Western Civilization*. San Francisco: Harper.

Balint, Michael. (1937), Early developmental states of the ego. Primary object-love. *International Journal of Psycho-Analysis* 18:265–73. Rpt. in: *Primary Love and Psychoanalytic Technique*, 2d ed. London: Tavistock, 1965, pp. 74–90.

Bannister, Roger. (1955), *First Four Minutes*. London.

Barbour, Ian G. (1974), *Myths, Models, and Paradigms: A Comparative Study in Science and Religion*. New York: Harper.

Batson, C. Daniel & Ventis, W. Larry. (1982), *The Religious Experience: A Social-Psychological Perspective*. New York & Oxford: Oxford University Press.

Bellak, Leopold. (1958) Creativity: Some random notes to a systematic consideration. *Journal of Projective Techniques* 22:363–80.

Berger, I. (1910), *Esser Tzachtzochoth*. Piotrkov [Hebrew].

Bergman, Anni & Wilson, Arnold. (1984), Thoughts about stages on the way to empathy and the capacity for concern. In: Joseph Lichtenberg, Melvin Bornstein, & Donald Silver (Eds.), *Empathy II*. Hillsdale, NJ: Analytic Press, pp. 59–80.

Bergmann, Martin S. (1971), Psychoanalytic observations on the capacity to love. In: John B. McDevitt & Calvin F. Settlage (Eds.), *Separation-Individuation: Essays in Honor of Margaret S. Mahler*. New York: International Universities Press, pp. 15–40.

Bharati, Agehananda. (1976), *The Light at the Center: Context and Pretext of Modern Mysticism*. Santa Barbara: Ross-Erikson.

———. (1980), *The Ochre Robe*, 2d ed. Santa Barbara: Ross-Erikson.

Birket-Smith, Kaj. (1953), *The Chugach Eskimo*. Nationalmuseets Skrifter, Ethnografisk Roekke 6. Copenhagen: Nationalmuseets Publikationsfond.

Blacker, Carmen. (1965), Initiation in the Sugendo: The passage through the ten states of existence. In: C. J. Bleeker (Ed.), *Initiation: Contributions to the Theme of the Study-Conference of the International Association for the History of Religions, Held at Strasburg, September 17th to 22nd 1964*. Leiden, Netherlands: E. J. Brill.

Blaustein, Alvin B. (1975), A dream resembling the Isakower phenomenon: A brief clinical contribution. *International Journal of Psycho-Analysis* 56:207–8.

Bleeker, C. Jouco. (1965), Initiation in ancient Egypt. In: C. J. Bleeker (Ed.), *Initiation: Contributions to the Theme of the Study-Conference of the International Association for the History of Religions, Held at Strasburg, September 17th to 22nd 1964*. Leiden, Netherlands: E. J. Brill.

Boesky, Dale. (1983), The problem of mental representation in self and object theory. *Psychoanalytic Quarterly* 52:564–83.

Bogoras, Waldemar. (1928), The shamanistic call and the period of initiation in northern Asia and North America. 23rd *International Congress of Americanists*, 441–44.

Boisen, Anton T. (1936), *The Exploration of the Inner World: A Study of Mental Disorder and Religious Experience*. Rpt. Philadelphia: University of Pennsylvania Press, 1971.

Bouyer, Louis. (1963), *Rite and Man: Natural Sacredness and Christian Liturgy*. Trans. M. Joseph Costellor. Notre Dame: University of Notre Dame Press.

Bowker, John. (1973), *The Sense of God: Sociological, Anthropological and Psychological Approaches to the Origin of the Sense of God*. Oxford: Clarendon Press.

Boyer, L. Bryce. (1979), *Childhood and Folklore: A Psychoanalytic Study of Apache Personality*. New York: Library of Psychological Anthropology.

Bradford, Terry. (1984), *The Experience of God: Portraits in the Phenomenological Psychopathology of Schizophrenia*. New York: Peter Lang.

Bråten, Stein. (1988), Dialogic mind: The infant and the adult in protoconversation. In: Marc E. Carvallo (Ed.), *Nature, Cognition and System*. Dordrecht, Boston & London: Kluwer Academic Publishers. Vol. 1, pp. 187–205.

Breen, Hal J. (1986), A psychoanalytic approach to ethics. *Journal of the American Academy of Psychoanalysis* 14(2):255–75.

Brierley, Marjorie. (1951), *Trends in Psycho-Analysis*. London: Hogarth Press & Institute of Psycho-Analysis.

Brown, Daniel P. & Engler, Jack. (1984), An outcome study of intensive mindfulness meditation. *Psychoanalytic Study of Society* 10:163–225.

Buber, Martin. (1947), *Tales of the Hasidim: The Early Masters*. Trans. Olga Marx. New York: Schocken.

———. (1956), *Tales of Rabbi Nachman*. Rpt. New York: Avon, 1970.

———. (1958), *I and Thou*, 2d ed. Trans. Ronald Gregor Smith. New York: Scribner.

———. (1965), *Between Man and Man*. New York: Macmillan.

———. (1985), *Ecstatic Confessions*. Trans. Esther Cameron. San Francisco: Harper.

Buie, Dan H. (1981), Empathy: Its nature and limitations. *Journal of the American Psychoanalytic Association* 29:281–307.

Burkert, Walter. (1987), *Ancient Mystery Cults*. Cambridge, MA: Harvard University Press.

Burtt, E. A. (Ed.). (1955), *The Teachings of the Compassionate Buddha*. New York: New American Library.

Butler, Dom Cuthbert. (1922), *Western Mysticism: The Teaching of Augustine, Gregory, and Bernard on Contemplation and the Contemplative Life*, 2d ed., with *Afterthoughts*. Rpt. New York: Harper Torchbooks, 1966.

Bychowski, Gustav. (1951), From catharsis to work of art: The making of an artist. In: George B. Wilbur & Warner Muensterberger (Eds.), *Psychoanalysis and Culture: Essays in Honor of Geza Roheim*. New York: International Universities Press, pp. 390–409.

Caird, D. (1987), Religion and personality: Are mystics introverted, neurotic, or psychotic? *British Journal of Social Psychology* 26:345–46.

Cartwright, Peter. (1856), *Autobiography of Peter Cartwright, the Backwoods Preacher*. Ed. W. P. Stickland. Cincinnati: Hitchcock & Walden; New York: Nelson & Phillips.

Carver, Alfred. (1924), Primary identification and mysticism. *British Journal of Medical Psychology* 4:102–14.

Chernus, Ira. (1982), *Mysticism in Rabbinic Judaism: Studies in the History of Midrash*. Berlin & New York: Walter de Gruyter.

Christiansen, Reidar Th. (1953), Ecstasy and arctic religion. *Studia Septentrionalia* 4:19–92.

Coe, George Albert. (1916), *The Psychology of Religion*. Rpt. Chicago: University of Chicago Press, 1925.

Cohn, Ruth C. (1968), Training intuition. In: Herbert Otto & John Mann (Eds.), *Ways of Growth*. New York: Grossman Publishers.

Combs, Allan & Mark Holland. (1990), *Synchronicity: Science, Myth, and the Trickster*. New York: Paragon House.

Committee on Psychiatry and Religion [Furst, Sidney S., Leavy, Stanley A., Lewis, Richard C., Lubin, Albert J., Ostow, Mortimer, & Zales, Michael R.]. (1976), *Mysticism: Spiritual Quest or Psychic Disorder?* Group for the Advancement of Psychiatry, Vol. 9, Publication No. 97, November 1976. New York: Group for the Advancement of Psychiatry.

Conze, Edward. (1956), *Buddhist Meditation.* London; rpt. New York: Harper, 1969.

————. (1959), *Buddhist Scriptures: Selected and Translated.* Harmondsworth, UK: Penguin.

————. (1962), *Buddhist Thought in India: Three Phases of Buddhist Philosophy.* London: George Allen & Unwin.

Corbin, Henry. (1954), *Avicenna and the Visionary Recital.* Trans. Willard R. Trask. Rpt. Irving, TX: Spring 1980.

————. (1969), *Creative Imagination in the Sufism of Ibn 'Arabi.* Trans. Ralph Manheim. Princeton: Princeton University Press.

————. (1971), *The Man of Light in Iranian Sufism.* Trans. Nancy Pearson. Rpt. Boulder, CO: Shambhala, 1978.

D'Alviella, Goblet. (1914), Initiation: Introductory and primitive. In: James Hastings with John A. Selbie & Louis H. Gray (Eds.), *Encyclopaedia of Religion and Ethics.* Edinburgh: T. & T. Clark; New York: Scribner.

Deikman, Arthur J. (1963), Experimental meditation. *Journal of Nervous and Mental Disease* 136:329–73.

————. (1966a), De-automatization and the mystic experience. *Psychiatry* 29:324–38.

————. (1966b), Implications of experimentally induced contemplative meditation. *Journal of Nervous and Mental Disease* 142(2):101–16.

————. (1982), *The Observing Self: Mysticism and Psychotherapy.* Boston: Beacon.

Deutsch, Helene. (1927), On satisfaction, happiness and ecstasy. (Ed.) Paul Roazen. *International Journal of Psycho-Analysis* 70 (1989): 715–23.

Devereux, George (Ed.). (1953), *Psychoanalysis and the Occult.* Rpt. New York: International Universities Press, 1973.

Dillon, John. (1977), *The Middle Platonists: A Study of Platonism 80 BC to AD 220.* London: Gerald Duckworth.

Dobh Baer of Lubavitch. (1963), *Tract on Ecstasy.* Trans. Louis Jacobs. London: Valentine, Mitchell.

Dorpat, Theo L. (1981), Basic concepts and terms in object relations theory. In: Saul Tuttman, Carol Kaye, & Muriel Zimmerman (Eds.), *Object and Self: A Developmental Approach. Essays in Honor of Edith Jacobson.* New York: International Universities Press.

Easson, William M. (1973), The earliest ego development, primitive memory traces, and the Isakower phenomenon. *Psychoanalytic Quarterly* 42:60–72.

Eckhart, Meister. (1941), *A Modern Translation*. Trans. Raymond Bernard Blakney. New York: Harper.

Economou, George D. (1972), *The Goddess Natura in Medieval Literature*. Cambridge, MA: Harvard University Press.

Ehnmark, Erland. (1935), *The Idea of God in Homer*. Uppsala: Almqvist & Wiksells.

———. (1939), *Anthropomorphism and Miracle*. Uppsala Universitets Arsskrift 1939:12. Uppsala: A.-B. Lundequistska.

Eisnitz, Alan J. (1980), The organization of the self-representation and its influence on pathology. *Psychoanalytic Quarterly* 49:361–92.

Eliade, Mircea. (1958), *Rites and Symbols of Initiation: The Mysteries of Birth and Rebirth*. [Originally titled: "Birth and Rebirth".] Trans. Willard R. Trask. Rpt. New York: Harper Colophon, 1975.

———. (1962), *The Forge and the Crucible*. Trans. Stephen Corrin. London: Rider; rpt. New York: Harper, 1971.

———. (1964), *Shamanism: Archaic Techniques of Ecstasy*. Trans. Willard R. Trask. New York: Bollingen Foundation/Pantheon.

Elkin, A. P. (1977), *Aboriginal Men of High Degree*, 2d ed. Rpt. New York: St. Martin's, 1978.

Emde, Robert N. (1988), Development terminable and interminable. I. Innate and motivational factors from infancy. *International Journal of Psycho-Analysis* 69:23–42.

Evagrius Ponticus. (1981), *The Praktikos. Chapters on Prayer*. Trans. John Eudes Bamberger. Kalamazoo, MI: Cistercian Publications.

Fairbairn, W. Ronald D. (1941), A revised psychopathology of the psychoses and psychoneuroses. Rpt. in: *Psychoanalytic Studies of the Personality*. 1952; rpt. London & New York: Tavistock/Routledge, 1990, pp. 28–58.

Fauteux, Kevin. (1994), *The Recovery of Self: Regression and Redemption in Religious Experience*. New York: Paulist.

Federn, Paul. (1926), Some variations in ego-feeling. *International Journal of Psycho-Analysis* 7:434–44.

———. (1932), The reality of the death instinct, especially in melancholia: Remarks on Freud's book: "Civilization and Its Discontents." *Psychoanalytic Review* 19:129–51.

Fenichel, Otto. (1945), *The Psychoanalytic Theory of Neurosis*. New York: Norton.

Ferenczi, Sandor. (1913), Stages in the development of the sense of reality. Rpt. in: *First Contributions to Psycho-Analysis*. 1916; rpt. New York: Brunner/Mazel, 1980.

Figueira, Dorothy M. (1994), *The Exotic: A Decadent Quest*. Albany: State University of New York Press.

Finn, Mark & John Gartner. (1992), *Object Relations Theory and Religion: Clinical Applications*. Westport, CT: Praeger/Greenwood.

Finney, Charles Grandison. (1876), *Memoirs of Rev. Charles G. Finney: Written by Himself*. New York: A. S. Barnes.

Fisher, David James. (1976), Sigmund Freud and Romain Rolland: The terrestrial animal and his great oceanic friend. *American Imago* 1976:1–59.

Fiske, S. T. & Linville, P. W. (1980), What does the schema concept buy us? *Personality and Social Psychology Bulletin* 6:543–57.

Flower, J. Cyril. (1927), *An Approach to the Psychology of Religion*. New York: Harcourt.

Flugel, J. C. (1945), *Man, Morals and Society: A Psycho-Analytical Study*. New York: International Universities Press.

Fodor, Nandor. (1959), *The Haunted Mind: A Psychoanalyst Looks at the Supernatural*. New York: Garrett.

Forman, Robert K. C. (Ed.). (1990), *The Problem of Pure Consciousness: Mysticism and Philosophy*. New York & Oxford: Oxford University Press.

———. (1996), *Samadhi* and Peter Wimsey: Mysticism, reading and Bruce Janz. *Studies in Religion/Sciences Religieuses* 25(2):193–207.

Fowler, III, James W. (1981), *Stages of Faith: The Psychology of Human Development and the Quest for Meaning*. San Francisco: Harper.

Frankl, Victor E. (1975), *The Unconscious God: Psychotherapy and Theology*. New York: Simon & Schuster.

Freeman, Kathleen (Trans.). (1978), *Ancilla to the Pre-Socratic Philosophers: A Complete Translation of the Fragments in Diels*, Fragmente der Vorsokratiker. Cambridge, MA: Harvard University Press.

Freemantle, Anne (Ed.). (1964), *The Protestant Mystics*. New York: New American Library, 1965.

French, Thomas Morton. (1937), Reality testing in dreams. *Psychoanalytic Quarterly* 6:62–77.

———. (1939), Insight and distortion in dreams. In: *Psychoanalytic Interpretations: The Selected Papers of Thomas M. French*. Chicago: Quadrangle, 1970.

———. (1952), *The Integration of Behavior*. Vol. 1, *Basic Postulates*. Chicago: University of Chicago Press.

———. (1954), *The Integration of Behavior*. Vol. 2, *The Integrative Process in Dreams*. Chicago: University of Chicago Press.

————. (1957), Analysis of the dream censorship. In: George E. Daniels, James P. Cattell, Williard M. Gaylin, Terry C. Rodgers, & Daniel Shapiro (Eds.), *New Perspectives in Psychoanalysis: Sandor Rado Lectures 1957–1963.* New York: Grune & Stratton, 1965. Rpt. in: *Psychoanalytic Interpretations.*

———— & Fromm, Erika. (1964), *Dream Interpretation: A New Approach.* New York: Basic.

———— & Whitman, Roy M. (1969), A focal conflict view. In: Milton Kramer, with Roy M. Whitman, Bill J. Baldridge, & Paul H. Ornstein (Eds.), *Dream Psychology and the New Biology of Dreaming.* Springfield, IL: Charles C. Thomas.

Freud, Sigmund. All references are to: *The Standard Edition of the Complete Psychological Works of Sigmund Freud,* 24 vols. Ed. James Strachey, with Anna Freud, Alix Strachey, & Alan Tyson. London: Hogarth Press. (Hereafter cited as *Standard Edition*).

————. (1900), The interpretation of dreams. *Standard Edition,* 4–5:1–625. London: Hogarth Press, 1958.

————. (1901), The psychopathology of everyday life. *Standard Edition,* 6:1–279. London: Hogarth Press, 1960.

————. (1905), Three essays on the theory of sexuality. *Standard Edition,* 7:130–243. London: Hogarth Press, 1953.

————. (1910), Leonardo da Vinci and a memory of his childhood. *Standard Edition,* 11:63–137. London: Hogarth Press, 1957.

————. (1913), Totem and taboo: Some points of agreement between the mental lives of savages and neurotics. *Standard Edition,* 13:xiii–162. London: Hogarth Press, 1958.

————. (1914), On narcissism: An introduction. *Standard Edition,* 14:78–102. London: Hogarth Press, 1957.

————. (1916–17), Introductory lectures on psycho-analysis. *Standard Edition,* 15–16:9–463. London: Hogarth Press, 1961–63.

————. (1921), Group psychology and the analysis of the ego. *Standard Edition,* 18:69–143. London: Hogarth Press, 1955.

————. (1923), The ego and the id. *Standard Edition,* 19:12–59. London: Hogarth Press, 1961.

————. (1927), The future of an illusion. *Standard Edition,* 21:5–56. London: Hogarth Press, 1961.

————. (1930), Civilization and its discontents. *Standard Edition,* 21:64–145. London: Hogarth Press, 1961.

————. (1933), New introductory lectures on psycho-analysis. *Standard Edition,* 22:7–182. London: Hogarth Press, 1964.

————. (1936), A disturbance of memory on the Acropolis. *Standard Edition*, 22:239–48. London: Hogarth Press, 1964.

————. (1939), Moses and monotheism: Three essays. *Standard Edition*, 23:6–137. London: Hogarth Press, 1964.

————. (1940), An Outline of Psycho-Analysis. *Standard Edition*, 23:144–207. London: Hogarth Press, 1964.

Furer, Manuel. (1967), Some developmental aspects of the superego. *International Journal of Psycho-Analysis* 48:277–80.

Gaddini, Eugenio. (1969), On imitation. *International Review of Psycho-Analysis* 50:475–84. Rpt. in: Adam Limentani (Ed.), *A Psychoanalytic Theory of Infantile Experience: Conceptual and Clinical Reflections*. London & New York: Tavistock/Routledge, 1992, pp. 18–34.

Gaensbauer, Theodore J. (1982), The differentiation of discrete affects: A case report. *Psychoanalytic Study of the Child* 37:29–66.

Galston, Miriam. (1990), *Politics and Excellence: The Political Philosophy of Alfarabi*. Princeton, NJ: Princeton University Press.

Garside, Bruce. (1972), Language and the interpretation of mystical experience. *International Journal of the Philosophy of Religion* 3:101–2.

Gaster, Theodor H. (1950), *Thespis: Ritual, Myth, and Drama in the Ancient Near East*. New York: Norton, 1977.

Gay, Volney Patrick. (1989), *Understanding the Occult: Fragmentation and Repair of the Self*. Minneapolis: Fortress.

————. (1992), *Freud on Sublimation: Reconsiderations*. Albany: State University of New York Press.

Geels, Antoon. (1982), Mystical experience and the emergence of creativity. In: Nils G. Holm (Ed.), *Religious Ecstasy*. Scripta Instituti Donneriani Aboensis XI. Stockholm: Almqvist & Wiksell International, pp. 27–62.

Gennep, Arnold van. (1960), *The Rites of Passage*. Trans. Monika B. Vizedom & Gabrielle L. Caffee. Chicago: University of Chicago Press.

Gibbon, Edward. (1932), *Autobiography*. London: J. M. Dent.

Gimello, Robert M. (1978), Mysticism and meditation. In: Steven T. Katz (Ed.), *Mysticism and Philosophical Analysis*. London: Sheldon.

Goodman, Stanley. (1965), Current status of the theory of the superego. *Journal of the American Psychoanalytic Association* 13:172–80.

Grof, Christina & Grof, Stanislav. (1990), *The Stormy Search for the Self: A Guide to Personal Growth through Transformational Crisis*. Los Angeles: Jeremy P. Tarcher.

Grof, Stanislav. (1975), *Realms of the Human Unconscious: Observations from LSD Research.* New York: Viking.

———— & Halifax, Joan. (1978), *The Human Encounter With Death.* New York: Dutton.

Grossman, Lee. (1993), The significance of religious themes and fantasies during psychoanalysis. *Journal of the American Psychoanalytic Association* 41(3):755–64.

Grossman, William I. (1982), The self as fantasy: Fantasy as theory. *Journal of the American Psychoanalytic Association* 30(4):919–37.

Grotstein, James. (1980–81), The significance of Kleinian contributions to psychoanalysis II. Freudian and Kleinian conceptions of early mental development. *International Journal of Psychoanalytic Psychotherapy* 8:393–428.

Hadewijch. (1980), *The Complete Works.* Trans. Mother Columba Hart, O.S.B. New York: Paulist.

Halifax, Joan. (1980), *Shamanic Visions: A Survey of Visionary Narratives.* New York: Dutton.

Happold, F. C. (1970), *Mysticism: A Study and an Anthology,* 2d ed. Harmondsworth: Penguin.

Hardin, Harry T. (1987), On the vicissitudes of Freud's early mothering. I: Early environment and loss. *Psychoanalytic Quarterly* 56:628–44.

————. (1988a), On the vicissitudes of Freud's early mothering. II: Alienation from his biological mother. *Psychoanalytic Quarterly* 57:72–86.

————. (1988b), On the vicissitudes of Freud's early mothering. III: Freiberg, screen memories, and loss. *Psychoanalytic Quarterly* 57:209–23.

Hardy, Sir Alister. (1979), *The Spiritual Nature of Man: A Study of Contemporary Religious Experience.* Oxford: Clarendon Press.

Harrison, Irving B. (1979), On Freud's view of the infant-mother relationship and of the oceanic feeling—Some subjective influences. *Journal of the American Psychoanalytic Association* 27:399–421.

————. (1986), On "merging" and the fantasy of merging. *Psychoanalytic Study of the Child* 41:155–70.

Hartmann, Heinz. (1939), *Ego Psychology and the Problem of Adaptation.* New York: International Universities Press, 1958.

————. (1960), *Psychoanalysis and Moral Values.* New York: International Universities Press.

Harvey, E. Ruth. (1975), *The Inward Wits: Psychological Theory in the Middle Ages and the Renaissance.* London: Warburg Institute-University of London.

Hawkes, Jacquetta. (1954), *Man on Earth.* London: Cresset Press.

Hazzaya, Joseph. (1934), Mystical treatise. *Woodbrooke Studies* 7:177–84.

Heiler, Friedrich. (1920), *Prayer: A Study in the History and Psychology of Religion.* Trans. Samuel McComb, with J. Edgar Park. Rpt. London: Oxford University Press, 1932.

Herdt, Gilbert R. (Ed.). (1982), *Rituals of Manhood: Male Initiation in Papua New Guinea.* Berkeley: University of California Press.

———— & Stoller, Robert J. (1990), *Intimate Communications: Erotics and the Study of Culture.* New York: Columbia University Press.

Herford, Charles Harold (Ed.). (1929), *Joseph Estlin Carpenter: A Memorial Volume.* Oxford: Clarendon Press.

Heschel, Abraham Joshua. (1962), *The Prophets*, 2 vols. New York: Harper.

Hesse, Mary. (1970), *Models and Analogies in Science.* Notre Dame: Notre Dame University Press.

Hillyer, Richard. (1966), *Country Boy: The Autobiography of Richard Hillyer.* London: Hodder & Stoughton.

Himmelfarb, Martha. (1993), *Ascent to Heaven in Jewish and Christian Apocalypses.* New York: Oxford University Press.

Hoens, D. J. (1965), Initiation in later Hinduism according to tantric texts. In: C. J. Bleeker (Ed.), *Initiation: Contributions to the Theme of the Study-Conference of the International Association for the History of Religions, Held at Strasburg, September 17th to 22nd 1964.* Leiden, Netherlands: E. J. Brill.

Hoffer, Abram & Humphry Osmond. (1968), *New Hope for Alcoholics.* New Hyde Park, NY: University Books.

Hoffman, Edward. (1992), *Visions of Innocence: Spiritual and Inspirational Experiences of Childhood.* Boston & London: Shambhala.

Hoffman, Martin L. (1978), Toward a theory of empathic arousal and development. In: Michael Lewis & Leonard A. Rosenblum (Eds.), *The Development of Affect.* New York: Plenum Press, pp. 227–56.

Hollenback, Jess Byron. (1996), *Mysticism: Experience, Response, and Empowerment.* University Park: Pennsylvania State University Press.

Holm, Gustav. (1912), Legends and tales from Angmagsalik. *Meddelelser om Gronland* 39(5).

Holt, Robert R. (1989), *Freud Reappraised: A Fresh Look at Psychoanalytic Theory.* New York: Guilford Press.

————. (1992), Freud's parental identifications as a source of some contradictions within psychoanalysis. In: Toby Gelfand & John Kerr (Eds.), *Freud and the History of Psychoanalysis.* Hillsdale, NJ: Analytic.

Horner, Thomas. M. (1985), The psychic life of the young infant: Review and critique of the psychoanalytic concepts of symbiosis and infantile omnipotence. *American Journal of Orthopsychiatry* 55(3):324–44.

————. (1992), The origin of the symbiotic wish. *Psychoanalytic Psychology* 9(1):25–48.

Hood, Jr., Ralph W. (1976), Conceptual criticisms of regressive explanations of mysticism. *Review of Religious Research* 17(3):179–88.

————. (1977), Differential triggering of mystical experience as a function of self actualization. *Review of Religious Research* 18(3):264–70.

Hopkins, P. (1940), Analytic observations on the *scala perfectionis* of the mystics. *British Journal of Medical Psychology* 18:198–218.

Horton, Paul C. (1974), The mystical experience: Substance of an illusion. *Journal of the American Psychoanalytic Association* 22:364–80.

Hultkrantz, Åke. (1978), The relation between the shaman's experiences and specific shamanistic goals. In: Louise Bäckman & Åke Hultkrantz. *Studies in Lapp Shamanism.* Stockholm: Almqvist & Wiksell, 1978, pp. 90–109.

————. (1983), The concept of the supernatural in primal religion. *History of Religions* 22(3):231–53.

Huxley, Aldous. (1954), *The Doors of Perception* and (1956), *Heaven and Hell.* Rpt. London: Granada, 1977.

————. (1962), Visionary experience. In: Gerhard S. Nielson (Ed.), *Clinical Psychology, Proceedings of the XIV International Congress of Applied Psychology*, Vol. 4. Copenhagen, Denmark: Munksgaard, pp. 11–35. Rpt. in: John White (Ed.), *The Highest State of Consciousness.* Garden City, NY: Anchor/Doubleday, 1972, pp. 34–57.

Idel, Moshe. (1988), *Kabbalah: New Perspectives.* New Haven: Yale University Press.

Inge, William Ralph. (1899), *Christian Mysticism.* New York: Meridian, 1956.

Isaac of Nineveh. (1923), *Mystical Treatises by Isaac of Nineveh: Translated from Bedjan's Syriac Text with an Introduction and Registers.* Trans. A. J. Wensinck. (Verhandelingen der Koninklijke Akademie van Wetenschappen te Amsterdam Afdeeling Letterkunde, Nieuwe Reeks, Deel XXII No. 1.) Amsterdam: Koninklijke Akademie van Wetenschappen.

Isakower, Otto. (1938), A contribution to the psychopathology of phenomena associated with falling asleep. *International Journal of Psycho-Analysis* 19:331–46.

Ivanhoe, Philip J. (1993), *Confucian Moral Self Cultivation.* New York: Peter Lang.

Jacobson, Edith. (1954a), Contribution to the metapsychology of psychotic identifications. *Journal of the American Psychoanalytic Association* 2:239–62.

————. (1954b), The self and the object world: Vicissitudes of their infantile cathexes and their influence on ideational and affective development. *Psychoanalytic Study of the Child* 9:75–127.

————. (1957), Normal and pathological moods: Their nature and functions. *Psychoanalytic Study of the Child* 12:73–113.

————. (1964), *The Self and the Object World*. New York: International Universities Press.

Jaki, Stanley L. (1988), *The Savior of Science*. Washington, DC: Regnery Gateway.

James, William. (1902), *The Varieties of Religious Experience: A Study in Human Nature*. Rpt. New York: New American Library, 1958.

Joffe, W. G. & Sandler, Joseph. (1965), Notes on pain, depression, and individuation. *Psychoanalytic Study of the Child* 20:394–424.

John of the Cross, St. (1973), *Collected Works*. Trans. Kieran Kavanaugh & Otilio Rodriguez. Washington, DC: Institute of Carmelite Studies.

Johnson, Raynor C. (1959), *Watcher on the Hills*. London: Hodder and Stoughton.

Jones, Ernest. (1916), The theory of symbolism. Rpt. in: *Papers on Psycho-Analysis*, 5th ed. London: Bailliere, Tindall & Cox, 1948.

Jones, Eli Stanley. (1968), *A Song of Ascents: A Spiritual Autobiography*. Nashville: Abingdon.

Jones, James W. (1991), *Contemporary Psychoanalysis and Religion: Transference and Transcendence*. New Haven: Yale University Press.

Josephs, Lawrence. (1989), Self psychology and the analysis of the superego. *Psychoanalytic Psychology* 6(1):73–86.

Jung, Carl Gustav. (1960), *Synchronicity: An Acausal Connecting Principle*. Trans. R. F. C. Hull. Rpt. Princeton: Princeton University Press, 1973.

————. (1968), *Psychology and Alchemy*, 2d ed. Collected Works, Vol. 12. Princeton: Princeton University Press.

————. (1970a), *Alchemical Studies*. Trans. R. F. C. Hull. Collected Works, Vol. 13. Princeton: Princeton University Press.

————. (1970b), *Mysterium Coniunctionis: An Inquiry into the Separation and Synthesis of Psychic Opposites in Alchemy*, 2d ed. Collected Works, Vol. 14. Princeton: Princeton University Press.

Kason, Yvonne, with Degler, Teri. (1994), *A Farther Shore: How Near-Death and Other Extraordinary Experiences Can Change Ordinary Lives*. New York: HarperCollins Publishers.

Kalupahana, David J. (1987), *The Principles of Buddhist Psychology*. Albany: State University of New York Press.

Kanzer, Mark. (1969), Sigmund and Alexander Freud on the Acropolis. *American Imago* 26(4):324–54.

Katraya, Dadisho. (1934), A treatise on solitude. Trans. A. J. Wensinck. *Woodbrooke Studies* 7:70–143.

Katz, Steven T. (1978), Language, epistemology, and mysticism. In: Steven T. Katz (Ed.), *Mysticism and Philosophical Analysis*. London: Sheldon Press, pp. 22–74.

————. (1982), Models, modeling and mystical training. *Religion* 12:247–75.

————. (1983), The 'conservative' character of mystical experience. In: Steven T. Katz (Ed.), *Mysticism and Religious Traditions*. Oxford: Oxford University Press, pp. 3–60.

Keiser, Sylvan. (1962), Disturbance of ego functions of speech and abstract thinking. *Journal of the American Psychoanalytic Association* 10:50–73.

Kernberg, Otto F. (1966), Structural derivatives of object relationships. *International Journal of Psycho-Analysis* 47:236–53. Rpt. in: *Object-Relations Theory and Clinical Psychoanalysis*. Northvale, NJ: Jason Aronson, 1990.

————. (1982), Self, ego, affects, and drives. *Journal of the American Psychoanalytic Association* 30(4):893–917.

————. (1991), Some comments on early development. In: Salman Akhtar & Henri Parens (Eds.), *Beyond the Symbiotic Orbit: Advances in Separation-Individuation Theory. Essays in Honor of Selma Kramer, M.D.* Hillsdale, NJ: Analytic, pp. 103–20.

Keter Shem Tov [Hebrew]. Zolkiew, 1794/1795.

King, Sallie B. (Trans.) (1993), *Passionate Journey: The Spiritual Autobiography of Satomi Myodo*. Albany: State University of New York Press.

Kirk, Russell. (1971), *Eliot and His Age*. New York: Random House.

Klein, Melanie. (1933), The early development of conscience in the child. Rpt. in: *Love, Guilt and Reparation: & Other Works 1921–1945*. New York: Delacorte/Seymour Lawrence, 1975, pp. 248–62.

————. (1936), Weaning. Rpt. in: *Love, Guilt and Reparation*, pp. 290–305.

————. (1937), Love, Guilt & Reparation. Rpt. in: *Love, Guilt and Reparation*, pp. 306–43.

Klein, Milton. (1981), On Mahler's autistic and symbiotic phases: An exposition and evaluation. *Psychoanalysis & Contemporary Thought* 4:69–105.

Knowles, David. (1967), *What Is Mysticism?* London: Sheed & Ward, 1979.

Kohn, Livia. (1991), *Taoist Mystical Philosophy: The Scripture of Western Ascension*. Albany: State University of New York Press.

Kohut, Heinz. (1971), *The Analysis of the Self: A Systematic Approach to the Treatment of Narcissistic Personality Disorders*. New York: International Universities Press.

————. (1977), *The Restoration of the Self*. New York: International Universities Press.

————. (1978), *The Search for the Self: Selected Writings of Heinz Kohut*, 2 vols. (Ed.). Paul H. Ornstein. New York: International Universities Press.

————. (1984), *How Does Analysis Cure?* Chicago: University of Chicago Press.

Kongtrul, Jamgön. (1996), *Creation and Completion: Essential Points of Tantric Meditation*. Trans. Sarah Harding. Boston: Wisdom.

Kopp, Richard R. (1995), *Metaphor Therapy: Using Client-Generated Metaphors in Psychotherapy*. New York: Brunner/Mazel.

Kris, Ernst. (1934), The psychology of caricature. Rpt. in: *Psychoanalytic Explorations in Art*. New York: International Universities Press, 1952, pp. 173–88.

———. (1939), On inspiration. Rpt. in: *Psychoanalytic Explorations in Art*, pp. 291–302.

———. (1950), On preconscious mental processes. *Psychoanalytic Quarterly* 19. Rpt. in: *Psychoanalytic Explorations in Art*. New York: International Universities Press, 1952, pp. 303–18.

Kristeva, Julia. (1987), *In the Beginning Was Love: Psychoanalysis and Faith*. Trans. Arthur Goldhammer. New York: Columbia University Press.

Laing, R. D. (1967), Family and individual structure. In: P. Lomas (Ed.), *The Predicament of the Family*. New York: International Universities Press, pp. 107–25.

Lamrimpa, Gen. (1992), *Samatha Meditation: Tibetan Buddhist Teachings on Cultivating Meditative Quiescence*. Trans. B. Alan Wallace. Ed. Hart Sprager. Ithaca, NY: Snow Lion.

Langer, Susanne K. (1957), *Philosophy in a New Key: A Study in the Symbolism of Reason, Rite, and Art*, 3rd ed. Cambridge, Mass.: Harvard University Press.

Langs, Robert. (1988), *Decoding Your Dreams*. New York: Henry Holt.

———. (1991), *Take Charge of Your Emotional Life: Self-analysis Day by Day*. New York: Henry Holt.

———. (1994), *The Dream Workbook: Simple Exercises to Unravel the Secrets of Your Dreams*. Brooklyn, NY: Alliance.

Laski, Marghanita. (1962), *Ecstasy: A Study of Some Secular and Religious Experiences*. Rpt. New York: Greenwood, 1968.

Lawrence of the Resurrection, Brother. (1977), *The Practice of the Presence of God*. Trans. John J. Delaney. Garden City, NY: Image/Doubleday.

Leary, David E. (Ed.). (1990), *Metaphors in the History of Psychology*. Cambridge: Cambridge University Press.

Leatherdale, W. H. (1974), *The Role of Analogy, Model, and Metaphor in Science*. New York: American Elsevier.

Lee, Harry B. (1948), Spirituality and beauty in artistic experience. *Psychoanalytic Quarterly* 17:487–523.

Lehmann, Herbert. (1983), Reflections on Freud's reaction to the death of his mother. *Psychoanalytic Quarterly* 52:237–49.

Lerner, Robert E. (1972), *The Heresy of the Free Spirit in the Later Middle Ages*. Berkeley: University of California Press.

Levy, Paul. (1957), *Buddhism: A 'Mystery Religion'?* London: Athlone; rpt. New York: Schocken, 1968.

Lewin, Bertram D. (1951), *The Psychoanalysis of Elation.* London: Hogarth.

Lichtenberg, Joseph D. (1983), *Psychoanalysis and Infant Research.* Hillsdale, NJ: Analytic.

Lidz, Theodore & Lidz, Ruth Wilmanns. (1989), *Oedipus in the Stone Age: A Psychoanalytic Study of Masculinization in Papua New Guinea.* Madison, CT: International Universities Press.

Lifton, Robert Jay. (1956), "Thought reform" of Western civilians in Chinese communist prisons. *Psychiatry* 19:173–95.

———. (1961), *Thought Reform and the Psychology of Totalism: A Study of "Brainwashing" in China.* New York: Norton; rpt. Chapel Hill: University of North Carolina Press, 1989.

Lin, Paul J. (1977) *A Translation of Lao Tzu's* Tao Te Ching *and Wang Pi's* Commentary. Ann Arbor: Center for Chinese Studies, University of Michigan.

Lindblom, Johannes. (1962), *Prophecy in Ancient Israel.* Philadelphia: Fortress.

Loewald, Hans W. (1951), Ego and reality. *International Journal of Psycho-Analysis* 32. Rpt. in: *Papers on Psychoanalysis.* New Haven: Yale University Press, 1980, pp. 3–20.

———. (1973), On internalization. *International Journal of Psycho-Analysis* 54:9–17.

———. (1978), *Psychoanalysis and the History of the Individual.* New Haven: Yale University Press.

———. (1988), *Sublimation: Inquiries into Theoretical Psychoanalysis.* New Haven: Yale University Press.

Loewenberg, Peter. (1985), *Decoding the Past: The Psychohistorical Approach.* Berkeley: University of California Press.

Lowe, C. Marshall & Braaten, Roger O. (1966), Differences in religious attitudes in mental illness. *Journal for the Scientific Study of Religion* 5(2):435–45.

Loyola, St. Ignatius. (1991), The Spiritual Exercises *and Selected Works* (Eds.). George E. Ganss, with Parmananda R. Divarkar, Edward Malatesta, & Martin E. Palmer. New York: Paulist.

MacCormac, Earl R. (1976), *Metaphor and Myth in Science and Religion.* Durham, NC: Duke University Press.

Madelung, Wilfrid. (1977), Aspects of Isma'ili theology: The prophetic chain and the god beyond being. In: Seyyed Hossein Nasr (Ed.), *Isma'ili Contributions to Islamic Culture.* Tehran: Imperial Iranian Academy of Philosophy, 1977.

Mahdi, Louise Carus, Foster, Steven, & Little, Foster (Eds.). (1987), *Betwixt and Between: Patterns of Masculine and Feminine Initiation.* La Salle, IL: Open Court.

Mahler, Margaret Schoenberger. (1952), On Child Psychosis and Schizophrenia: Autistic and Symbiotic Infantile Psychoses. *Psychoanalytic Study of the Child* 7:286–305.

———. (1958), Autism and Symbiosis, Two Extreme Disturbances of Identity. *International Journal of Psycho-Analysis* 39:77–83.

———, with Manuel Furer. (1968), *On Human Symbiosis and the Vicissitudes of Individuation: Infantile Psychosis*. New York: International Universities Press.

Maréchal, Joseph. (1927), *Studies in the Psychology of the Mystics*. Trans. Algar Thorold. London: Burns, Oates & Washbourne; rpt. Albany: Magi, 1964.

Maslow, Abraham H. (1968), *Toward a Psychology of Being*, 2d ed. Rpt. New York: D. Van Nostrand, n.d.

Masson, J. Moussaieff & Masson, T. C. (1978), Buried memories on the Acropolis: Freud's response to mysticism and anti-Semitism. *International Journal of Psycho-Analysis* 59:199–208.

Matt, Daniel C. (1990), *Ayin*: The concept of nothingness in Jewish mysticism. In: Robert K. C. Forman (Ed.), *The Problem of Pure Consciousness: Mysticism and Philosophy*. New York: Oxford University Press, pp. 139–45.

Mavromatis, Andreas. (1987), *Hypnagogia: The Unique State of Consciousness Between Wakefulness and Sleep*. London & New York: Routledge.

Maxwell, Meg & Tschudin, Verena (Eds.). (1990), *Seeing the Invisible: Modern Religious and Other Transcendent Experiences*. London: Penguin Books.

McDargh, John. (1983), *Psychoanalytic Object Relations Theory and the Study of Religion: On Faith and the Imagining of God*. Lanham, MD: University Press of America.

McDevitt, John B. (1979), The role of internalization in the development of object relations during the separation-individuation phase. *Journal of the American Psychoanalytic Association* 27:327–43.

Mechthild of Magdeburg. (1953), *The Revelations of Mechthild of Magdeburg (1210–1297), or, The Flowing Light of the Godhead*. Trans. Lucy Menzies. London: Longmans, Green.

Meissner, W. W. (1984), *Psychoanalysis and Religious Experience*. New Haven: Yale University Press.

———. (1992), *Ignatius of Loyola: The Psychology of a Saint*. New Haven: Yale University Press.

Merkur, Dan. (1984), The nature of the hypnotic state: A psychoanalytic approach. *International Review of Psycho-Analysis* 11/3:345–54.

———. (1988a), Adaptive symbolism and the theory of myth: The symbolic understanding of myths in Inuit religion. *Psychoanalytic Study of Society* 13:63–94. Eds. L. Bryce Boyer & Simon A. Grolnick. Hillsdale, NJ: Analytic.

176   *Books Cited*

———. (1988b), Prophetic initiation in Israel and Judah. *Psychoanalytic Study of Society* 12:37–67. Eds. L. Bryce Boyer & Simon A. Grolnick. Hillsdale, NJ: Analytic.

———. (1991ₐ), The induction of mystical union: Two Hasidic teachings. *Studia Mystica* 14(4):70–76.

———. (1991b), *Powers Which We Do Not Know: The Gods and Spirits of Inuit Religion.* Moscow, ID: University of Idaho Press.

———. (1992a), *Becoming Half Hidden: Shamanism and Initiation Among the Inuit*, 2d ed. New York: Garland.

———. (1992b), Spirit and the problem of social instincts: Exceptions to Freud's critique of religion. *Psychoanalytic Study of Society* 17:249–87. Eds. L. Bryce Boyer & Ruth Boyer. Hillsdale, NJ: Analytic.

———. (1993a), *Gnosis: An Esoteric Tradition of Mystical Visions and Unions.* Albany: State University of New York Press.

———. (1993b), Mythology into metapsychology: Freud's misappropriation of romanticism. *Psychoanalytic Study of Society* 18:345–60. Eds. L. Bryce Boyer, Ruth M. Boyer, & Stephen M. Sonnenberg. Hillsdale, NJ: Analytic.

———. (1995–96), "And he trusted in Yahweh": The transformation of Abram in Gen 12–13 and 15. *Journal of Psychology of Religion* 4–5:65–88.

———. (1996), The numinous as a category of values. In *The Sacred and Its Scholars: Comparative Methodologies for the Study of Primary Religious Data.* Eds. Thomas A. Idinopulos and Edward A. Yonan. Leiden, Netherlands: E. J. Brill, pp. 104–23.

———. (1997), Transpersonal psychology: Models of spiritual awakening. *Religious Studies Review* 23(2):141–47.

———. (1998a), *The Ecstatic Imagination: Psychedelic Experiences and the Psychoanalysis of Self-Actualization.* Albany: State University of New York Press.

———. (1998b), Reflections on the meaning of theosophy. *Theosophical History* 7(1):18–34.

Milrod, David. (1990), The ego ideal. *Psychoanalytic Study of the Child* 45:43–60.

Miller, Arthur, Isaacs, Kenneth S., & Haggard, Ernest A. (1965), On the nature of the observing function of the ego. *British Journal of Medical Psychology* 38:161–69.

Modell, Arnold H. (1958), The theoretical implications of hallucinatory experiences in schizophrenia. *Journal of the American Psychoanalytic Association* 6:442–80.

———. (1968), *Object Love and Reality: An Introduction to a Psychoanalytic Theory of Object Relations.* New York: International Universities Press.

Morrison, Andrew P. (1983), Shame, ideal self, and narcissism. *Contemporary Psychoanalysis* 19(2):295–318.

Morse, Melvin, with Paul Perry. (1992), *Transformed by the Light: The Powerful Effect of Near-Death Experiences on People's Lives.* New York: Villard.

Moxon, Cavendish. (1920), Mystical ecstasy and hysterical dream-states. *Journal of Abnormal Psychology* 15:329–34.

Muir, Willa. (1968), *Belonging: A Memoir.* London: Hogarth.

Mullen, Jr., E. Theodore. (1980), *The Divine Council in Canaanite and Early Hebrew Literature.* Chico, CA: Scholars Press.

Muller, Friedrich Max. (1879), *The Upanisads.* Rpt. New York: Dover, 1962.

Murray, Lynne. (1991), Intersubjectivity, object relations theory, and empirical evidence from mother-infant interactions. *Infant Mental Health Journal* 12(3):219–32.

Needleman, Jacob. (1980), *Lost Christianity: A Journey of Rediscovery to the Centre of Christian Experience.* New York: Doubleday; rpt. Rockport, MA: Element Books, 1993.

Netton, Ian Richard. (1989), *Allah Transcendent: Studies in the Structure and Semiotics of Islamic Philosophy, Theology and Cosmology.* London: Routledge.

Neubauer, Peter B. (1995), On Wolfson's Crossing gender boundaries. In: Mortimer Ostow (Ed.), *Ultimate Intimacy: The Psychodynamics of Jewish Mysticism.* Madison, CT: International Universities Press, pp. 338–47.

Newman, Francis W. (1852), *The Soul; Its Sorrows and Aspirations,* 3rd ed.

Newman, Louis I. (Ed.). (1963), *The Hasidic Anthology: Tales and Teachings of the Hasidim,* with Samuel Spitz. New York: Schocken.

Niederland, William G. (1969), Freud's 'déjà vu' on the Acropolis. *American Imago* 26(4):373–78.

Nunberg, Herman. ([1932] 1955), *Principles of Psychoanalysis: Their Application to the Neuroses.* Trans. Madlyn Kahr & Sidney Kahr. New York: International Universities Press.

O'Brien, John A. (Ed.). (1949), *The Road to Damascus: The Spiritual Pilgrimage of Fifteen Converts to Catholicism.* Garden City, NY: Doubleday.

Oliver, Thomas. (1779), *The Arminian Magazine.* Ed. John Wesley. London: J. Fry and Company.

Otto, Rudolf. (1931), *Religious Essays: A Supplement to 'The Idea of the Holy'.* Trans. Brian Lunn. London: Oxford University Press – Humphrey Milford.

———. (1932a), *Mysticism East and West: A Comparative Analysis of the Nature of Mysticism.* Trans. Bertha L. Bracey & Richenda C. Payne. Rpt. New York: Macmillan, 1970.

———. (1932b), The sensus numinis as the historical basis of religion. *Hibbert Journal* 30:283–97, 415–30.

———. (1950), *The Idea of the Holy: An inquiry into the non-rational factor in the idea of the divine and its relation to the rational,* 2d ed. London: Oxford University Press.

Otto, Walter F. (1954), *The Homeric Gods: The Spiritual Significance of Greek Religion.* Trans. Moses Hadas. Rpt. London: Thames & Hudson, 1979.

Owen, H. P. (1971), Christian mysticism: A study in Walter Hilton's *The Ladder of Perfection. Religious Studies* 7, 31–42.

Pahnke, Walter N. & Richards, William A. (1966), Implications of LSD and experimental mysticism. *Journal of Religion and Health* 5(3):175–208.

Paffard, Michael. (1973), *Inglorious Wordsworths: A Study of Some Transcendental Experiences in Childhood and Adolescence.* London: Hodder and Stoughton.

Paper, Jordan. (1980), From shaman to mystic in Ojibwa religion. *Studies in Religion/Sciences Religieuses* 9(2):185–99.

———. (1982), From shamanism to mysticism in the Chuang-tzu. *Scottish Journal of Religious Studies* 3:27–45.

Parkin, Alan. (1985), Narcissism: Its structures, systems and affects. *International Journal of Psycho-Analysis* 66:143–56.

Patrick, Catharine. (1935), Creative thought in poets. *Archives of Psychology* 26(178):1–74.

———. (1937), Creative thought in artists. *Journal of Psychology* 4:35–73.

———. (1938), Scientific thought. *Journal of Psychology* 5:55–83.

Peterfreund, Emanuel. (1978), Some critical comments on psychoanalytic conceptualizations of infancy. *International Journal of Psycho-Analysis* 59:427–41.

Peters, Larry G. (1982), Trance, initiation, and psychotherapy in Tamang shamanism. *American Ethnologist* 9:21–46.

Pfister, Oskar. (1932), Instinctive psychoanalysis among the Navahos. *Journal of Nervous and Mental Disease* 76:234–54.

Piaget, Jean. (1937), *The Construction of Reality in the Child.* Rpt. New York: Basic, 1954.

———. (1951), *Play, Dreams and Imitation in Childhood.* Trans. C. Gattegno & F. M. Hodgson. Rpt. London: Routledge & Kegan Paul, 1972.

Pike, Nelson. (1965), Comments. In: W. H. Capitan & D. D. Merill (Eds.), *Art, Mind and Religion.* Pennsylvania: University of Pittsburgh Press.

Pine, Fred. (1981), In the beginning: Contributions to a psychoanalytic developmental psychology. *International Review of Psycho-Analysis* 8:15–33.

———. (1986), The "symbiotic phase" in light of current infancy research. *Bulletin of the Menninger Clinic* 50(6):564–69.

———. (1990), *Drive, Ego, Object, and Self: A Synthesis for Clinical Work.* New York: BasicBooks/HarperCollins.

Piontelli, Alessandra. (1992), *From Fetus to Child: An Observational and Psychoanalytic Study.* London & New York: Tavistock/Routledge.

Poulain, Augustin Francois. (1910), *The Graces of Interior Prayer: A Treatise on Mystical Theology.* Trans. Leonora L. Yorke Smith. London: Paul, Trench & Trubner; rpt. London: Routledge & Kegan Paul, 1950.

Powys, John Cowper. (1934), *Autobiography.* London: J. Lane, The Bodley Head.

Pratt, James Bissett. (1921), *The Religious Consciousness: A Psychological Study.* New York: Macmillan.

Prince, Raymond. (1979–80), Religious experience and psychosis. *J. Altered States Cs.* 5(2):167–81.

———— & Savage, Charles. (1965), Mystical states and the concept of regression. In: *Personality Change and Religious Experience,* pp. 36–52. Montreal: R. M. Bucke Memorial Society; rpt. *Psychedelic Review* 8 (1966):59–81.

Pruyser, Paul. (1974), *Between Belief and Unbelief.* New York: Harper & Row.

————. (1983), *The Play of Imagination: Toward a Psychoanalysis of Culture.* New York: International Universities Press.

Pseudo-Dionysius the Areopagite. (1987), *The Complete Works.* Trans. Colm Luibheid. New York & Mahwah: Paulist Press.

Rado, Sandor. (1928), The problem of melancholia. *International Journal of Psycho-Analysis* 9:420–38.

Rambo, Louis R. (1993), *Understanding Religious Conversion.* New Haven: Yale University Press.

Rank, Otto & Sachs, Hans. (1916), *The Significance of Psychoanalysis for the Mental Sciences.* Nervous & Mental Disease Monograph Series, No. 23. New York; rpt. *American Imago* 21(1-2) (1964).

Rasmussen, Knud. (1929), *Intellectual Culture of the Iglulik Eskimos.* Report of the Fifth Thule Expedition 1921–24, 7(1).

Reich, Annie. (1953), Narcissistic object choice in women. Rpt. in: *Annie Reich: Psychoanalytic Contributions.* New York: International Universities Press, 1973, pp. 179–208.

Reid, Forrest. (1912), *Following Darkness.* London: Edward Arnold.

————. (1926), *Apostate.* London: Constable.

Reik, Theodor. (1959), *Mystery on the Mountain: The Drama of the Sinai Revelation.* New York: Harper.

————. (1960), *The Creation of Woman.* New York: Braziller.

————. (1961), *The Temptation.* New York: Braziller.

Richard of St. Victor. (1979), *The Twelve Patriarchs. The Mystical Ark. Book Three of the Trinity.* Trans. Grover A. Zinn. New York: Paulist.

Rizzuto, Ana-Maria. (1974), Object relations and the formation of the image of God. *British Journal of Medical Psychology* 47:83–99.

———. (1979), *The Birth of the Living God: A Psychoanalytic Study*. Chicago: University of Chicago Press.

Róheim, Géza. (1943–44), *War, Crime and the Covenant*. In: *Journal of Criminal Psychopathology* 4(4), 5:1–34 [1943–44]. Rpt. Journal of Clinical Psychopathology Monograph Series No. 1. Monticello, NY: Medical Journal Press, 1945.

Rose, Gilbert J. (1964), Creative imagination in terms of ego 'core' and boundaries. *International Journal of Psycho-Analysis* 45:75–84.

———. (1972), Fusion states. In: Peter L. Giovacchini (Ed.), *Tactics and Techniques in Psychoanalytic Therapy*. London: Hogarth, pp. 170–88.

Ross, Nathaniel. (1968), Beyond "The future of an illusion." *Journal of the Hillside Hospital* 17:259–76.

———. (1975), Affect as cognition: With observations on the meanings of mystical states. *International Review of Psycho-Analysis* 2:79–93.

Rowe, William L. (1975), *The Cosmological Argument*. Princeton, NJ: Princeton University Press.

Rubin, Jeffrey. (1992), Psychoanalytic treatment with a Buddhist meditator. In: Mark Finn & John Gartner (Eds.), *Object Relations Theory and Religion: Clinical Applications*. Westport, CT: Praeger.

Ruysbroek, Jan van. (1953), *The Spiritual Espousals*. Trans. Eric Colledge. Rpt. Westminster, MD: Christian Classics, 1983.

Sacks, Howard L. (1979), The effect of spiritual exercises on the integration of self-system. *Journal of the Scientific Study of Religion* 18(1):46–50.

Sandbach, F. H. (1975), *The Stoics*. London: Chatto & Windus.

Sandler, Joseph. (1981), Character traits and object relationships. *Psychoanalytic Quarterly* 50:694–708.

——— & Rosenblatt, Bernard. (1962), The concept of the representational world. *Psychoanalytic Study of the Child* 17:128–45.

Schafer, Roy. (1959), Generative empathy in the treatment situation. *Psychoanalytic Quarterly* 28:342–73.

Schein, Edgar H. (1956), The Chinese indoctrination program for prisoners of war: A study of attempted "brainwashing." *Psychiatry* 19:149–72.

———. (1959), Brainwashing and totalitarianization in modern society. *World Politics* 11:430–41.

Schmidt, Wilhelm. (1931), *The Origin and Growth of Religion: Facts and Theories*. Trans. H. J. Rose. New York: Cooper Square, 1972.

Scholem, Gershom G. (1954), *Major Trends in Jewish Mysticism*, 3rd ed. Rpt. New York: Schocken, 1961.

Books Cited   181

——. (1965), *Jewish Gnosticism, Merkabah Mysticism and Talmudic Tradition*, 2d ed. New York: Jewish Theological Seminary of America.

——. (1971), *Devekut*, or communion with God. In: *The Messianic Idea in Judaism: And Other Essays in Jewish Spirituality*. New York: Schocken.

——. (1974), *Kabbalah*. New York: Quadrangle/New York Times.

Schroeder, Theodore. (1922), Prenatal psychisms and mystical pantheism. *International Journal of Psycho-Analysis* 3:445–66.

Searles, Harold F. (1960), *The Nonhuman Environment: In Normal Development and in Schizophrenia*. New York: International Universities Press.

Sefer Ha-Bahir: Haniqra Midrasho shel R. Nehunia' ben Haqanah [Hebrew]. (Ed.). Reuben Moshe Margoliot. Jerusalem: Mossad Ha-Rav Kook, 5711.

Segal, Hanna. (1991), *Dream, Phantasy and Art*. London: Tavistock/Routledge.

Settlage, Calvin F. (1993), Therapeutic process and developmental process in the restructuring of object and self constancy. *Journal of the American Psychoanalytic Association* 41(2):473–92.

Sherman, Spencer. (1972), Brief report: Very deep hypnosis. *Journal of Transpersonal Psychology* 4:87–91.

Shor, Ronald E. (1959), Hypnosis and the concept of the generalized reality orientation. *American Journal of Psychotherapy* 13:582–602.

Siegelman, Ellen Y. (1990), *Metaphor and Meaning in Psychotherapy*. New York: Guilford.

Silberer, Herbert. (1912), On symbol-formation. Rpt. in: David Rapaport (Ed.), *Organization and Pathology of Thought: Selected Sources*. New York: Columbia University Press, 1951.

Silverman, Lloyd H. (1978), Unconscious symbiotic fantasy: A ubiquitous therapeutic agent. *International Journal of Psycho-Analytic Psychotherapy* 7:562–85.

——. (1979), The unconscious fantasy as therapeutic agent in psychoanalytic treatment. *Journal of the American Psychoanalytic Association* 7(2):189–218.

——, Lachmann, Frank M., & Milich, Robert H. (1982), *The Search for Oneness*. New York: International Universities Press.

Slochower, Harry. (1970), Freud's *déjà vu* on the Acropolis: A symbolic relic of 'mater nuda'. *Psychoanalytic Quarterly* 39:90–102.

Smart, Ninian. (1965), Interpretation and mystical experience. *Religious Studies* 1:75–87.

——. (1968), *The Yogi and the Devotee*. London: George Allen & Unwin.

——. (1983), The purification of consciousness and the negative path. In: Steven T. Katz (Ed.), *Mysticism and Religious Tradition*. Oxford: Oxford University Press.

Solnit, Albert J. (1959), The vicissitudes of ego development in adolescence. *Journal of the American Psychoanalytic Association* 7:523–36.

Spanos, N. P. & Moretti, P. (1988), Correlates of mystical and diabolical experiences in a sample of female university students. *Journal for the Scientific Study of Religion* 27:105–16.

Spitz, René A. (1957), *No and Yes: On the Genesis of Human Communication.* New York: International Universities Press.

———, with Cobliner, W. Godfrey. (1965), *The First Year of Life: A Psychoanalytic Study of Normal and Deviant Development of Object Relations.* New York: International Universities Press.

Stace, W. T. (1960), *Mysticism and Philosophy.* Philadelphia & New York: Lippincott.

Starbuck, Edwin Diller. (1911), *The Psychology of Religion: An Empirical Study of the Growth of Religious Consciousness,* 3rd ed. London & New York: Walter Scott.

Stark, Rodney. (1965), A taxonomy of religious experience. *Journal for the Scientific Study of Religion* 5(1):97–116.

Sterba, Richard. (1968), Remarks on mystic states. *American Imago* 25:77–85.

Stern, Daniel N. (1983), The early development of schemas of self, other, and "self with other". In: Joseph D. Lichtenberg & Samuel Kaplan (Eds.), *Reflections of Self Psychology.* Hillsale, NJ: Analytic, pp. 49–84.

———. (1985), *The Interpersonal World of the Infant: A View from Psychoanalysis and Developmental Psychology.* New York: Basic.

Strauss, Leo. (1952), *Persecution and the Art of Writing.* Westport, CT: Greenwood Press, Publishers, 1973.

Streeter, B. H. & Appasamy, A. J. (1922), *The Sadhu: A Study in Mysticism and Practical Religion.* London: Macmillan.

Suso, Henry. (1952), *The Life of the Servant.* Trans. James M. Clark. London: James Clark.

———. (1953), *Little Book of Eternal Wisdom* and *Little Book of Truth.* Trans. James M. Clark. New York: Harper.

Sutherland, Cherie. (1992), *Reborn In the Light: Life After Near-Death Experiences.* [Originally titled: *Transformed By the Light.*] Sydney, Australia & Auckland, New Zealand: Bantam; rpt. New York: Bantam, 1995.

Sutherland, J. D. (1963), Object-relations theory and the conceptual model of psychoanalysis. *British Journal of Medical Psychology* 36:109–24.

Tart, Charles T. (1970), Transpersonal potentialities of deep hypnosis. *Journal of Transpersonal Psychology* 2(1).

———. (1979), Measuring the depth of an altered state of consciousness, with particular reference to self-report scales of hypnotic depth. In: Erika Fromm & Ronald E. Shor (Eds.), *Hypnosis: Developments in Research and New Perspectives,* 2d ed. New York: Aldine, pp. 567–601.

Tauler, Johann. (1961), *Spiritual Conferences*. Trans. & ed. Eric Colledge & Sister M. Jane. Rpt. Rockford, IL: Tan, 1978.

Teresa of Jesus [of Avila], St. (1946), *Complete Works*, 3 vols. Trans. E. Allison Peers. London: Sheed & Ward.

Thouless, Robert H. (1924), *An Introduction to the Psychology of Religion*, 2d ed. Cambridge: University Press.

Ticho, Ernst A. (1972), The development of superego autonomy. *Psychoanalytic Review* 59:217–33.

Tolpin, Marian. (1971), On the beginnings of a cohesive self: An application of the concept of transmuting internalization to the study of the transitional object and signal anxiety. *Psychoanalytic Study of the Child* 26:316–52.

Trevor, John. (1897), *My Quest for God*. London: "Labour Prophet" Office.

Tufail, Abu Bakr Muhammad bin. (1982), *The Journey of the Soul: The Story of Hai bin Yaqzan*. Trans. Riad Kocache. London: Octagon.

Turner, Victor W. (1969), *The Ritual Process: Structure and Anti-Structure*. Rpt. Ithaca, NY: Cornell University Press, 1977.

Tyson, Phyllis & Tyson, Robert L. (1990), *Psychoanalytic Theories of Development: An Integration*. New Haven: Yale University Press.

Underhill, Evelyn. (1910), *Mysticism: A Study in the Nature and Development of Man's Spiritual Consciousness*. Rpt. New York: New American Library, 1955.

van der Leeuw, Gerardus. (1938), *Religion In Essence and Manifestation*, 2 vols. Rpt. Gloucester, MA: Peter Smith, 1967.

Vinacke, William Edgar. (1952), *The Psychology of Thinking*. New York: McGraw-Hill.

von Franz, Marie-Louise. (1980), *On Divination and Synchronicity: The Psychology of Meaningful Chance*. Toronto: Inner City.

Wallas, Joseph. (1926), *The Art of Thought*. New York: Harcourt.

Watt, William Montgomery (Trans.). (1953), *The Faith and Practice of Al-Ghazali*. Rpt. Oxford: Oneworld Publications, 1994.

Weiss, Eduardo. (1932), Regression and projection in the super-ego. *International Journal of Psycho-Analysis* 13:449–78.

Werblowsky, R. J. Zwi. (1990), God as 'nothing' in kabbalah. In: Robert E. Carter (Ed.), *God, the Self, and Nothingness: Reflections Eastern and Western*. New York: Paragon House.

Werman, David S. (1977), On the occurrence of incest fantasies. *Psychoanalytic Quarterly* 46:245–55.

Whiting, John W. M., Kluckhohn, Richard, & Anthony, Albert. (1958), The function of male initiation ceremonies at puberty. In: Eleanor E. Maccoby, Theodore M.

Newcomb, & Eugene L. Hartley (Eds.), *Readings in Social Psychology*, 3rd ed. New York: Holt.

Widengren, Geo. (1961), Researches in Syrian mysticism: Mystical experiences and spiritual exercises. *Numen* 8(3):161–98.

Wilber, Ken. (1977), *The Spectrum of Consciousness*, 2d ed. Rpt. Wheaton, IL: Theosophical, 1993.

———. (1983), *Eye to Eye: The Quest for the New Paradigm*. Garden City, NY: Anchor Press/Doubleday.

Willson, A. Leslie. (1964), *A Mythical Image: The Ideal of India in German Romanticism*. Durham, NC: Duke University Press.

Winnicott, Donald W. (1958), The capacity to be alone. *International Journal of Psycho-Analysis* 39:416–20. Rpt. in: *The Maturational Processes and the Facilitating Environment: Studies in the Theory of Emotional Development*. New York: International Universities Press, 1963, pp. 29–36.

———. (1963), Communicating and not communicating leading to a study of certain opposites. Rpt. in: *The Maturational Processes and the Facilitating Environment*, pp. 179–92.

Wolfson, Elliot R. (1987), Circumcision, vision of God, and textual interpretation: From midrashic trope to mystical symbol. *History of Religions* 27:189–215. Rpt. in: *Circle in the Square*.

———. (1994), *Through a Speculum that Shines: Vision and Imagination in Medieval Jewish Mysticism*. Princeton, NJ: Princeton University Press.

———. (1996), Iconic visualization and the imaginal body of God: The role of intention in the rabbinic conception of prayer. *Modern Theology* 12(2):137–62.

Wolfson, Harry Austryn. (1935), The internal senses in Latin, Arabic, and Hebrew philosophic texts. *Harvard Theological Review* 28(2):69–133.

Wolters, Clifton (Trans). (1978), *The Cloud of Unknowing and Other Works*. Harmondsworth: Penguin.

Wuthnow, Robert. (1978), Peak experiences: Some empirical tests. *Journal of Humanistic Psychology* 18(3):59–75.

Yu-Lau, Fung. (1953), *A History of Chinese Philosophy*, Vol. 2, *The Period of Classical Learning (From the Second Century B.C. to the Twentieth Century A.D.)*. Trans. Derk Bodde. Princeton: Princeton University Press.

Zaehner, Robert Charles. (1957), *Mysticism Sacred and Profane: An Inquiry Into Some Varieties of Preternatural Experience*. Rpt. London: Oxford University Press, 1961.

———. (1970), *Concordant Discord: The Interdependence of Faiths*. Oxford: Clarendon Press.

———. (1972), *Zen, Drugs and Mysticism*. New York: Random, 1974.

Something More, 72, 76, 93, 97–98, 100, 102–104, 107, 109, 142, 151
spiritual awakening, 67, 139. *See also* conversion
spiritual emergency, 61–62. *See also* acting-out; mystical union and hysterical spells
spiritual transformation, 125–127
Stace, W. T., 6
Starbuck, Edwin Diller, 127
Stern, Daniel N., 53–54
Sterba, Richard, 111–112, 136
Stoicism, 39
sublimation, defined, 59–60. *See also* mystical union as sublimation
Sufism, 13–14, 15, 67, 68
superego, 64, 111–113, 121–123, 128, 131, 136, 137, 150–151, 152
Suso, Henry, 5, 10, 14–15, 25, 80, 85
symbol formation, random, 156–157
symbols, regressive and adaptive, 104–108, 110
Syriac Mystery of the Cross, 88–91

Taoism, 22
Tauler, Johann, 80
Tennyson, Alfred, 3–4, 10
Teresa of Avila, St., 12, 13, 16
theistic thinking, 80, 93, 95
Thouless, Robert H., 3
Ticho, Ernest A., 42
typical fantasies, 29
trance, 81, 83; and reification, 103
transcendent, idea of, 76–78, 79–80, 86, 93–94, 102; and ecstatic death, 87; and miracles, 151; and mystical nothingness, 86; and self-transcendence, 86–87; in world religions, 78–79. *See also* Something More

Underhill, Evelyn, 1, 34, 68
unitive experiences, numinosity of, 75–78
unitive experiences, types of
  beauty, 41–42
  energy, 45–46, 49
  identification, 32–33, 48
  inclusion, 31–32, 49, 120–121
  incorporation, 28–30, 48
  loving presence, 46–47, 49, 95–102, 107, 109, 120
  omnipresence, 47–48, 49
  propriety, 35–38, 119–120
  relatedness, 33–34, 49, 118
  self-transcendence, 86–87
  solitary self, 3–4, 27–28, 48, 57, 63, 66, 74–75, 76–77, 80, 94
  vitality, 44–45
unitive thinking, and symbol formation, 75; experience of miracles as, 150; in metaphysics, 44–48, 49, 66, 67, 71; in morality, 41–44, 49, 66, 71; in science, 38–41 49, 66, 71; theistic thinking as, 80, 93–95

van der Leeuw, Gerardus, 73–74
Ventis, W. Larry, 61
via negativa, 85

Wallas, Joseph, 30–31
Wholly Other, 72, 99–100, 102–103
Wilber, Ken, 62, 80, 86
Winnicott, Donald W., ix, 28, 48, 113–114

Zaehner, R. C., 9, 10, 18